Dangerous Dossiers

ALSO BY HERBERT MITGANG

BIOGRAPHY

LINCOLN AS THEY SAW HIM

THE FIERY TRIAL: A LIFE OF LINCOLN

THE MAN WHO RODE THE TIGER: THE LIFE AND TIMES OF JUDGE SAMUEL SEABURY

REPORTAGE

FREEDOM TO SEE: TELEVISION AND THE FIRST AMENDMENT

CRITICISM

WORKING FOR THE READER: A CHRONICLE OF CULTURE, LITERATURE, WAR AND POLITICS IN BOOKS

HISTORY (Editor)

THE LETTERS OF CARL SANDBURG

AMERICA AT RANDOM: TOPICS OF THE TIMES

WASHINGTON, D.C. IN LINCOLN'S TIME

SPECTATOR OF AMERICA

CIVILIANS UNDER ARMS: STARS & STRIPES, CIVIL WAR TO KOREA

FICTION

THE RETURN

GET THESE MEN OUT OF THE HOT SUN

THE MONTAUK FAULT

KINGS IN THE COUNTING HOUSE

PLAY

MISTER LINCOLN

Dangerous Dossiers

Herbert Mitgang

DONALD I. FINE BOOKS
New York

DONALD I. FINE BOOKS

Published by the Penguin Group
Penguin Books USA Inc., 375 Hudson Street, New York, New York 10014, U.S.A.
Penguin Books Ltd, 27 Wrights Lane, London W8 5TZ, England
Penguin Books Australia Ltd, Ringwood, Victoria, Australia
Penguin Books Canada Ltd, 10 Alcorn Avenue, Toronto, Ontario, Canada M4V 3B2
Penguin Books (N.Z.) Ltd, 182–190 Wairau Road, Auckland 10, New Zealand

Penguin Books Ltd, Registered Offices: Harmondsworth, Middlesex, England

Primus paperback edition published in 1996 by Donald I. Fine Books, an imprint of Penguin Books USA Inc.

1 3 5 7 9 10 8 6 4 2

Copyright © 1988 by Herbert Mitgang

Chapter XVI copyright © 1989 by Herbert Mitgang

Introduction to the Primus paperback edition copyright © 1996 by Herbert Mitgang

All rights reserved

ISBN: 1-55611-485-0
CIP data is available

Printed in the United States of America

Without limiting the rights under copyright reserved above, no part of this publication may be reproduced, stored in or introduced into a retrieval system, or transmitted, in any form, or by any means (electronic, mechanical, photocopying, recording, or otherwise) without the prior written permission of both the copyright owner and the above publisher of this book.

CONTENTS

They [the framers of the Constitution] conferred, as against the Government, the right to be let alone—the most comprehensive of rights and the right most valued by civilized men.

—Associate Justice Louis D. Brandeis,
Olmstead v. United States, 1928.

In darkling street they seek and hide,
The game grows wild and drunken;
They spy upon the other side,
Keep secrets in a punkin.

—E. B. White, "I Spy"

INTRODUCTION TO THE PRIMUS PAPERBACK EDITION

Authors and artists do not boast that they have a right to keep and bear arms. But they do cherish the right to keep and bear pens and brushes, word processors and easels. No book has ever been written with an Uzi or Glock and no oil been painted with a Magnum or sawed-off shotgun.

This hyperbolic thought comes to mind because personal arsenals and private militias are suddenly in the air, encouraged by the rabid voices of demagogues who spew venom over the public airwaves as never before in the history of broadcasting.

There is nothing in the United States Constitution that encourages or permits the worst elements in American life to blow up federal installations with fertilizer bombs or to terrorize the public. As a new millennium looms on the horizon, serious issues of right and regulation are raised anew by wrongful activities in a free society.

How do we balance lawful acts and police powers? When

should the government weigh in with all its might against the constitutional protections of individual citizens? What distinctions should be made between informing the public and suppressing information? And—the underlying aim of this book—what access should be allowed to government records so that illegal activities can be examined under the Freedom of Information Act and exposed by journalists, authors and historians?

There is a delicate balance in the Bill of Rights between the powers of the state and the rights of the people. From the time of the Federalist Papers and the Constitutional Convention, the balance has tipped in favor of the people. That is one of the lessons contained in this study of the reckless dossiers maintained on American and European authors and artists, particularly during the long reign of J. Edgar Hoover as the witch-hunting director of the Federal Bureau of Investigation.

In recent times, home-grown gunslingers and foreign terrorists have surfaced, here and abroad. It comes as a shock to our sensibilities and sense of history that Pennsylvania Avenue, the route of Presidents for two centuries, has had to be barricaded in front of the White House to protect the Chief Executive/Commander in Chief from would-be assassins.

In the wake of the bombings of the World Trade Center in New York City and of the federal building in Oklahoma City, most Americans would agree that the F.B.I. and other Government police agencies should be well-armed with information about actual and potential murderers and assassins. Fanatical and misguided organizations with personal arsenals who seek to take the law into their own hands—including such weekend warriors as the Michigan Militia, the Christian Patriots Defense League and the innocent-sounding Blue Ridge Hunt Club—represent the dangerous underside of America. In the tradition of the Ku Klux Klan, their literature boasts that they train to combat the usual white-supremacist and anti-Semitic targets. These unamerican creatures live under rocks and come out at night in camouflage clothing and combat boots to play soldier. But they have larger aims—to attack federal officials and buildings, the United Nations and the so-called New World Order.

Where should the government draw the line on surveillance and maintaining dossiers on the citizenry? This book discloses that secret files were kept on many of the most distinguished authors and artists and writers' organizations—time, energy, manpower and resources that might well have been better spent pursuing organized crime and real criminality under the federal statutes.

It is important to note that not one of the half-dozen Nobel laureates whose files I obtained under the Freedom of Information Act and are related here—Sinclair Lewis, Pearl S. Buck, William Faulkner, Ernest Hemingway, John Steinbeck, Thomas Mann—ever threatened the President, the United States government or its institutions. As their dossiers sadly show, it is the government that found them suspect. Despite thousands of pages in their files, none was ever convicted, let alone accused, of violating federal or state laws. By contrast, today a genuine enemy exists from within: the armed fanatics and their sub-rosa organizations that threaten the United States and its people.

To avoid invading the privacy of innocent Americans for their personal or political beliefs, speeches and writings—and not just authors or other persons in the public eye—it is always wise to turn to the Bill of Rights for guidance.

Three Amendments in the Bill of Rights are relevant. The First Amendment says that Congress shall make no law establishing or prohibiting any religion. In addition, freedom of speech and of the press are guaranteed. The Fourth Amendment guarantees the right of privacy. It says that the right of the people to be secure in their "persons, houses, papers, and effects" against unreasonable searches and seizures shall not be violated. Both amendments have been tested and upheld, again and again, by the Supreme Court of the United States.

It is the Second Amendment that has caused the greatest confusion—and the greatest threat to freedom today. The National Rifle Association's lobbyists and the members of scattershot private militias maintain that there is an absolute right to bear arms.

Not so.

The Second Amendment, ratified in 1791 and never altered, says: "A well regulated Militia, being necessary to the security of a free State, the right of the people to keep and bear Arms, shall not be infringed."

The crystal-clear phrase preceding the right is absolutely necessary to understand and interpret the reasoning behind, and the limitations of, the Second Amendment. The phrase governs the right. It specifically provides a right to keep a gun to bear arms on behalf of a free state. Private ownership for personal needs—not mentioned in the Constitution—is neither allowed nor forbidden.

Furthermore, ownership of small arms as part of a militia is not merely to be regulated by the government but "well regulated." The framers of the Constitution did not choose their words lightly. Every word carries weight and purpose.

The unregulated, misnamed militias obviously are anti-free state and anti-federal government. A real militia, not these bogus private militias, is very much a part of the Constitution. The President is recognized as head of the various state militias when called into federal service as well as the regular armed forces. The constitutionally recognized militias are out in the open. By contrast, the private militias are paramilitary groups. They should not be confused with the citizens who picked up hunting rifles and muskets and fought for freedom in the Revolution.

Since the demise of FBI Director Hoover and the fall of the Nixon Administration, I have been told by federal officials that the old practices of surveillance of authors and artists and the buildup of their dossiers are a thing of the past. One hopes so. At the same time, let us hope that responsible and sophisticated law-enforcement officers, under the Department of Justice, are tracking the paramilitary leaders and their organizations. It is *their* dossiers that deserve attention. The true enemy within must be exposed to the light by federal agencies and then exposed to the public under the Freedom of Information law.

The case histories in this book indicate—to paraphrase the title of Sinclair Lewis's antifascist novel of the nineteen-thirties—that it can almost happen here.

—HERBERT MITGANG

I.

THE RIGHT OF PRIVACY

Early in this century, the United States Supreme Court was called upon to decide a case that foreshadowed dire events: domestic surveillance of citizens, political espionage of dissidents, unauthorized wiretapping and electronic eavesdropping, information banks and the panoply of offenses summed up in the word *Watergate*.

In testimony before the Senate Judiciary Committee, Professor Arthur R. Miller of the Michigan and Harvard law schools once spoke darkly of a time of approaching "dossier dictatorship."

The two concepts—privacy and dossiers—inevitably collide.

The purpose of this book is to demonstrate by example that, in most cases, government dossiers are constitutionally unsound, fruitless and dangerous—dangerous not only to the individual who is harmed by having an unnecessary government record that follows him, and possibly his family, forever, but also to the nation's values and traditions of personal independence.

Dossiers are a heritage of hysteria about radicalism and of the cold war. In the last decade much of the FBI's Hooverian paranoia has evaporated, thanks to congressional oversight and increased public awareness of the dangers of secret subgovernments. Nevertheless, in more recent times, lawlessness has been revealed on other, more radical levels that recall Sinclair Lewis's warning novel, *It Can't Happen Here.* The Iran-Contra hearings showed an interlocking network of official spies, mercenaries, former generals, opportunists and cold war profiteers operating within government precincts but outside the Constitution and institutions of government.

The history of the cold war and of secret government dossiers runs on parallel tracks that then converge. Taking the long view, the cold war began long before Winston Churchill's post-World War II "Iron Curtain" speech in Fulton, Missouri, that became a watershed in international relations during the Truman presidency. The mutual suspicion between the Western nations and the new Soviet government can be said to have started toward the end of World War I. It coincided with the beginning of the Bolshevik takeover of the Russian Revolution seventy years ago. During the Wilson presidency, the little remembered point of contact was at Archangel, in northern Russia. In a largely forgotten episode in the annals of American arms, a force of British, French and American troops occupied Archangel. Their avowed aim was to prevent war supplies from falling into the hands of the Germans; presumably, the expedition was not directed against the Bolsheviks. But the expedition soon began attacking local Soviets and it was not withdrawn until a year after the Armistice. The Allies more or less openly supported the counter-revolutionary leaders, including several monarchist generals, against the Bolsheviks. They feared that the radical revolution could be exported to their own nations. That did not happen, but the cold war die was cast.

By the middle of the 1920's the European states began to recognize the Soviet government as the legitimate rulers of Russia; the United States did not do so until 1933, during the first term of President Franklin D. Roosevelt. This did not endear Roosevelt to J. Edgar Hoover, who had made his reputation by compiling FBI dossiers on all those he considered to be "Reds," and therefore "un-American." Roosevelt's New Deal, designed to pull Americans out of the Depression, was not immune from Hoover's unlegislated concept of who or what was "un-American." The FBI Director told his Hollywood friend, the actor George Murphy, later Senator Murphy from California and a Republican political cohort of Governor Ronald Reagan, that Roosevelt's New Deal was engineered by the Communists—so Murphy stated in an interview with Robert Scheer in the Los Angeles *Times.* Serving under Attorney General A. Mitchell Palmer, Hoover decided to save America from those he regarded as alien and homegrown Bolsheviks. The infamous raids against so-called Reds lumped together alleged radicals, Socialists, anarchists, members of the International Workers of the World, and militant trade unionists. Reckless arrests and deportations became the order of the day.

Two benchmarks that frequently appear in the following dossiers are the Sacco-Vanzetti case in 1927 and the Spanish Civil War ten years later. The two Italian-born anarchists were convicted of murdering a guard and paymaster during a payroll holdup in South Braintree, Massachusetts; their defenders felt that they were being framed because of their political philosophy. The case polarized the country until they were executed by the Commonwealth of Massachusetts. Those who protested—including scores of authors and artists as well as people from other walks of life—were subjected to harassment and having their names inscribed in police and domestic intelligence files. The Spanish Civil War, which pitted Generalissimo Franco's Fascist insurgents against the Republican government's Loyalists, also divided the world on the eve of the Second World War. Supporting Franco on the battlefield were elements of the armed forces of Fascist Italy and Nazi Germany. In the United States, those who joined the Abraham Lincoln Brigade or were open supporters of the Loyalists could count on having a black mark placed against their names in dossiers as (in the cock-eyed view of the FBI) disloyal and suspicious Americans. To this day, some revisionist historians and neoconservative American writers and editors are trying to clean up Franco's dictatorial act and atrocities in the "realpolitik" of anti-Communism.

On their side, the Soviet government for a time attempted to expand its influence through the Communist International; but the Comintern became one of the Soviet Union's major failures. Only tanks and guns and a visibly symbolic Berlin Wall could contain the boundaries of Soviet hegemony. Anyone who has gone through Checkpoint Charlie into and out of East Berlin, as this writer has done a half-dozen times, sees and senses that the Wall can have little popular demand as a Communist export product now or in the future.

And on our side, during these cold war years, the United States has propped up "our" dictatorships—the Colonels' regime in Greece, the generals in Chile and elsewhere in Latin America—with arms and sometimes CIA subversion, all in the name of their anticommunism (that imprisons the freedoms) and our supposed security.

In the 1980's among the most startling of many comments by President Reagan was his call—in the aftermath of the lawlessness exposed by the Iran-Contra scandal about his Administration—for a return of the House Committee on Un-American Activities. The clear implication was that those who questioned the Reagan regency might well deserve to be policed by Congressional Red-hunters. By contrast to this invocation of the worst days of the cold war are the words of Professor Marshall Shulman, the retired director of the Russian Institute at Columbia University. In his book, *Beyond the Cold War,* the scholar-diplomat wrote:

"The cold war has changed its character not only because Soviet policy has been evolving in response to change in the world environment, but because the United States and its Western Allies are becoming aware that anti-Communism is not an adequate response to the total situation in which we live."

International amity and progress—with legal safeguards and without fear—can yet be attained because of universal knowledge that we live in an interdependent nuclear and economic world. Before the dawn of a new century, new thinking is required about the role of government in people's lives, in this and other lands.

The hundreds of individual and organizational names mentioned here, based upon thousands of pages of documents obtained under the Freedom of Information-Privacy Act and from archives in Washington, mainly cover authors, dramatists and artists; but the principles apply to other professions and fields of activity as well.

In recent years, and especially during the reign of Richard M. Nixon, revelations have emerged of an increasing intrusion by the federal government into private lives and careers. If a person did not have a file with the Federal Bureau of Investigation, chances were good that he would be included in the computerized information bank of the Central Intelligence Agency, one of the congressional security committees, the Passport Office, the Department of Justice's Division of Internal Security, the intelligence branches of the armed services, or any of a dozen other federal, state and city police agencies. The Massachusetts State Police Division of Subversive Activities, for example, is reported to have done thousands of security name-checks, some in response to private inquiries, on "peace groups, civil rightists and other such groups." Today, in addition to its ordinary benefits, the computer has opened up a new and improved era of electronic snooping and recordkeeping.

The landmark Supreme Court case, *Olmstead v. United States*, was argued and decided in 1928 during Prohibition and a year before the great Wall Street Crash. It involved two different approaches to the law and to the notion of privacy—a word that, as such, does not appear in the Constitution but is inherent in the Bill of Rights and in the due process clauses of the Fifth and Fourteenth amendments. In the Olmstead case, evidence had been obtained of private telephone conversations between defendants who were accused of conspiracy to violate the National Prohibition Act. The evidence was obtained by means of tapping wires running from residences of some of the defendants to the office from which the conspiracy was directed. The defendants had been convicted of unlawfully importing, possessing and selling intoxicating liquors and maintaining nuisances. Bootlegging, with the repeal a few years later of Prohibition, has faded in memory, but the issue of constitutionally protected privacy that was raised by the case remains.

In Olmstead, the question arose whether evidence gained by wiretapping, in violation of state law, was admissible. The convicted defendants appealed to the high court on grounds that such evidence was not only illegal but unethical because it violated the Fourth Amendment to the Constitution. That amendment—one of the strongest roots of our theory of privacy—provides that "the right of the people to be secure in their persons, houses, papers, and effects, shall not be violated, and no warrants shall issue, but upon probable cause, supported by oath or affirmation, and particularly describing the place to be searched, and the persons or things to be seized."

Taking a very narrow view of the Fourth Amendment, the majority opinion by Chief Justice Taft upheld the government's lawmen. He ruled that the Fourth Amendment did not prohibit wiretapping because there was "no searching" and "no seizure," and "no entry of the houses or offices" of the defendants. "The evidence was secured by the sense of hearing and that only," said Chief Justice Taft, forgetting that neither telephones nor tapped wires existed when the Constitution was framed, that messages were delivered by horse couriers, and homes invaded at the point of foreign bayonets.

We remember the Olmstead case today not because of the majority ruling but because of the relevance of the words of the dissenting opinion by Justice Brandeis, in which he was joined by Justices Holmes, Butler and Stone. The significance of the dissenting language for privacy and government dossiers echoes down to our own time.

Against the background of the dossiers kept on authors during the past half-century, it is useful to consider the legal perspective provided by Justice Brandeis in his dissenting opinion:

> Subtler and more far-reaching means of invading privacy have become available to the government. Discovery and invention have made it possible for the government, by means far more effective than stretching upon the rack, to obtain disclosure in court of what is whispered in the closet. . . . The progress of science in furnishing the government with means of espionage is not likely to stop with wiretapping. Ways may some day be developed by which the government, without removing papers from secret drawers, can reproduce them in court,

> and by which it will be enabled to expose to a jury the most intimate occurrences of the home. . . . The evil incident to invasion of the privacy of the telephone is far greater than that involved in tampering with the mails. Whenever a telephone line is tapped, the privacy of the persons at both ends of the line is invaded, and all conversations between them upon any subject, and although proper, confidential, and privileged, may be overheard. Time and again this Court, in giving effect to the principle underlying the Fourth Amendment, has refused to place an unduly literal construction upon it. [Such "literal construction" of the law is at the hard core of the Reagan-Meese view of the Constitution and their effort to place political idealogues on the federal bench. The only difference is that the Reagan-Meese phrase for turning the Constitution into a dead document after two centuries is the confining "original intent."]

Justice Brandeis then got to the heart of privacy in measured words that have become part of our living language:

> The makers of our Constitution undertook to secure conditions favorable to the pursuit of happiness. They recognized the significance of man's spiritual nature, of his feelings and of his intellect. They knew that only a part of the pain, pleasure and satisfactions of life are to be found in material things. They sought to protect Americans in their beliefs, their thoughts, their emotions and their sensations. They conferred, as against the government, the right to be let alone—the most comprehensive of rights and the right most valued by civilized men. To protect that right, every unjustifiable intrusion by the government upon the privacy of the individual, whatever the means employed, must be deemed a violation

> of the Fourth Amendment. . . . The greatest dangers to liberty lurk in insidious encroachment by men of zeal, well-meaning but without understanding.

Governmental institutions, including investigative and intelligence agencies, have voracious appetites for information. Much of their pursuit of information, yesterday and today, has been justifiable. The Federal Bureau of Investigation does have an important, defined role to play. It was created in 1908 as the Justice Department's investigative arm. In the main, the FBI has been responsible for enforcing federal criminal statutes. Its two primary areas have been security operations and general investigations. Director Hoover built up an antiradical division within the bureau during the First World War and extended its power by keeping long lists of radical groups and people in the early 1920s. The raids on radicals and deportations of aliens made his name and earned Hoover the top job in the FBI. Over the years the bureau has been criticized for not doing enough to expose major criminal syndicates; to which it has responded by claiming lack of jurisdiction even though it has encouraged the public perception of indomitable G-men. There is, though, general agreement that the bureau did a creditable job in preventing sabotage during the Second World War, and the bureau traditionally helps other law-enforcement agencies with technical assistance and provides name-checks on individuals being considered for government jobs.

However, during Hoover's reign—when most of the files were built up—the bureau was criticized for its excesses, rivalries with other agencies, political intrusion and actual violation of the laws that led to the exposure of its illegal extracurricular activities on the political front to suppress dissent. What has been undeniable—according to the memoirs of some of his own former colleagues in the bureau—is that the FBI was shaped in the image of one individual, J. Edgar Hoover. He was recognized as a fanatic on the subject of radicals, Communists, leftists and liberals, drawing hardly any distinction among them. As the files secured for this book indicate, many authors were categorized as internal security risks and branded Communists.

Hoover was also a racist, as evidenced by his voyeuristic pursuit of Martin Luther King, Jr., lack of any significant number of blacks in the bureau, and outright stalling before he was forced to help the Justice Department handle civil rights cases in the South. He was a politician without portfolio who kept private files on public officials to blackmail them. And he turned himself into a self-proclaimed diety. The favorite Hoover story told behind his back by his special agents was that he vetoed a plan by his sidekick, Clyde Tolson, to buy adjoining cemetery plots. Hoover was unwilling to pay his share because he only expected to use the plot for three days.

That Hoover crossed the line of his jurisdictional boundaries and tried to set up his own anti-free press manipulation agenda can be seen in a document in my possession that turned up—inadvertently, I believe, because it is not marked "declassified" and is not censored—in one of the author files. The subject is labeled: *"Molders of Public Opinion in the United States."*

The FBI document, written "For the Information of the Director," is an exchange of views between two of Hoover's top assistants, written in 1959, after the demise of McCarthyism but before the end of the second Eisenhower administration. Part of the document reads: "The director expressed his concern about the prevalence of articles in publications which are severely and unfairly discrediting our American way of life and praising directly or indirectly the Soviet system. The director questioned whether there might not be some subversive factors in the backgrounds of some of the prominent columnists, editors, commentators, authors, et cetera, which could be influencing such slanted views."

The document goes on: "In accordance with the director's concern in this matter, immediate research was conducted concerning a representative cross section of prominent molders of opinion. One hundred names of prominent individuals in this category were considered. A preliminary analysis resulted in the immediate elimination of twelve individuals who had no known subversive connections. File reviews were conducted on the remaining eighty-eight. Of these, forty were determined to have pertinent factors in their backgrounds which could have a bearing on their reporting of political, economic, and social aspects of world affairs. In preparing the write-ups on these individuals, public source material was used wherever possible; however, confidential material from bureau files was also necessarily utilized. The material was carefully paraphrased and prepared, with a brief introduction, in blind memorandum form to conceal the bureau as the source. This was done in the event the director should desire to make available to appropriate persons some of the information on an informal and confidential basis."

Here is a direct example of how the FBI used its dossiers on "columnists, editors, commentators, authors, et cetera" to knife them furtively and possibly to harm them professionally. None was accused of being a Communist; rather, in KGB-style, they were simply and vaguely charged with "discrediting our American way of life." Hoover had a list of friendly hack columnists—as suggested without much subtlety in the document—who were slipped tidbits from the files and then ran them in their cooperative newspapers and magazines.

In this respect, Representative Don Edwards of California, chairman of the House Subcommittee on Civil and Constitutional Rights, recently brought me up to date on the FBI and the current concerns of his committee. As a former FBI agent he speaks with added authority:

"The FBI's war against Americans who were not criminals but who did not measure up to Director Hoover's idea of an acceptable citizen is a blot on our claim to be a free society. Beginning in some cases in the 1920s and '30s, and continuing until the sensational disclosures in 1973–74 by the Senate Church Committee and the House Pike Committee, the FBI engaged in a pattern of misbehavior, some of it criminal, that harassed not only writers but even more aggressively civil rights leaders, black organizations, peace activists, native Americans and feminists."

He went on to say that in 1975, the House Subcommittee on Civil and Constitutional Rights ordered an audit by the General Accounting Office of the domestic security files of the ten largest FBI offices. The audit found that there were 19,700 open cases in those ten offices where Americans were being investigated by the FBI. About nineteen percent of the agency's total investigative efforts were being expended on these "subversive" cases. Yet of the thousands of investigations, criminal conduct was discovered in only four—none of which involved national security, espionage or terrorism.

Heeding the national outrage at this epidemic of surveillance, in 1976 Attorney General Edward H. Levi put forth new guidelines for FBI domestic security investigations. These required that cases be terminated after ninety days if violation of federal criminal laws was not found. Attorney General William French Smith weakened these guidelines in 1983, but the criminal law standard still applies. The effect of the Levi guidelines was to hasten a trend that had begun several years earlier with the realization, within the bureau, that most of its domestic security cases were worthless. From an estimated 160,000 open files on subversive matters in

1975, twelve years later there were about 25 full investigations continuing in the domestic security area.

Congressman Edwards added, "Among the FBI activities that we are now trying to stop are the recruitment of librarians as informants, a massive expansion of the FBI's computerized information-sharing system, the launching of undercover operations without court authorization and the lengthy delays and extensive excisions in response to Freedom of Information Act requests."

The latest threat—surveillance of library patrons—is another direct example of invasion of privacy that has nothing to do with radicals, liberals, conservatives or neoconservatives. The FBI calls it the "Library Awareness Program." The idea is to cultivate librarians to keep an eye on borrowers and see what they are reading, thereby turning librarians into informants. The FBI, of course, has a duty to discover foreign agents and possible terrorists. But to turn librarians into secret subagents is to break down the free library system in this country—a peacetime variation on the Vietnam War's cynical innocence: "The village had to be destroyed in order to save it."

In certain authoritarian countries we justifiably criticize, surveillance by neighbors and functionaries is assumed. But not here. The American Library Association has accused the FBI of attempting to infringe the First Amendment rights of library patrons. The association has warned its librarian-members to beware of approaches by federal agents trying to find out what use is being made of libraries by foreigners. The FBI wants to know what foreigners are gaining access to information that might be "potentially harmful to our national security." The librarians take the position that all library readers—even foreigners—have a right to keep what they read a private matter between reader and author.

At a modern reenactment of the First Continental Congress that was held in Philadelphia, the proposal was made that another constitutional amendment was needed "to guarantee forever that the people have the right to personal privacy and freedom from undue government interference." It's not a bad idea, but one that is hardly necessary. The "right to be let alone," for authors and everyone else with or without allegedly damning dossiers, is already there: in the spirit of the Constitution and in the minds of fearless men.

II.

POLICING AMERICA'S WRITERS

For a great part of the twentieth century, the federal government policed many of the most revered American authors and playwrights and also watched well-known writers from other countries who are read and admired here. Furthermore, the practice of maintaining dossiers that cast a shadow of criminality over certain prominent literary personalities continues up to our own time.

Few of these authors were aware that they had been tracked as suspicious characters—like foreign agents of some cold war state—for supposed crimes as serious as espionage and as vague as subversion. Yet documents that I have unearthed during the last several years under the Freedom of Information law, and through other sources, tell another story. Thousands of pages of government records in my possession, and official files that I have been allowed to read without disclosing their origin, reveal that these authors often came under suspicion because of the themes—fiction as well as fact—they chose for their books; professional writers' guilds they belonged to and writers' meetings they attended; petitions they signed and publications they subscribed to; and the places where they traveled in their own country and abroad.

Among them are authors who have received the Nobel Prize in Literature and the highest honors conferred for writing achievement in the United States: membership in the American Academy and Institute of Arts and Letters, and receipt of the National Book Award and the Pulitzer Prize. Of even greater significance, these authors have written books that are studied in almost every college classroom and are recognized throughout the world as a part of our cultural fabric and national heritage. In their ranks can be found some of the main shapers of American thought and literature.

To quickly note a mere dozen of these treasured authors—among the scores who have files (most of them still heavily censored)—that I have found during the course of my enquiry: Pearl S. Buck, Theodore Dreiser, William Faulkner, Dashiell Hammett, Ernest Hemingway, Sinclair Lewis, Thomas Mann, John Dos Passos, Carl Sandburg, John Steinbeck, Thornton Wilder, Tennessee Williams. And more.

What all of these icons of literature and learning have in common is a "record." It is maintained on them, to this day, by the Federal Bureau of Investigation and, in some cases, by other government agencies and archives in Washington. Under the Freedom of Information Act, I could only obtain the files of deceased authors; but, unofficially, I have seen government documents specifically listing many living authors and playwrights in internal security files. To respect their privacy, I do not include their names here. However, several old friends, including Bill Mauldin, the artist and author who won the Pulitzer Prize twice—for his wartime and more recent political cartoons—sent me their FBI files after reading my article on this theme in the New Yorker magazine entitled "Annals of Government: Policing America's Writers." E.L. Doctorow, the novelist, told me that to have a dossier in the company of the half-dozen Nobel laureates included here amounted to being on an American "honors list."

When I asked several of the most eminent authors in the United States if they thought they had an FBI record, one replied that it had never entered his mind that he might have a file but he had never tried to find out if one actually did exist. "I have always thought myself beyond criminality—too subversive for confinement in a pigeonhole or filing cabinet," he said. "But one never knows what others are thinking." (I have since found that his name does appear in an internal security file.) Another greatly honored American writer also answered that he had never asked to see if he had a file. "I guess I haven't yet wanted to look back on my own past," he said. "Maybe the day will come." (He, too, appears in an internal security file.) I recently obtained John Cheever's file. Surely it would have amazed the late novelist and New Yorker writer to learn that the CIA passed on to the FBI information that made him a subject of "internal security interest." The reason why is censored in the CIA document.

Of course, there is no official government stamp on what is written or printed in the United States. American authors are not subjected to Soviet-style psychological pressure to conform or exiled because of what they attempt to publish. Instead, in a book world increasingly dominated by American conglomerates and European ownership of New York publishing houses designed in part to circumvent foreign antitrust laws, American authors encounter economic pressures that also can seriously affect the contents of their writings.

Although no imprimatur is required here, a censorious, antilibertarian tone, emanating from the White House, reverberates through the federal government. It is particularly evident in the Department of Justice under Attorney General Edwin Meese—whose jurisdiction includes the Federal Bureau of Investigation. Rather late in the dusk of the second term of the Reagan administration, even naïve and sycophantic journalists and commentators have discovered that information and disinformation are regularly linked in statements provided to the press and the public; when caught, high-ranking officials hail deception as a necessary "bodyguard of lies."

In this atmosphere, book-branders and book-burners in ignorant and hypocritical corners of the land are encouraged to do their worst with evangelical fervor. The American Library Association keeps a long list of books that have been challenged, removed from school shelves or otherwise imprisoned—from *Huckleberry Finn* to *Slaughterhouse-Five,* from *The Wizard of Oz* to *The Diary of Anne Frank.* In an obscenity-obsessed time, coifed teleministers, dressed to kill, are courted politically; and with almost equal passion they condemn certain books while praising the Lord and the Defense Department's ammunition. The absurd list of banned books has lengthened during the Reagan era.

Today, authors' organizations and individual authors concerned with freedom of expression fear that certain themes—especially those of an investigatory nature that expose government policies or take on powerful companies that have unlimited funds for litigation—will be vetted and rendered comatose in advance of publication or even avoided altogether by publishers. They anticipate illiberal interpretations on libel and other writer perils from a Reagan-dominated Supreme Court of the future.

AGENT "T-10"

The attitude of the Reagan administration on the use of incriminating FBI files can be measured by the fact that Mr. Reagan himself surfaced as a onetime FBI source with a code number of his own: Confidential Informant "T-10." He has not denied the facts found in a 1985 report, based upon Justice Department records obtained under a Freedom of Information request, that originally appeared in the San Jose *Mercury News,* a California daily, and was underplayed or ignored nationally. The documents apparently were released after four decades because of Mr. Reagan's public status and because there were no high-level objections to what could be interpreted, by Mr. Meese's Justice Department and the White House's spear carriers, as politically admirable and advantageous. As I write, before me is the 156-page heavily blacked-out file of "Ronald Reagan, Movie Actor."

These documents disclose that at the same time Mr. Reagan was active in the Screen Actors Guild in the 1940s and its elected president in 1947 he had played a second, real-life role as an informer against his own professional colleagues. J. Edgar Hoover had passed on information to George Murphy, another actor who later went to Washington as a senator from California, about Communists taking over Hollywood. Murphy told Reagan. Thereafter, Reagan was visited by three FBI agents (Reagan described them only as representatives of "a well-known government agency"). "I got to admire these men: they never accused anyone of being a Communist unless they had every last bit of evidence which would stand up against the most vicious court assault," Reagan wrote. "They were extremely careful never to smear anyone or guess even on good but less than complete evidence." To protect himself against alleged enemies during labor unrest in Hollywood while he was busy in the Screen Actors Guild, Reagan carried a loaded .32 caliber Smith & Wesson pistol concealed in a shoulder holster, as he noted in his book, *Where's the Rest of Me?* The future governor and president said, "I learned how much a person gets to lean on hardware like that."

Mr. Reagan's name first appeared on an FBI document in 1941, when an agent in the Los Angeles bureau cited him as a source with whom he had become "intimately acquainted." Another document mentions that he and his then wife, actress Jane Wyman, were interviewed by the FBI in 1947 about the Hollywood Independent Citizens Committee of the Arts, Sciences and Professions. Mr. Reagan had quit that organization the year before because of its alleged Communist leadership. The Reagans provided the FBI with "information regarding the activities of some members of the [Screen Actors] Guild who they suspected were carrying on Communist party work."

The FBI memorandum said: "Reagan and Jane Wyman advised [that] for the past several months there are two cliques of members, one headed by [name deleted] and [name deleted] which on all questions of policy that confront the Guild follow the Communist party line."

Confidential Informant "T-10" was particularly active, while Guild president, secretly working for the FBI and the Hollywood producers behind the backs of his fellow actors. In 1947, an FBI memorandum stated:

"T-10 advised Special Agent [name deleted] that he has been made a member of a committee headed by Mayer [Louis B. Mayer, head of MGM], the purpose of which allegedly is to 'purge' the motion-picture industry of Communist party members, which committee was an outgrowth of the Thomas [Representative J. Parnell Thomas, New Jersey Republican, chairman of the House Committee on Un-American Activities] committee hearings in Washington and subsequent meetings of motion-picture producers in New York City.

"T-10 stated it is his firm conviction that Congress should declare, first of all, by statute, that the Communist party is not a legal party, but is a foreign-inspired conspiracy. Secondly, Congress should define what organizations are Communist-controlled so that membership therein could be construed as an indication of disloyalty. He felt that lacking a definite stand on the part of the government, it would be very difficult for any committee of motion-picture people to conduct any type of cleansing of their own household."

Spurred on by its president, the Screen Actors Guild passed a resolution in 1947 asking members to sign an affidavit saying that they were not Communists before they could be eligible to hold any Guild office. Despite the resolve and cooperation of Mr. Reagan, FBI Director J. Edgar Hoover expressed his dissatisfaction with a report from his Los Angeles bureau on the motion-picture industry. He scrawled a note across the bottom: "It is outrageous that House Un-American Activities Committee got 'cold feet' and dropped Hollywood investigation. The picture industry still continues to be a stinking mess."

Contributing to this judgment—because of his role as a conduit to the FBI while simultaneously furthering his career with the studio heads—was Confidential Informant "T-10."

THE PROFESSIONALS

Although I am acquainted with many writers, here and abroad, and have served as a president of the Authors Guild, it came as a shock to me that such extensive records had been maintained on the nation's most influential men and women of letters. But I was not surprised to learn that the Authors Guild, the Dramatists Guild and the Authors League were all investigated by the FBI.

The Authors Guild is a voluntary organization established early in this century that includes most of the professional book writers in the country. It is linked to the Dramatists Guild, which includes most of the country's professional playwrights. Together the two guilds make up the Authors League of America, which came into existence in 1912. Among authors and dramatists who have served as president of the guilds or league are Oscar Hammerstein II, Pearl S. Buck, William L. Shirer, Rex Stout, John Hersey, Moss Hart, Elmer Rice, Leon Edel, Elizabeth Janeway, Harrison E. Salisbury, John Brooks and Madeleine L'Engle.

In addition to establishing professional standards, for many years the three organizations have defended the First Amendment and freedom of expression before Congress, the courts and the country. They have gone on record against blacklisting by the television networks and the Hollywood studios. At least since the beginning of the cold war, the reign of terror of the House Un-American Activities Committee and Senator McCarthy's governmental inquisition, the guilds and league have been watched.

Responding to my request, William M. Baker, the FBI's assistant director, Office of Congressional and Public Affairs, admitted: "The investigation relating to these organizations was conducted to determine whether or not there was Communist influence, infiltration or control in these groups. In January of 1956 the case was closed due to the lack of information indicating Communist party activity."

Nevertheless, the files on the three organizations—including their leadership and positions on freedom and other issues—continue to exist in Washington. Those affiliated with these professional organizations, in the past and present, remain names in government files. False records are rarely corrected or purged; in the wrong hands in Washington, these authors and dramatists are not above suspicion.

The dossiers on individual authors and dramatists indicate that, in some cases, they were hounded for years. Once accused by unnamed informants, their activities or appearances in print were monitored up to and sometimes even after their deaths. What the files do not disclose is that careers were hobbled and lives unhinged because of these records—and that the authors did not know they were under government surveillance, and could not challenge their accusers because of what they had said, signed or written.

This additional point must be underscored: despite the tens of millions of dollars spent in investigative man-hours and recordkeeping to spy on authors—time and effort and funds that might otherwise have been devoted to pursuing real lawbreakers in violation of United States codes—not one of the more than a hundred men and women whose names appear in these dossiers was ever convicted of any of the suspected crimes attributed to them by the FBI or other investigative agencies.

One of the freedoms any American is believed to enjoy—if not specifically in the Bill of Rights, then in the due process clause of the Fourteenth Amendment and by adjudicated law—is the freedom not to have a dossier kept on him. Freedom of expression and freedom to write cannot exist unfettered if files are maintained by federal investigative arms on what authors say on platforms or in their books. In a time of officially ordained antilibertarianism in the White House and Justice Department—implicitly endorsed by toadying neoconservative foundations, columnists and publications—there can hardly be clean finger-pointing at the condition of writers in those countries where authors and their words are routinely policed and censored.

No statute of limitations exists on police mentality and administrative bureaucracy in the FBI or elsewhere in Washington. The officeholders change; the files continue. Which is why yesterday's outrages can serve as tomorrow's cautionary tales.

IN THE WEB: E.B. WHITE

After E.B. White died in October, 1985, I had a farfetched notion: to see if he—of all beloved American writers—had a file kept on him in Washington. Because of his children's books, *Charlotte's Web* and *Stuart Little,* his guide to clear and forceful writing, *Elements of Style,* and his bold editorial comments and essays in the New Yorker that are studied as models of independence and individuality, he was universally regarded as one of the most influential writers of our time. His honors included a Presidential Medal of Freedom from President Kennedy (which he later declined to accept in person from President Johnson in Washington). In the "Notes and Comments" column in the New Yorker in 1953 he had attacked Senator Joseph McCarthy and McCarthyism in this fashion:

"[A] very great majority of loyal Americans are deeply worried, not because they have a skeleton in their closet or because they disapprove of fact-finding in Congress, but because they see and feel in their daily lives the subtle change that has already been worked by a runaway loyalty-checking system in the hands of a few men who, to say it in a whisper, are not ideally equipped to handle the most delicate and dangerous job in the nation, that is, the questioning of values of one's fellow citizens. A couple of these committeemen [Senator McCarthy was chairman of the Permanent Subcommittee on Investigations] don't know a fact from a bag of popcorn anyway."

A year later, when Senator McCarthy was riding high on network television during his investigation of disloyalty in the army, White again wrote a "Talk of the Town" column, saying that the junior senator from Wisconsin had "succeeded only in making the country less secure" and in keeping the nation "in an uproar just when it should have a firm grasp on itself." White's daring words were read by newspaper editorial writers and television news commentators who did not have the courage, or the approval of their publishers and station owners, to be as boldly outspoken as the New Yorker during the McCarthy era. What some future historians would call the "hidden-hand" presidency of General Eisenhower also remained hidden from the American public and press at that time when it might have most counted.

During this period there were strong links between McCarthy and Hoover. Hoover's disinherited heir apparent, William C. Sullivan, who had served in the FBI for thirty years, wrote him a bitter letter in 1971, saying that "you had us preparing material for McCarthy regularly, kept furnishing it to him while you denied publicly that we were helping him." E.B. White proved prescient about the McCarthy-Hoover relationship. Undoubtedly noted by the FBI, McCarthy's staff and senatorial committee members in Washington were these words by White:

"The twenty-years-of-treason junket, the use of the word 'guilt' in hearing rooms where nobody is on trial and where no judge sits, the Zwicker inquisition, the willingness to shatter an army to locate a dentist, the sly substitution of the name 'Alger' for the name 'Adlai,' the labeling of the majority of the press as 'extreme Left Wing,' the distortion of facts and figures, the challenge of the power of the White House, the use of the grand elision in the phrase 'Fifth Amendment

Communists,' the queer notion that he, and he alone, is entitled to receive raw information that it is illegal for others to have in their possession, the steady attack on national confidence and national faith, as though confidence were evil and suspicion were good—the score is familiar and need not be recited in its long detail. Whatever else can be said for and against the senator, it has become obvious that he dislikes a great many things about our form of government. To disapprove of those well-loved principles and rules is not a crime, but neither is it a help in performing the duties of a committee chairman in the United States Senate."

After waiting for several months, I received a letter from Emil P. Moschella, the chief of the FBI's Freedom of Information-Privacy Acts Section, Records Management Division, saying that there was "no information to indicate that E.B. White was ever the subject of an investigation by this bureau."

This ambiguously worded response was typical of those that I had obtained regarding other authors. Such phrasing, I had discovered, did not necessarily mean that E.B. White's name was not in a government police file; rather, that no deep check had been made on his activities by the bureau. The phrase, which I had seen before for other authors, was a covering device to protect the FBI that went back to Mr. Hoover's long, authoritarian rule. Mr. Moschella then added that he had located two pages on E.B. White in a "miscellaneous file."

One of the two file-pages was devoted to: "Subject: White, Elwyn Brooks." It was dated August 2, 1956. The category, checked against certain possible references in his file in the Records section, was listed as: "Main: Subv. References Only & Summaries." No explanation was offered by the FBI about why the search was only confined to a "Subv." (that is, subver-

In 1947, while he was president of the Screen Actors Guild, Ronald Reagan testified on communism in Hollywood before the House Committee on Un-American Activities. At the same time—and unknown to the membership of the Guild—he was an informant for the FBI, under the code name "Agent T-10." In 1987, President Reagan, in the aftermath of Iran-Contra revelations that exposed the lawlessness in his Administration, spoke nostalgically of the need for a return of the discredited House Committee on Un-American Activities.

6

Reagan – "T-10"
Wyman – "T-9"

CONFIDENTIAL

LA 100-15732

does not pertain to request

b7D

C. The Screen Actors' Guild

On December 3, 1947, Source T-9, a well known motion picture actress, advised the following information:

The Screen Actors' Guild appears to be waging a successful fight to keep out radical actors and actresses from executive positions. She said that there were a few, however, who mysteriously seemed to remain in positions of prominence within the organization, which enabled the radical group to bring about discord. Some of the radical actors and actresses identified as possible Communists were [redacted]

[redacted] was of the opinion that RONALD REAGAN, executive officer of the Guild, had "seen the light" and was sincere in his efforts to keep the radical members out of controlling positions.

b7C

does not pertain to request

b7C,D

b7C,D

CONFIDENTIAL

-22-

100-138754-367

Agent "T-9" was Jane Wyman, then wife of Agent "T-10," Ronald Reagan, president of the Screen Actors Guild. In this internal FBI memorandum between the Los Angeles office of the FBI and Washington headquarters, Mr. Reagan is identified as having "seen the light." While supposedly representing the actors, he was reporting on their political beliefs to the FBI as an informant.

E.B. White, author of the children's books *Charlotte's Web* and *Stuart Little*, and an outstanding advocate of the right of privacy in the pages of The New Yorker, wrote of the McCarthy Senate Subcommittee on Investigations that its committeemen "don't know a fact from a bag of popcorn." The FBI checked him at one point as a possible "Subv." (Subversive). He is shown here at his farm in North Brooklin, Maine.

Herbert Mitgang

Fede. Bureau of Investigation
Records Section

______________, 1956

- [ ] Name Check Unit - Room 6523
- [ ] Service Unit - Room 6524
- [ ] Forward to File Review
- [ ] Attention ______________
- [ ] Return to ______________

Supervisor Room Ext.

Type of References Requested:

- [ ] Regular Request (Analytical Search)
- [ ] All References (Subversive & Nonsubversive)
- [ ] Subversive References Only
- [ ] Nonsubvessive References Only
- [x] Main *Subv.* References Only

+ summaries

Type of Search Requested:

- [ ] Restricted to Locality of ______________
- [ ] Exact Name Only (On the Nose)
- [ ] Buildup [ ] Variations
- [ ] Check for Alphabetical Loyalty Form

Subject *White, Elwyn Brooks*
Birthdate & Place ______________
Address ______________

Localities ______________

R ______ Date *8/2* Searcher Initials *L71*

FILE NUMBER SERIAL

NR
Elwyn B.
NR
Elwyn
NR
E.B.
NR
E. Brooks
NR
Brooks
NR

A page from E.B. White's FBI file. Arrow points to notation indicating a search was made to see if he was a subversive.

sive) file. In any case, *this particular page in his record was more than thirty years old.*

A second page, dated August 8, 1956, clarified somewhat his record. It indicated that a "name-check" had been requested on him by the United States Information Agency and a search made in the FBI's "main files only." The reason for the request for an FBI file-check was for a presidential program called "People-to-People Partnership." The document noted: "The foregoing information is furnished to you as a result of your request for an FBI file-check and is not to be construed as a clearance or a nonclearance of the individual involved. This information is furnished for your use and should not be disseminated outside of your agency."

By his brief FBI dossier (assuming that this was all that did indeed exist on him, which I cannot say with certainty), even an E.B. White could not be, strictly speaking, considered altogether "clean."

Although I made a further inquiry about the possibility that his name might be found in a nonsubversive file, the FBI did not respond. The documents on him showed no knowledge of his life or career. They simply stated that he had been born on July 11, 1899, in Mount Vernon, New York. Next to his name someone had written, in ink or pencil, "author."

In at least one respect the hollowness of his file was truly astonishing. It contained no reference to anything that he had ever written. Apparently the New Yorker was not on the FBI's required reading list. Of greater significance, his record was maintained even after his death. After calling the FBI's Records Management division, I was told that his death normally would not be noted, unless someone happened to clip a notice of his obituary from a newspaper, since he was not regarded as a well-known public figure.

I could not help wishing that E.B. White was still around to make a lighthearted subversive comment—for he was one of the most "subversive" writers in the country when it came to any government or corporate intrusion, especially by record-keeping, upon any American's personal freedom—had he discovered that he was a possible "Subv." in Mr. Hoover's book.

HALF-FREEDOM FILES

In nearly all the documents I obtained under the Freedom of Information Act, material is blacked out. The usual reason given for such censorship—or denying of access altogether—is an all-encompassing clause in Title 5 of the United States Code, Section 552 (b) (1) that reads: "Information which is currently and properly classified pursuant to Executive Order 12356 in the interest of national defense or foreign policy, for example, information involving intelligence sources or methods." But there are a dozen other exemptions that can be used to censor material in a dossier.

Whenever such documents were blacked out (actually, a brown ink, which appears gray-black on photocopies, is used by those censoring the FBI files before deciding they can be partially released), I appealed to a subdivision of the Department of Justice's Office of Legal Policy, the Office of Information and Privacy. My grounds for appeal usually were that the authors or playwrights were public figures and had never been accused or convicted of any crimes. Occasionally my routine letters of appeal resulted in the release of a few more pages. Under the law the FBI, CIA and other agencies had to offer "judicial review" of their rulings in the United States District Court in which the petitioner resides or in the District of Columbia. But I did not avail myself of this costly judicial review because a case could continue for years on the federal calendars and, even if successful, might produce only some zealous person's concept of secrecy on a document of relative unimportance.

The degree of compliance with my requests varied greatly in time and in what was provided. Generally there has been more delay and stonewalling during the Reagan presidency. Sometimes the FBI was more helpful than the CIA or State Department. For instance, in the case of a thirty-five-year-old document concerning Pearl S. Buck, the Nobel laureate, it took almost two-and-a-half years after my appeal before the State Department would release it. In some cases I am still waiting to receive records more than a year after the FBI acknowledged that a file did exist.

President Reagan's Executive Order 12356, issued in 1982, slowed down the declassification process and access to information. The order eliminated previous requirements that government officials must consider the public's right to know before classifying documents, and that classification must be based on "identifiable" potential damage to the national security. The order also eliminated the ban on reclassification of documents and information already released; created a presumption that intelligence sources and methods were classified; removed the requirement that doubts be resolved in favor of declassification, and curtailed declassification review practices in the National Archives and all executive agencies and departments.

The Freedom of Information Act was further tightened by President Reagan and his attorney general in October, 1986. A revision in the law gave law-enforcement agencies new authority to withhold documents that, in their view, might compromise certain investigations. In one of the key provisions, agencies for the first time were given authority to refuse either to confirm or deny that certain records existed at all. Fortunately, most of my requests under the Act were made before this revision; even where material was withheld or blacked out, at least I was informed that a file did exist.

In effect, these changes have caused a partial gutting of the Freedom of Information Act that, originally, came into existence in the wake of Watergate's revelations about domestic surveillance and lawbreaking during the Nixon administration.

Among the experts I consulted to confirm some of my findings was Athan G. Theoharis, professor of History at Marquette University, who served as a consultant to Senator Frank Church's Select Committee to Study Governmental Operations with Respect to Intelligence Activities, which issued its final report in 1976. Professor Theoharis, author of *Spying on Americans: Political Surveillance from Hoover to the Houston Plan,* recently told me:

"I can't say with certainty that similar espionage on authors and other Americans is not going on today. The bureau once tried to shape public opinion. Some, but not all, of the files were purified. I'm sure there has been a down-scaling of Freedom of Information Act requests that have been fulfilled under the Reagan administration. I think that the FBI under William Webster was more wholesome than during the reign of J. Edgar Hoover. But I wouldn't be surprised if the FBI is still pursuing some of the old cases. One thing about investigations—they never seem to die."

Congressional aides and attorneys working in the field of justice and privacy told me that no matter who serves as attorney general or FBI director, the patterns of the past are deeply embedded in the bureau. The dossiers on authors continue to exist and tell their own sad tales. They are alarm bells that reverberate for the future through the dark corners of government.

III.

THE NOBEL LAUREATES

Among America's Nobel laureates in literature whose FBI files I was able to obtain were: Sinclair Lewis (who received the award in 1930); Pearl S. Buck (1938); William Faulkner (1949); Ernest Hemingway (1954); John Steinbeck (1962); and Thomas Mann (the German-born novelist who won the prize in 1929, left Nazi Germany and emigrated to the United States in 1938, and became an American citizen in 1944).

SINCLAIR LEWIS

Sinclair Lewis (1885–1951) had no fewer than 150 pages in his dossier. It was heavily censored. A 1951 document stamped *Secret* said that subject's name was also found as S. Lewis, Sinclaire Lewis and Saint Clair Lewis. FBI agents are not necessarily novel readers, a notion that struck me as somewhat contradictory since so many of the files revealed that, in some cases, the bureau labored assiduously in the realm of fiction.

The Nobel laureate—the first American author to be so honored—came out of Sauk Centre, Minnesota, and frequently found his themes in smalltown hypocrisy and puritanism. *Main Street, Babbitt, Arrowsmith, Dodsworth* and *Elmer Gantry* all portrayed a changing America that bore little resemblance to the roseate glow of *Saturday Evening Post* covers. Then, in the 1930s, Lewis warned against homegrown fascism taking root in the White House in his novel *It Can't Happen Here.*

There is at least one revelation in the Lewis file that indicates the FBI chief's political predilections: the author was among those who were being watched by the FBI because of his support of President Franklin D. Roosevelt's wartime fourth term.

The FBI also took peripheral interest in a book club and its subscribers because Lewis was involved with it. When "The Reader's Club" was starting, an FBI report—also on a page stamped *Secret*—noted that on March 5, 1941, it received an open letter on the letterhead of "Clifton Fadiman, Sinclair Lewis, Carl Van Doren, Alexander Woollcott," from 41 East 57th Street, New York, enclosing a four-page circular. It said that these "famous men of books" will help you discover some of the best already-published books for only one dollar a copy.

Over a year later, on July 17, 1942, the FBI was still keeping tabs on this club and its bookmen. The documents reveal that the FBI used false names as subscribers to the club in order to find out what was being published and by whom. The FBI's Birmingham bureau received two letters with two pamphlets enclosed that solicited membership. "Since the letters were addressed to the fictitious names used by the bureau for subscriptions," reads the page stamped *Secret,* "it appeared that the publication 'In Fact' furnished a mailing list to 'The Reader's Club.' "

In censoring the Lewis material that I received, apparently someone forgot to cross out the fact that false names were used as subscribers and that the Birmingham bureau was used to receive the book club data. Usually the FBI and other intelligence agencies censored anything that revealed internal methods. (This writer had some small knowledge about these procedures, having served in a wartime air force counterintelligence unit at an airfield in the States that used coded names and afterward, in North Africa, handled American and Allied secret documents.) The 'In Fact' referred to was an iconoclastic newsletter, edited and published by George Seldes, that started in 1940 and regularly criticized the shortcomings of the American press for the next ten years before winking out.

The report on the book club continued: "From a review of these pamphlets, it appeared that 'The Reader's Club' would be similar in operation to the well-known 'Book of the Month Club.' The committee designated to select the books that were to be made available to the members of the club included Sinclair Lewis."

It is noteworthy that the FBI was doing this at a time when America had already gone to war and, presumably, all its governmental resources were directed toward building the armed forces and tracking pro-Nazi and pro-Fascist groups in the United States, not pursuing book-club judges.

An early entry in the Lewis dossier was made almost by accident in 1936, the year after his novel *It Can't Happen Here* was published. J. Edgar Hoover invited Lewis and his wife to take a special tour of the bureau. In a friendly letter three years later Hoover sent Lewis his fingerprint impressions and two photographs that were placed in the "civil files of the Bureau"—as a souvenir. Lewis cordially thanked him.

An internal FBI memorandum written in 1939 by L.B. Nichols, a top Hoover aide, quoted Lewis as saying that "Mr. Hoover would make a great fictional character for a novel depicting what can be done through the application of intelligence, training and science." In passing, the FBI noted that "Lewis does not reside with his wife"—that he lived at the Hotel Lombardy in Manhattan, while his wife, the columnist Dorothy Thompson, lived at 88 Central Park West, telephone TRafalgar 4-4121.

In addition to noting the divided marital arrangement, the FBI was not above reporting a little domestic gossip as, no doubt, a part of its domestic intelligence to protect the United States from its enemies. When Mr. Nichols said that sometimes Miss Thompson had not spoken favorably about the FBI, Mr. Lewis said that if she also visited the bureau they should first butter her up, indicating that was his own style. Lewis advised: "In greeting her she should be told by the person who is designated to see her that he enjoys reading her writings, admires her, that her columns are thought-provoking, even though he does not believe everything she writes, and then 'proceed to give Hitler hell,' whereupon she would get her peeve against Hitler out of her system and would then settle down and enjoy herself for the day."

Lewis then felt the need to classify himself as a liberal but said there was "a line between liberalism and communism." He said that he now feels badly if the *Daily Worker* does not castigate him at least once a week. From the tone of the memorandum the FBI and Lewis were both complimenting each other. Lewis was told that Hoover emphasized "civil liberties" and urged law enforcement "to respect the rights of others." As part of its image-making with a celebrity, the FBI provided Lewis and his niece, Marcella Powers, with a car and driver for a pleasure trip to Mount Vernon.

But suddenly, in 1940, the FBI's attitude toward Lewis

changed. The bureau's Philadelphia office received information from one (censored) that apparently concerned possible espionage activities by Sinclair Lewis. In addition, the office noted: "[name blacked out] novelist, Sinclair Lewis, are active as organizers for Communist party." In the same year the Cleveland office also raised the matter of "Espionage, Subversive Activities" by Lewis. The matter was dropped after the informant failed to produce evidence. Although Hoover said that no further investigation was needed and the espionage matter be considered closed, it was not. Eleven years later, Hoover passed on information (censored) about Lewis to the army chief of Intelligence at the Pentagon. Air Force Intelligence also tracked the author.

In a 1941 entry, a special agent of the FBI reported that after Lewis spoke at a Jewish temple in Jacksonville, Florida, he engaged in a gambling game at a "notorious joint" where he lost 160 dollars and was drunk. Lewis reported his loss to the police and tried to get his money back. He did not press charges in what the FBI called a "flim flam."

Despite the surface friendliness in the past, in 1947 the FBI got involved in the subject and contents of one of his novels, *Kingsblood Royal.* A letter from a correspondent in Madera, California, called Mr. Hoover's attention to the novel, branding it "the most incendiary book" since *Uncle Tom's Cabin.* The communique to Assistant Attorney General Theron L. Caudle advised that *Kingsblood Royale* (sic) was published by Random House, was deemed by an informant to be "incendiary" because "Lewis discusses the Negro question in a manner which, according to [name censored], is intended to inflame Negroes against whites. The book was stated to be 'propaganda for the white man's acceptance of the Negro as a social equal.' "

Clearly subversive stuff.

The Senate Internal Security Committee, then headed by

Senator Patrick McCarran, was given material in 1951 stamped *Secret* and labeled "Re: Sinclair Lewis Security Matter—C." (Senator McCarran was coauthor of the McCarran-Walter Act that is used to bar entry to foreign authors who are considered dangerous because of their political beliefs and writings.) The Lewis paragraphs that might explain why he was a "C" (FBI shorthand for Communist) security case are blacked out. The censored document says that "no reference should be made to the McCarran Committee nor should there be any indication that the documents emanated from G-2."

This G-2 (Army Intelligence) source revealed that a detailed investigation had been made into Lewis' affiliations and writings for a long time—possibly even longer than the FBI's surveillance. One reference going back to 1928 showed that Lewis was a member of an international committee endorsing an announcement by the Viking Press, which published *The Letters of Sacco and Vanzetti.* A 1929 bulletin was found stating that Lewis' name appeared as a member of a book committee of the American Society for Cultural Relations with Russia. A Los Angeles report to the FBI named him as a member of various committees for cultural exchange with Russia. A 1929 pamphlet was discovered, entitled "Cheap and Contented Labor," written and copyrighted by Lewis and published by the United Textile Workers of America and Women's Trade Union League, Philadelphia. In the pamphlet Lewis wrote that "there could only be one answer on the part of workers—a militant and universal organization of trade unions." The page on which this observation appeared (which foretold the mainstream Congress of Industrial Organizations) was stamped *Secret.*

In 1930—the year Lewis received the Nobel Prize—his name turned up before a Special Committee to Investigative Communistic Activities in the House of Representatives, 71st Congress, because he was listed as a member and correspondent of the Federated Press, which published Labor News. It was also stamped *Secret.* The same House committee named him a member of the American Birth Control League, which published the Birth Control Review—and this, *too,* was stamped *Secret* in his file.

While supposedly investigating Communists, the House committee listed four of Lewis' books—*Elmer Gantry, Main Street, Babbitt* and *Arrowsmith*—as suspect because they were distributed by the Workers Library. This library, which put out inexpensive paperback editions for workers, was described as a means of "awakening organization, leading the masses in their struggle against the bosses, against the misleaders of labor, and against the system that is at the root of exploitation, oppression and war." Obviously no one had read the four Lewis novels to see if their themes matched the grandiose aims of the Workers Library. But the novels became tarred by association.

During the Spanish Civil War, authors siding with the democratically elected republican government against *Generalissimo* Franco's insurgents—who were backed up by Mussolini's Fascist troops and tanks and Hitler's Nazi bombers—became suspect, at least to the FBI and other so-called Red-hunting agencies. (In this respect, little has changed; to the neoconservatives of the 1980s, baldly trying to rewrite history, those who sided with the Loyalists against Franco's columns are considered naïve and suspect.)

Sinclair Lewis' name was flagged as a member of the North American Committee to Aid Spanish Democracy and also as a sponsor of the Motion Picture Artists (Spanish Aid) for medical help to the Loyalists. His file shows that, during that war, his name appeared in an advertisement in the New York *Times* in 1937, appealing for contributions to buy medical supplies for the American Base Hospital outside Madrid.

Scores of other American and British writers supported the Loyalists; some went there to report and bear witness, others, to die in battle.

To the Lewis file in 1939 was added an article from People's World, in which he praised his wife, Miss Thompson, for her verbal slap against the German-American Bund and its leader, Fritz Kuhn, who conducted a pro-Nazi meeting in New York. Lewis is quoted: "These gangsters are trying to corrupt America. It is astounding that such meetings are permitted in this country. What will happen next?" Lewis' anti-Nazi stand entered his file.

Several documents, the sources unnamed in the file, report that his play version of *It Can't Happen Here* was controversial and opposed in some communities. (Praise for a book or play is rarely found in the government files on authors and playwrights.)

A New York bureau memorandum to Hoover reported that on September 21, 1944, a rally was held at Madison Square Garden sponsored by the Independent Voters Committee of the Arts and Sciences for President Roosevelt. Why a political campaign, out in the open, should have been the concern of the FBI appears puzzling—unless it is understood that the FBI was engaged in its own cold war crusade during World War II and before the actual cold war began in the postwar years. This is how the FBI reported the event, as it appears in the Lewis file on a page stamped *Secret*:

"At this meeting Sinclair Lewis was reported to have criticized Thomas E. Dewey [Governor Dewey of New York, the Republican presidential candidate], saying that despite Roosevelt being referred to as a tired old man, Roosevelt had accomplished more in one month than Dewey could in a year. He said that he believed that the reason Winston Churchill and Joseph Stalin were such sincere friends of America was because of President Roosevelt."

The mere reading of Sinclair Lewis' novels aroused suspicion. A Kansas City bureau report stated that (censored) was a Communist party sympathizer because he "assigned Sinclair Lewis' *Babbitt* to his class as a 'masterpiece' for reading." Once Lewis' name was on the FBI watch-list, even a book review about one of his novels was placed in the file. In 1947, the Boston Bureau noted that *Kingsblood Royal* was reviewed in Temple Israel, in Hull, Massachusetts, in a program sponsored by the American Jewish Congress. Incredibly, the book review is stamped *Secret.* Similarly, the Los Angeles bureau forwarded to Washington a leaflet called "The Scourge of Bigotry." It linked Laura Z. Hobson's *Gentlemen's Agreement* and Sinclair Lewis' *Kingsblood Royal* as the latest recruits of an organization called Friends of Democracy, that "allegedly fights native Fascist groups, Communists and other enemies of democracy."

The FBI was not the only agency keeping an eye on Lewis. Abroad, he was watched by military intelligence. In 1950, he came under surveillance by the Office of Special Investigations, the Inspector General, Department of the Air Force. In a report stamped *Secret* the directorate of Intelligence, Headquarters USAF, notes: "The files of several reliable government agencies reflect Sinclair Lewis to be a member and sponsor of many Communist-front organizations, including the American Society for Cultural Relations with Russia, Motion Picture Artists Committee, North American Committee to Aid Spanish Democracy and the Medical Bureau to Aid Spanish Democracy."

By 1951, the Lewis file had grown so "voluminous" that the FBI recommended that the material about him be placed in the "Correlation Section." A summary had been prepared that showed "no information indicating that Sinclair Lewis has been involved in espionage activities or that any current espionage investigation is warranted. All available data on

Sinclair Lewis has been referred to the Internal Security Unit in the form of a correlation summary for a determination as to whether an investigation of Lewis is warranted."

The Lewis documents fail to show whether or not such an investigation was ever made—or how long surveillance of the American Nobel laureate and his writings continued—before his death that year. After tracking him for a quarter of a century in his own country and in Europe, the FBI, the army and the air force failed to catch their man doing anything illegal. They might, more profitably, have read his books.

PEARL S. BUCK

The file on Pearl S. Buck (1892–1973) is even thicker than that of Sinclair Lewis. Although 203 pages were released to me, I was denied 77 pages. In addition to the FBI files, her name appears in records of the State Department, army and navy. After I made appeals for the denied material, the army supplied a few more pages; the navy refused to give up anything.

Her novel, *The Good Earth,* was widely admired because of its human portrait of the Chinese people. One additional matter is worth mentioning with respect to Miss Buck: she once served as a president of the Authors Guild, with a strong personal belief (that I heard her express several times in her apartment in Manhattan at Authors Guild Council meetings) about the organization's aims of protecting and advancing the rights of American writers. It is now known that the Authors Guild, and many of its members, came under FBI scrutiny during her lifetime.

Miss Buck's file begins in 1938, the same year that she won the Nobel Prize. Like Lewis, she was invited by Mr.

Hoover to take a special tour of FBI facilities in Washington. His invitation mentioned that he admired her novel. It is not known if she ever took up his offer; he invited many celebrities and journalists to see the headquarters, especially if there was a chance thereby to promote himself and his domain. (Hoover, like Reagan, was a master of photo opportunity.)

In any case, Pearl Buck aroused the FBI in 1941 and 1942 after they discovered that she had written articles for the Post War World Council entitled "Freedom for All." The pamphlet with these articles found their way into her FBI dossier. In one section she wrote: "The discriminations of the American army and navy and air forces against colored soldiers and sailors, the exclusion of colored labor in our defense industries and trade unions, all our social discriminations, are of the greatest aid today to our enemy in Asia, Japan."

Underlined passages cover her point of white exploitation of Asians and repeat the theme of Japanese propaganda that colored troops are exploited. Her warning was against race prejudice. Miss Buck's prescient remarks—that even after victory in World War II colonialism would have to end because "the deep patience of colored peoples is at an end"—caused someone in the FBI to write "Sabotage" and "Lies" over her words, again and again.

After the end of the war Mr. Hoover no longer offered the red-carpet treatment. Instead, a background check was made on her in 1946 that spelled out every detail of her life, affiliations, marriage, divorce, children and publications where her work appeared. Now she was referred to as "the well-known authoress."

The blacked-out report that I obtained more than ten years after her death is marked *Confidential.* It accused her of having "Communist affiliation" in these words: "Although it is not believed from the information available that Miss Buck is a Communist, her active support of all programs advocating racial equality has led her to associate with many known Communists and other individuals of varying shades of political opinions."

Her membership in the American Civil Liberties Union was listed under "Communist-Front Organizations." The ACLU was and is anything but, yet racial equality and civil liberties remained dirty and suspicious words in the FBI lexicon.

Like many distinguished American authors during World War II who wished to enlist their talents in the cause of freedom even if they were not eligible to serve in uniform, Pearl Buck was a member of the Writers' War Board. Its chairman was Rex Stout, creator of the Nero Wolfe detective novels and wartime president of the Authors Guild. This is how the voluntary board is described—and individual authors and the Authors League stigmatized—in the FBI files:

"The Writers' War Board was formed in December, 1941, by a group of members of the Authors League of America, Inc., to serve as a means by which members of the Authors League of America could aid in the war effort. [The next seven lines are censored.] Such members as Pearl S. Buck, Clifton Fadiman, Quentin Reynolds, Louis Adamic, Louis Bromfield, Dorothy Canfield Fisher, Carl Van Doren and Clifford Odets are familiar in this regard [referring to the blacked-out lines]. It is significant to note that the name of Langston Hughes appears with the advisory council. On August 10, 1943, the Writers' War Board arranged a radio forum broadcast on the subject, 'Can America get along with Russia now and after the war?' Arthur Upham Pope and Walter Duranty were the speakers. These two men are well known for their pro-Russian sympathies. Pope [censored] has written articles for the *Daily Worker* [the Communist party newspaper]."

Miss Buck's mail was watched. Her file reads: "On May 25 and July 4, 1944, the Office of Censorship advised the bureau that Pearl S. Buck had received copies of the publication 'Voks' through the mail from Soviet Russia."

Even a comic strip was studied by the FBI and became a suspicious fact in her dossier: "The East and West Association, of which Pearl Buck is president, cooperates in the preparation of a comic sheet entitled 'The Twain Shall Meet.' This copyrighted feature has for its purpose the featuring of understanding between peoples of the world. While no information has been received that this comic strip is Communist propaganda, it is definitely the type of material the Communist party would capitalize on and use if possible."

The FBI also kept an eye on the books Miss Buck wrote—as well as on those who read them. Her file reads: *"Fighting Angel* in 1942 was on the approved reading list of an organization known as the Southern School for Workers. This school was reportedly organized and operated by the Communist party." Nevertheless, in 1952, the FBI decided not to place her on its "Security Index" because no evidence was found that "subject has advocated overthrow of the government of the United States." This boilerplate language, applied to her life and career, displayed total ignorance of Miss Buck's writings.

Thinking, as usual, of its own public image, the FBI noted in a memorandum from the Philadelphia office to Hoover in Washington: "No interview is contemplated at this time since it is felt that such an interview of a person of Miss Buck's prominence might result in repercussions and adverse publicity for the bureau." However, the FBI refused to give up its opinions, as if to prove that the years of pursuing her proved something. Lacking a case, the file weakly notes: "She is an outspoken person whose political sympathies at times paralleled those of the Communist party."

Once her name was on record, the bureau kept tracking her personal life. In 1958, she and her husband adopted an eight-year-old child who was half-Japanese, half-black. The FBI saw fit to put a clipping from the New York *Herald Tribune* about the adoption in her file.

In response to a name-check of American Nobel laureates, the FBI informed the White House about all the things they found wrong about her beliefs: "This bureau's files contain many allegations in her writings and speeches that have been against universal military training, militarism, racial segregation, and has been critical of the government of Chiang Kai-shek."

The censored pages in her file continued right up to her death in 1973. After I appealed, the Army Intelligence and Security Command at Fort Meade, Maryland, released a few pages of an antidraft letter she had written in 1952 on behalf of the Women's International League for Peace and Freedom. The United States Navy, however, denied my appeal to see its Pearl Buck documents. Rear Admiral B.A. Harlow, acting judge advocate, informed me: "Even after the passage of thirty-four years, release of the withheld information would jeopardize the government's interest in preventing the unwarranted invasion of personal privacy of an individual about whom the government maintains information in its files. This letter constitutes a final denial of your request. You are further advised of your right to seek judicial review of this decision."

I did not bring a costly lawsuit. Had I done so, I would have made this point: as a matter of justice, informers who accuse others of felonious conduct that violates federal laws should not be allowed to shield their names. All the material in her extensive dossier was assembled behind her back. The main fact about Miss Buck was that, despite the accusations and suspicions caused by her speeches, articles and novels, the labors of the army, navy, State Department and FBI could not even produce an unpaid parking ticket.

WILLIAM FAULKNER

William Faulkner's dossier is comparatively light—eighteen pages. But it is telling about what could arouse FBI suspicions, because part of the file concerns his political and civil rights views; indeed, in the most fundamental sense, the characters in his Southern novels also reflect attitudes about social class and segregation in the Deep South. Speaking of his own favorite black character, Dilsey Gibson, in *The Sound and the Fury,* Faulkner described her as "much more brave and honest and generous than me." The narrator in that novel says: "I learned that the best way to take all people, black or white, is to take them for what they think they are, then leave them alone." A similar phrase about the right to individuality, regardless of color, had been expressed by Lincoln during his senatorial contest with Douglas in 1858.

Faulkner's attitude hardly coincided with the prejudiced view toward blacks of J. Edgar Hoover. All through the time of beatings and shootings of civil rights workers in the Deep South, Hoover avoided any role for his men, even in federal interstate crimes. Some of his informants were members of the Ku Klux Klan, according to several retired FBI agents. The director had a cool explanation for failing to uphold civil rights laws in Faulkner's Mississippi: "The FBI is not a police organization—it's purely an investigative organization, and the protection of individual citizens, either natives of this state or coming into this state, is a matter for local authorities. The FBI will not participate in such protection." It was only after Hoover was gone that blacks and women were recruited actively to the FBI's ranks; Hoover, a bachelor, had personal problems dealing with both.

An FBI document stamped *Confidential* and dated March 12, 1957—seven years after Faulkner had won his Nobel laurels—informed an unnamed person (with a copy to the State Department) that "no investigation had been made of 'William Faulkner, born Sept. 24, 1897, New Albany, Mississippi.'" But, it added, "the files of this bureau reflect the following information." The information reads:

"A confidential informant who has furnished reliable information in the past advised in March 1951 that the Civil Rights Congress in New York City had expressed their pleasure with the work of a committee of women which included the procuring of a statement from William Faulkner, Nobel Prize winner, in behalf of Willie McGee. It is to be noted that Willie McGee was convicted of raping a woman in Laurel, Miss., in 1945 and sentenced to die. Numerous appeals were filed, the last of which was to the United States Supreme Court in March 1951, at which time the full Supreme Court refused to review the case. McGee was executed on May 8, 1951. The Civil Rights Congress has been designated by the Attorney General of the United States pursuant to Executive Order 10450." All of which left the implication that Faulkner was tied to a Communist or Communist-front organization.

In its usual phrasing to cover the bureau in case something more "subversive" turned up in Faulkner's record, the FBI document added: "The foregoing information is furnished to you as a result of your request and is not to be construed as a clearance or nonclearance of the individual involved. This information is furnished for your use and should not be disseminated outside of your agency."

Actually, Faulkner's views about equality and progress for blacks emerged in his public expressions as well as in his stories. Long before it had become acceptable to Southern

Sinclair Lewis and Ernest Hemingway, two American Nobel Laureates in Literature, both with FBI dossiers that deplored their political views as too liberal and too anti-Fascist. Lewis's novel *It Can't Happen Here* warned of a possible American dictator deceiving the people into putting him into the White House in the future. Hemingway established an anti-Nazi network in Cuba and used his fishing boat to patrol and report U-boat activity. The FBI attempted to destroy his reputation and curtail his anti-Nazi activities. In this photograph, Hemingway and Lewis, on separate vacations, shake hands before boarding a steamship bound for Havana in 1940.

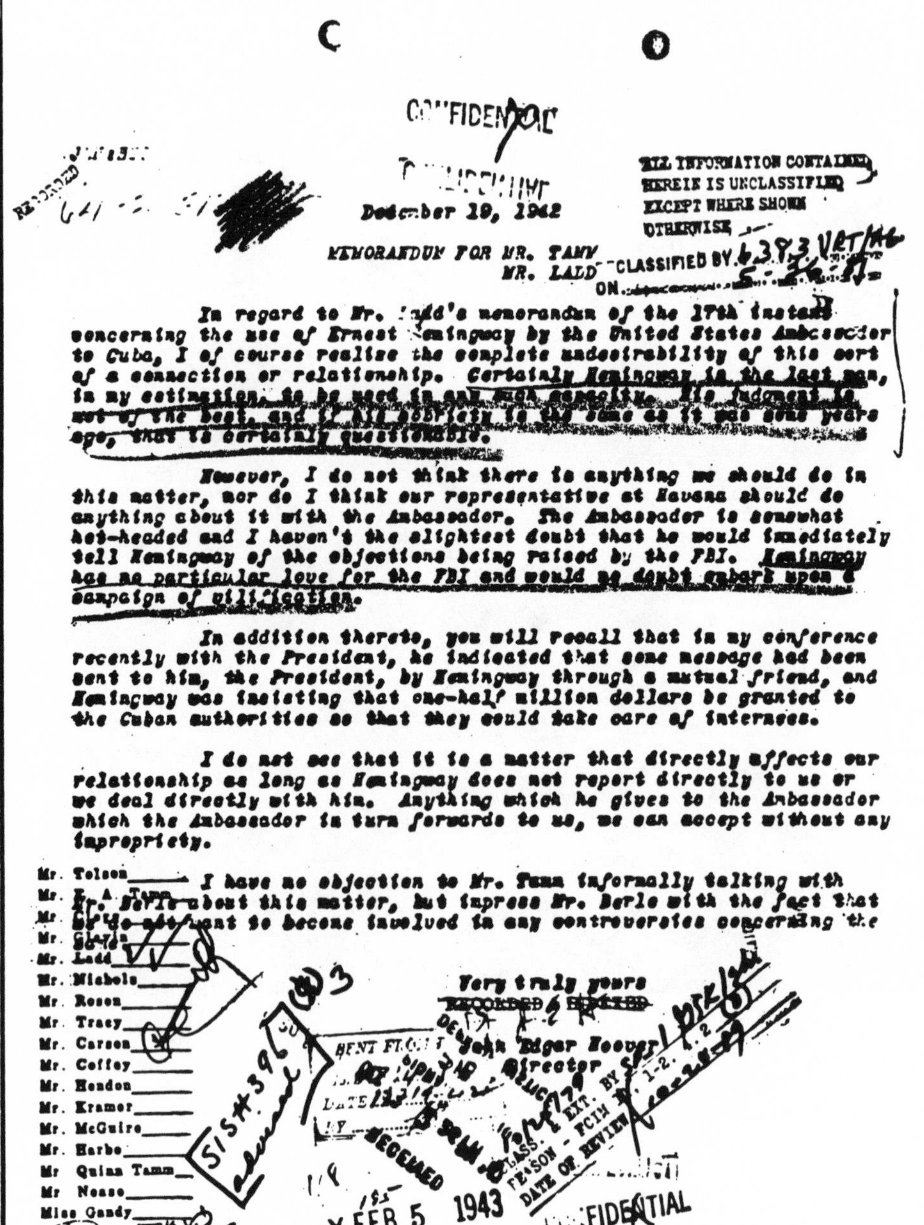

CONFIDENTIAL

December 19, 1942

MEMORANDUM FOR MR. TAMM
MR. LADD

In regard to Mr. Ladd's memorandum of the 17th instant concerning the use of Ernest Hemingway by the United States Ambassador to Cuba, I of course realize the complete undesirability of this sort of a connection or relationship. Certainly Hemingway is the last man, in my estimation, to be used in any such capacity. His judgment is not of the best, and if his sobriety is the same as it was some years ago, that is certainly questionable.

However, I do not think there is anything we should do in this matter, nor do I think our representative at Havana should do anything about it with the Ambassador. The Ambassador is somewhat hot-headed and I haven't the slightest doubt that he would immediately tell Hemingway of the objections being raised by the FBI. Hemingway has no particular love for the FBI and would no doubt embark upon a campaign of vilification.

In addition thereto, you will recall that in my conference recently with the President, he indicated that some message had been sent to him, the President, by Hemingway through a mutual friend, and Hemingway was insisting that one-half million dollars be granted to the Cuban authorities so that they could take care of internees.

I do not see that it is a matter that directly affects our relationship as long as Hemingway does not report directly to us or we deal directly with him. Anything which he gives to the Ambassador which the Ambassador in turn forwards to us, we can accept without any impropriety.

I have no objection to Mr. Tamm informally talking with Mr. Berle about this matter, but impress Mr. Berle with the fact that we do not want to become involved in any controversies concerning the

Very truly yours

John Edgar Hoover
Director

J. Edgar Hoover's man in Havana, the legal attaché at the consulate, kept an eye on Ernest Hemingway. Hemingway had enlisted some of his old Loyalist friends from the Spanish Civil War to spy on pro-Nazi elements in Cuba during World War II. Hoover, jealous of Hemingway's volunteer force, maligned him and said, in this confidential memorandum, that Hemingway was "the last man" to be trusted and that he had "no particular love for the FBI."

Pearl S. Buck, winner of the 1938 Nobel Prize in Literature, was greatly admired for her portrait of the Chinese people in her novel *The Good Earth.* In the same year she won the Nobel, the FBI began a file on her that added up to nearly 300 pages. The FBI did not admire her stand against racism. Her name also appeared in the files of the Authors Guild because she had once served as president.

William Faulkner, who received the 1950 Nobel Prize in Literature, had a comparatively light FBI file—only 18 pages—but it revealed what could arouse the suspicions of the Federal agents, particularly his stand on civil rights. No mention is made in his dossier of any of his novels or writings.

Ralph Thompson/Random House

1 - Mr. Belmont
1 - Mr. Rosen
1 - Name Check Section
1 - Mr. Woods

December 12, 1961

Summary 41/20

WILLIAM FAULKNER

No investigation pertinent to your inquiry has been conducted by the FBI concerning the captioned individual However, the files of this Bureau reveal the following information which may relate to the subject of your inquiry.

An informant who has furnished reliable information in the past advised in March, 1951, that the Civil Rights Congress Headquarters in New York City had expressed their pleasure with the work of a committee of women, which included the procuring of a statement from William Faulkner, Nobel Prize winner, in behalf of Willie McGee. It is to be noted that Willie McGee was convicted of raping a woman in Laurel, Mississippi, in 1945 and sentenced to die Numerous appeals were filed, the last of which was to the United States Supreme Court in March, 1951, at which time the full Supreme Court refused to review the case. McGee was executed on May 8. 1951.

The Civil Rights Congress has been designated pursuant to Executive Order 10450. (40-0-17974)

Enc to AG memo 12-13-61 captioned "Name Check Requests" WFW:fjb.

WFW:wap
(6)

Tolson
Belmont
Mohr
Callahan
Conrad
DeLoach
Evans
Malone
Rosen
Sullivan
Tavel
Trotter
Tele. Room
Ingram
Gandy

MAIL ROOM ☐ TELETYPE UNIT ☐

62-57-9972

ENCLOSURE

A number of the pages in William Faulkner's file delved into the author's personal life and a possible blackmail action. On this page, the FBI revealed that it kept informed of his activities on behalf of a black man accused of raping a white woman in Mississippi. He did so in cooperation with the Civil Rights Congress, which was designated as a Communist front.

John Steinbeck, winner of the Nobel Prize in Literature in 1962, was one of the few authors who guessed—correctly—that the FBI was tailing him. One reason why is that they considered his famous novel *The Grapes of Wrath* a rabble-rousing, un-American document. The FBI, the CIA and the Army all had files on him, adding up to over a hundred pages released but with some twenty-five more pages denied. This photograph shows him in California in 1938, while he was still at work on *The Grapes of Wrath*.

The Viking Press

U.S. Postal Service

Despite the fact that the Army denied John Steinbeck a commission as a lieutenant during World War II because of his FBI dossier, he was honored in 1979 with a postage stamp.

Thomas Mann, Germany's greatest 20th century novelist and winner of the 1929 Nobel Prize in Literature, went into voluntary exile from Nazi Germany, where his books were banned and burned. He became an American citizen. At the same time that his two sons, Klaus and Golo, were serving in the Army against Hitler's Third Reich, Mann was being watched, and Red-baited, by the FBI as a possible subversive. There were 800 pages in his FBI dossier. This photograph was taken by his publisher, Alfred A. Knopf—who also had an FBI dossier.

liberals, he had said that blacks ought to be enrolled at the University of Mississippi. "If the race problems were just left to the children, they'd be solved soon enough," Faulkner said. "It's the grown-ups and especially the women who keep the prejudices alive."

At the time when Washington dispatched regular army troops to Little Rock to maintain order and escort blacks into the Arkansas schools, Faulkner wrote: "We, because of the good luck of our still unspent and yet unexhausted past, may have to be the rallying point for all men, no matter what color they are or what tongue they speak, willing to federate into a community dedicated to the proposition that a community of individual free men not merely must endure, but can endure." The language echoed his stirring Nobel address: "I believe that man will not merely endure: he will prevail." Faulkner had allowed the three black tenant families who operated his farm to keep whatever profits they made, saying that "the Negroes don't always get a square deal in Mississippi."

Segregationists in the Deep South denounced Faulkner as "small-minded Willie, the Nigger-lover." In a visit to West Point, Faulkner said that the South would change its attitude because "life is motion and the only alternative to motion is stasis—death."

A more personal matter appeared in the FBI's Faulkner file in 1957. It referred to his relationship with Jean Stein, daughter of Jules Stein, the head of Music Corporation of America. Miss Stein, twenty-two, was described as a friend with whom he dined when in New York. A case of blackmail was reported; a telephone caller had attempted to expose their friendship to Estelle Faulkner, the author's wife, and that "this information would be worth five hundred dollars." Mrs. Faulkner told the caller that she was not interested in the information. After a complaint by Faulkner himself, a Random House managing partner, Donald Klopfer, got in touch with the FBI to report the phone calls. Both Faulkners were then interviewed by the FBI to obtain the details.

The FBI agent reported: "Mr. William Faulkner advised that he is a close personal friend of Miss Stein and that he and Miss Stein have mutual interests in television, radio and literary matters and that through Miss Stein he has made many writer contacts in New York City." The matter was dropped after the United States Attorney in Memphis decided that, on the available facts, there had been no violation of the federal extortion statue.

Miss Stein had conducted an interview with Faulkner in New York in 1956, and it appeared in *Writers at Work: The Paris Review Interviews,* in 1959. Faulkner had memorably said, "The writer's only responsibility is to his art. He will be completely ruthless if he is a good one. He has a dream. It anguishes him so much he must get rid of it. He has no peace until then." Of course, this did not appear in his FBI file—nor did anything else of a literary nature that might have rounded out the picture of the man's character and interests, even in an official record.

In 1954 Faulkner went to Lima and Sao Paulo for an international writers' conference and in 1955 he was sent by the State Department to Japan and Manila. President Eisenhower asked him to head the writers' section of a People-to-People program in 1956 (a fact not reflected in his dossier) that, more or less, was designed to sell the American Way behind the Iron Curtain. Faulkner accepted, attempted to enlist other authors, and discovered that they were as individualistic as he was in opposing any program that smacked of propaganda writing. Faulkner soon lost interest in the undertaking.

A name-check was made on Faulkner in 1961—a year before his death—for Attorney General Robert F. Kennedy, the president's brother. No reason was given other than that the request originated with Richard N. Goodwin, formerly of the White House staff. Apparently Faulkner and other Nobel laureates were being scrutinized before being invited to the Executive Mansion or to go on a government assignment. The information supplied to Attorney General Kennedy repeated Faulkner's statement of approval on behalf of Willie McGee to the Civil Rights Congress. In addition, the namecheck included a list of other Nobel laureates in various fields. Seven of them had once had similar checks and their names existed in the FBI files; one unnamed individual was singled out as a "prominent Quaker pacifist," a description that sounded accusatory.

Otherwise, the Faulkner documents contain nothing at all about what he was known for—his stories and novels. Not even in passing is one of Faulkner's books mentioned in his dossier.

ERNEST HEMINGWAY

The 122-page, heavily censored file on Ernest Hemingway apparently was opened in Havana in October, 1942, the first full year of America's entry into World War II. But there is evidence in the documents that the FBI, the State Department and other agencies were tracking his activities as a correspondent and Loyalist supporter during the Spanish Civil War.

While living in Cuba the novelist and short-story writer created what he called his "Crook Factory"—a group of twenty-six informants, six working full time and twenty undercover, to provide intelligence information and possibly spot German submarines operating in the Caribbean. Hemingway worked as a volunteer out of his home and used his fishing boat, the *Pilar,* for patrolling. He received some help from the US embassy in Havana. After the private "Crook Factory" was dissolved in April 1943 and replaced by American intelligence agents, Hemingway continued to patrol on the *Pilar* with machine guns and grenades supplied by the navy.

The purpose of patrolling in the submarine-infested waters was to lure one of the German U-boats to surface. The *Pilar,* disguised as a fishing boat, was heavily armed. Once the German submarine ordered Hemingway's boat alongside, according to the plan, the crew of nine would use their weapons to destroy it. The FBI and other Hemingway-bashers said that it was a wild scheme, designed to give him fuel so that he could fish, and that no submarine was ever spotted. This was later disputed by Winston Guest, Hemingway's second-in-command. "We did sight a submarine once," Guest recalled. "We got our glasses out and you could see it was a submarine. I think 740-class. But it speeded up and went directly on the course north-northwest. That was the submarine that ended up at New Orleans. I think they landed three men at the mouth of the Mississippi River. Ernest made a report back in Havana, which they thought incredible. But two days later they called him and said he was completely right, that it had been a submarine, and that several tankers had sighted it on the same course."

Jealous of its authority, the FBI tried to discredit Hemingway. Hoover considered him a rival, not a patriot trying to help his country at war in a self-assigned dangerous role. Hemingway's information was downgraded, and he was accused of being a Communist and a drunk. Furthermore, he had once committed the unpardonable sin of calling the FBI the American "Gestapo." An FBI memorandum in his file said: "Hemingway's investigation began to show a marked hostility to the Cuban police and in a lesser degree to the FBI."

Of necessity, Hemingway's operation was political. His informants were recruited from among Loyalist refugees he knew who had fled the Franco dictatorship. Hemingway enlisted them to keep an eye on the pro-Franco Spaniards in Cuba, who sided with the German-Italian Axis. He was authorized to set up his own network by Spruille Braden, ambassador to Cuba, and given expenses of one thousand dollars a month to pay his men plus an allotment of scarce fuel. In his postwar memoirs, Braden wrote that Hemingway built up an excellent network and did "an A-1 job."

Hoover had his own man, Raymond Leddy, the legal attaché inside the embassy, serving as his liaison and reporting back to him. At the same time that Hemingway was helping the Allied cause by watching the pro-Nazi elements on the island, Leddy was watching Hemingway. In the Hemingway file appears this letter from Hoover to Leddy: "Any information which you may have relating to the unreliability of Ernest Hemingway as an informant may be discreetly brought to the attention of Ambassador Braden." In another letter Hoover wrote Leddy: "Hemingway's judgment is not of the best, and if his sobriety is the same as it was some years ago, that is certainly questionable."

At the time he volunteered his intelligence work without pay or military rank, Hemingway had turned down 150,000 dollars to write a script for a "March of Time" program on the Flying Tigers in the Pacific Theatre, according to a letter marked *Confidential* from Leddy to Hoover in 1942. Hemingway had obtained a promise that his civilian network would be considered war casualties for purposes of indemnity to their families in case they died. He asked nothing for himself.

Nevertheless, the Hemingway file includes another *confi-*

dential memorandum written for Hoover by D.M. Ladd, one of his top aides in Washington, that is hostile to Hemingway because he opposed *Generalissimo* Franco. (At this time, the German navy and Luftwaffe were using Franco's Spanish bases to refuel submarines and to bomb American and Allied forces in North Africa, a fact ignored or unknown to the new wave of Franco apologists in American neoconservative publications in the 1980s.) The internal FBI memorandum goes:

"Hemingway, it will be recalled, engaged actively on the side of the Spanish Republic during the Spanish Civil War, and it is reported that he is very well acquainted with a large number of Spanish refugees in Cuba and elsewhere. Hemingway, it will be recalled, joined in attacking the bureau early in 1940, at the time of the 'general smear campaign' following the arrests of certain individuals in Detroit charged with violation of federal statutes in connection with their participation in Spanish Civil War activities. It will be recalled that Hemingway signed a declaration, along with a number of other individuals, severely criticizing the bureau in connection with the Detroit arrests. Hemingway has been accused of being of Communist sympathy, although we are advised that he has denied and does vigorously deny any Communist affiliation or sympathy."

Hoover responded with a memorandum to Ladd that underscored what he had told Leddy, his man in Havana: "Certainly Hemingway is the last man, in my estimation, to be used in any such capacity. His judgment is not of the best, and if his sobriety is the same that it was some years ago, that is certainly questionable." Again, Hoover looked out for his public image. After saying that the Bureau should not get involved or raise objections to Hemingway's work, Hoover added: "Hemingway has no particular love for the FBI and would no doubt embark on a campaign of vilification."

The FBI director continued to be near-obsessed by Hemingway. In 1943, less than a year later, he asked for another memorandum on Hemingway. This time Ladd's report extended "Communist sympathy" to embrace "liberal" views: "Mr. Hemingway, it will be noted, has been connected with various so-called Communist-front organizations and was active in aiding the Loyalist cause in Spain. Despite Hemingway's activities, no information has been received which would definitely tie him with the Communist party or which would indicate that he has been a party member. His actions, however, have indicated that his views are 'liberal' and that he may be inclined favorably to Communist political philosophies." (Liberal and Communist, in the subworld of dangerous dossiers, were clearly linked if not interchangeable.)

This FBI memorandum concludes with a typical half-truth: "The bureau has conducted no investigation of Hemingway, but his name has been mentioned in connection with other bureau investigations and various data concerning him have been submitted voluntarily by a number of different sources."

Although claiming that Hemingway had not been investigated, his dossier includes a detailed fourteen-page, single-spaced memorandum, complete with table of contents. It mentions the names of every organization he belonged to, comments about his personal life and marriages, details about his trips, the titles of his books (apparently more revealing than Faulkner's), the magazines he wrote for. This *confidential* memorandum, dated April 27, 1943, is still heavily censored, with entire paragraphs blacked out, more than four decades after it was written and long after Hemingway's death. It is an example of evasion under the Freedom of Information Act. Nevertheless, it includes personal matters and indicates what the FBI pursued:

"He has also contributed to Scribner's, Atlantic Monthly, New Republic, Esquire, Cosmopolitan [a Hearst Corporation publication], and other magazines. In addition, he has had articles published in the New Masses, his 'Fascism is a Lie' having appeared therein on June 22, 1937. In 1937 and 1938, he covered the Spanish Civil War for the North American Newspaper Alliance.

"With reference to the first Mrs. Hemingway it was reported in June 1940 that [censored]. Hemingway allegedly had a passionate love affair with Martha Gellhorn which subsequently led to his divorce from his first wife. [The FBI erred here: Miss Gellhorn was Hemingway's third wife.] After the divorce Hemingway married Martha Gellhorn, who is said to be a journalist in her own right and a contributor to Collier's Magazine."

The memorandum also included a statement that Hemingway and Lillian Hellman, the playwright, served on a committee to raise funds for anti-Fascist refugees in French camps. "Lillian Hellman, who together with Ernest Hemingway is cochairman, is an outright Communist. Hemingway who is on the outs with the Communists, apparently is serving as an innocent friend." Others mentioned in the Hemingway memorandum to aid the Spanish Republic and the Abraham Lincoln Brigade were Pearl S. Buck and Vincent Sheean.

A part of the shaky Hemingway memorandum is called: "Possible Connections with the Communist Party." It is replete with wrong factual information, such as calling him a "speciality writer" for the Communist *Daily Worker* and a "New York" writer. The facts in the memorandum are attributed to a "confidential source" (supposedly giving them an aura of credibility as well as secrecy); actually, the mistakes expose the quality of the FBI files and the ignorance of the bureau on factual literary and creative matters.

The long memorandum branding the author a "propagandist" goes on: "In the fall of 1940 Hemingway's name was included in a group of names of individuals who were said to be engaged in Communist activities. These individuals were reported to occupy positions on the 'intellectual front' and were said to render valuable service as propagandists. According to the informant, those whose names were included on this list loaned their efforts politically as writers, artists and speakers and traveled throughout the country supporting and taking part in Communist-front meetings and in the program of the party generally. They were alleged to be particularly active in the then paramount Communist party objective, defeat of the preparedness program."

The effort to link Hemingway to the Communist party continued: "Hemingway, according to a confidential source who furnished information on Oct. 4, 1941, was one of the 'heads' of the Committee for Medical Aid to the Soviet Union. This informant alleged that the above-mentioned committee was backed by the Communist party." Again: "In January 1942, it was reported that the American Russian Cultural Association of New York City put out a small pamphlet soliciting support. The name of Ernest Hemingway appeared therein as a member of the Board of Honorary Advisors. This group was purportedly organized to foster better relations between the United States and Russia."

For an author who supposedly had not been investigated, the FBI had still more in the Hemingway file under "Miscellaneous Activities."

The fact that Hemingway had once written an "article against war which appeared in Esquire Magazine" and was placed in his dossier proved that his themes were policed. The file reads: "This article was later incorporated in a pamphlet prepared by the American Youth Congress" and "one individual was arrested for distributing these on Nov. 11, 1935, in Seattle, Washington."

It was noted that he took part in the Congress of American Writers on June 4, 1937, in Carnegie Hall, with Archibald

MacLeish presiding. A "confidential informant" reported that Hemingway was close to the Communist party, but that he had no knowledge of Hemingway's actual membership. Hemingway was also pointed out as a vice-president and member of the board of directors of the League of American Writers, Inc., "which is reportedly a Communist-front organization." In 1941, this organization had solicited individuals who had fought with the Loyalists in the Spanish Civil War. Another "confidential informant" in the same year reported that Hemingway had "broken all ties with the Communists."

A section in the dossier that follows is labeled "Mexican Trip." It is totally censored—an indication that Hemingway was being watched by FBI informants and probably customs officials whenever he crossed an American border or traveled to Africa or Europe.

Hemingway engaged a good deal of attention from Hoover's top aides as well as from the chief himself in the midst of World War II. An internal dispute developed between C.H. Carson and E.A. Tamm about whether or not to expose him, the file notes, for "the phoney that he is." Carson recommended caution: "The legal attaché at Havana expresses his belief that Hemingway is fundamentally hostile to the FBI and might readily endeavor at any time to cause trouble for us. Because of his peculiar nature, it is the belief of the legal attaché that Hemingway would go to great lengths to embarrass the bureau if any incident should arise. In view of his prestige as a literary man, accepted by large sections of public opinion in matters not related to writing, it is the recommendation of the legal attaché at Havana that great discretion be exercised in avoiding an incident with Ernest Hemingway."

But E.A. Tamm did not concur: "I don't care what his contacts are or what his background is—I see no reason why we should avoid exposing him for the phoney that he is. I don't think we should go out of our way to do this, but most certainly if in the protection of the bureau's interest it is necessary to meet him head-on, I don't think we should try to avoid such an issue."

The FBI makes no mention of Hemingway's wartime reporting as a correspondent in France and Germany, respected by army officers and the press camp and welcomed by the soldiers who recognized him in the battle areas.

Five years after the end of the war, the FBI furnished a name-check on him to the secretary of defense. It repeated much of the material about his hostility to the FBI—quoting him as calling the bureau "antiliberal, pro-Fascist, and dangerous of developing into an American Gestapo"—and noted his affiliations with groups supporting aid to Spanish refugees.

In 1954, the year he won the Nobel Prize, the FBI continued to hound Hemingway on nonsensical matters. In a gossipy letter to Hoover stamped *Secret,* the legal attaché (the FBI's Man in Havana) reported a dispute between Hemingway and Edward Scott, a British columnist for the Havana *Post.* The columnist mentioned an argument with Mary Hemingway, his fourth wife, about whether lion steaks were "delectable," as she claimed. Scott challenged Hemingway to a duel; he declined, saying he was too busy writing and had no time for dueling. The incident is inconclusive; most of it is blacked out by the FBI. That same year, the FBI supplied information about Hemingway to President Eisenhower's chief of staff, Sherman Adams, who was later to resign because of corruption.

A name-check was provided in 1955 to the State Department and the army. It repeated that Hemingway had supported the Loyalists, nearly twenty years before, and had contributed to the Lincoln Brigade publication, "Among Friends."

The FBI file included a 1959 memorandum from the State

Department's Office of Security about Hemingway's sympathies toward Cuba and the Castro government. Returning to his home outside Havana after a visit to Spain, Hemingway said he hoped that Cubans would not regard him as a "Yanqui," and he "kissed" a Cuban flag. "Hemingway's remarks have been strongly played by Prensa Latina, and given wide publicity locally," reported Minister-Counselor Daniel M. Braddock. "It is unfortunate that a person of his position and reputation should publicly take a position which displays (1) strong criticism of his government and compatriots or (2) a remarkable ignorance concerning developments in Cuba since the first of the year."

After his death in 1961, the FBI file shows only one comment on him as a writer—by Westbrook Pegler, the venomous columnist who was a Roosevelt hater and Hoover favorite, in the New York *Journal American* of July 19, 1961. Dancing on the grave, the Pegler column went, "It has been my stubborn opinion that Ernest Hemingway was actually one of the worst writers in the English language during his time. It can be conceded that he invented a 'style,' but to me it was an ugly style, so barren of ordinary literary embellishment or amenity that it was confused and often incomprehensible."

Today, hardly anyone remembers Pegler or his vituperation and reactionary views. Hemingway remains a significant force in American and world literature. No hint of this would be apparent if one judged him by the malignant material in his FBI dossier.

During the last twenty years of his life, Hemingway suspected that he was a target of the FBI. His longtime lawyer, Alfred Rice, recently told me: "Whenever Ernest and I were at the Floridita in Cuba, he would sit at the end of the bar, protecting his back. Once he said to me, 'You see those three guys over there? They're agents, keeping an eye on me.' It sounded a little strange at the time, but you know something? He may have been right."

JOHN STEINBECK

Just as the FBI tried to judge Hemingway by his drinking instead of by his important writing (and his anti-Fascism), leaving the impression that he was something of a nut case whose patriotism was questionable, so too the dossier on John Steinbeck reveals an effort to challenge his Americanism and to judge him negatively because he undertook themes of social and economic justice. To the rigid minds of Hoover's sleuths, writing about the Oakies and other subjects showing the underside of the American dream made Steinbeck a radical, and thereby suspect.

The FBI provided me with ninety-four pages on Steinbeck but withheld twenty-three pages; the army gave up twenty pages; the CIA, which had two documents, withheld them entirely, despite my appeal, on grounds of "national defense or foreign policy."

Although Steinbeck won his Nobel Prize in 1962 and lived another six years, no mention can be found in his file that he ever received this international literary honor. His social novels—*The Grapes of Wrath, In Dubious Battle, Tortilla Flat*—made Americans aware of the migratory farm workers, trade union struggles, and the ravages of the Depression. A play and film were made of his 1942 novel, *The Moon is Down,* about the Nazis in Scandinavia. After serving as a war correspondent, he wrote *Once There was a War.* His *Russian Journal* appeared in 1948, and his rediscovery of the country, *Travels With Charley,* in 1962.

Steinbeck was one of few American authors who suspected

that the FBI was tailing him; but he had no idea to what extent. In his file there appears a letter Steinbeck wrote to Attorney General Francis Biddle in 1942 that reads in part: "Do you suppose you could ask Edgar's boys to stop stepping on my heels? They think I am an enemy alien. It's getting tiresome." Biddle forwarded the letter to Hoover, who replied that Steinbeck "was not being and never had been investigated."

As usual, when confronted by one of his theoretical superiors in the Justice Department, Hoover covered up. "Never had been investigated" did not mean that Steinbeck was not being watched. The euphemism overlooked the fact that the FBI had maintained a detailed record on him. It simply indicated that the bureau had not rolled out its heavy artillery for a full-scale investigation. In the FBI file on Steinbeck, dated March 10, 1954, this heading appears: "Instances Wherein America's Enemies Have Used or Attempted to Use Steinbeck's Writings and Reputation to Further Their Causes."

A number of examples are cited where Steinbeck's books are indicted as dangerous to the Republic if not to the Republic of Letters. So here the FBI had made a literary judgment on the author's fictional themes to challenge his personal loyalty.

The FBI cast itself in the role of book critic. The bureau labeled his writings propaganda and guilty of association on bookshelves. Their judgments sounded as if they were devised by cultural commissars before sentencing an author to the gulag. His file reads:

"Steinbeck's book, *Grapes of Wrath,* was among the periodicals and books sold from the literature table at a Communist party May Day meeting held on May 1, 1940, in Los Angeles, California [source censored].

"Bureau files reflect that because many of Steinbeck's writings portrayed an extremely sordid and poverty-stricken side of American life, they were reprinted in both German and Russian and used by the Nazis and Soviets as propaganda against America.

"A booklet announcing the courses of the Workers School of New York City, official Communist party school, for the winter term, 1943, stated that the works of leading dramatic writers, including Steinbeck, would be used in the discussions of history of social institutions as they had been reflected by writers of all times. [The source was a California Committee on Un-American Activities, a Red-hunting body that smeared reputations with an even broader brush than the House Committee on Un-American Activities in Washington; it was a frequently cited source in the FBI files.]

"During March 1945, a copy of a recommended reading list used by the American Youth for Democracy (cited by the attorney general) indicated that listed books were available from the New Jersey State office of that organization at a discount. The list included Steinbeck's *The Moon is Down.* [The informant's name is blacked out, but otherwise the source is listed as 'state headquarters of the Communist Political Association, Newark, New Jersey.']"

What is particularly noteworthy here is a fundamental omission: that *The Moon is Down* is about the Norwegian Resistance to the Nazi Occupation; in other words, Steinbeck was being condemned for an anti-Nazi novel during a war against the Nazis.

One of the more absurd statements in the Steinbeck file is an illustration of what might be branded guilt by possible reader association. In 1944, at a time when merchant seamen were transporting troops and supplies through submarine-infested oceans, the House Un-American Activities Committee stated that the National Maritime Union of America "toed the Communist party line." The FBI then concludes: "These ships of the American Merchant Marine are being supplied with libraries for the seamen to read while at sea. John Steinbeck's *Grapes of Wrath* is naturally present, as it would be in any Communist selection."

Similarly, a "confidential informant who has furnished reliable information in the past [name censored; this phrase often referred to ex-Communists who had presumably seen the light]" advised the FBI in 1945 that the American Youth for Democracy, in a recommended reading list, included Steinbeck's *The Moon is Down.* This item is followed by a statement that American Youth for Democracy is on the attorney general's list as "Communist or Communist-controlled."

In addition, the file notes that on June 2, 1953, an admitted former Communist party member testified before the House Un-American Activities Committee that "Steinbeck has done more through his novel about the agricultural workers than anyone else for the Communist party." After this reference to *The Grapes of Wrath,* the former party member said that Steinbeck appeared at odds with the Communists between 1937–1939, but could not state how or why.

Even before writing *The Grapes of Wrath* Steinbeck came under scrutiny. His file notes that "during the Fall of 1936 a group of liberal and Communistic writers issued a call for a conference to be held in San Francisco on November 13, 1936, which conference continued throughout the following day. This report indicated that one of the sponsors of the Western Writers Congress was John Steinbeck." (As usual, the FBI made no distinction between liberal and Communist writers; nor did the report say into which group Steinbeck supposedly fit.)

Like most major American authors and dramatists, Steinbeck belonged to writers' organizations. It was noted that he was a contributor—along with 417 other American writers—

to a pamphlet called "Writers Take Sides," published by the League of American Writers in New York in 1939. These were letters in support of the Loyalists during the Spanish Civil War. (Similarly, "Authors Take Sides on the Spanish War, 1937," was published by writers and poets of England, Scotland, Ireland and Wales. Among the many distinguished authors writing for the Spanish Republic and against the Franco insurgents were W.H. Auden, Samuel Beckett, Cyril Connolly, Ford Maddox Ford, Aldous Huxley, Sean O'Casey, V.S. Pritchett, Herbert Read, Stephen Spender.) Steinbeck was named president of the anti-Franco group in this country. He was also one of the signers of a letter urging the United States to lift the embargo so that arms could flow to the besieged Republic. The California Committee on Un-American Activities branded the Washington Committee to Lift Spanish Embargo a Communist front.

How all this negative information in his file affected Steinbeck personally emerged when he was trying to get into uniform and being considered for a commission in 1943 by Army Intelligence. He was rejected after an investigation conducted in Los Angeles; at the time he was living in Sherman Oaks. Army G-2 wrote: "In view of substantial doubt as to Subject's loyalty and discretion, it is recommended that Subject not be considered favorably for a commission in the Army of the United States."

Incredibly, Steinbeck was turned down. Yet his file shows that he had been employed in 1942—without pay—as a special consultant to the secretary of war, and assigned to the commanding general of the army air corps. As a volunteer he wrote an official book on flying and training. After completing this assignment he worked for the Office of War Information as a foreign news editor at an annual salary of thirty-six hundred dollars a year. Steinbeck told friends, who were questioned about him, that he was not a Communist. He did admit that he was concerned about "the lower-class working people regardless of their political creed." Friends in his file described him as a patriot, a registered Democrat, and a citizen with pro–New Deal instincts.

The writers' groups he belonged to also made him suspect. These included the Western Writers Congress, the League of American Writers and, most surprising of all, the National Institute of Arts and Letters. The Institute is the most prestigious in the United States; it is patterned after the French and British Academy and is now called the American Academy and Institute of Arts and Letters. The investigation of him that led to his rejection for the service reads:

"Subject has associated with individuals who are known to have a radical political and economic philosophy, and with some members of the Communist party." Also, "Subject received large volume of Communist literature and possessed books expressing radical political and economic views in his library." The FBI told Army Intelligence that Steinbeck subscribed to People's World. Among the sources of this information was the American Legion Radical Research Bureau in San Francisco; the legion said his book, *The Grapes of Wrath,* had been branded "Red propaganda."

During World War II, when the United States and the Soviet Union were allied against a common enemy, Steinbeck's reading and travels were monitored for pro-Soviet leanings. A mail-watch listed him as an individual who received Soviet literature. It was noted that on February 23, 1944, at a time when the Russians were fighting the Wehrmacht on the Eastern Front, the Steinbecks attended a reception at the Russian embassy in Mexico City that celebrated the twenty-sixth anniversary of the founding of the Soviet Army. This, of course, went into his file. And not in a flattering sense.

At the beginning of the cold war the Steinbeck dossier

shows that he wrote a series for the New York *Herald Tribune,* after visiting the Soviet Union, that became the basis for his 1948 book, *A Russian Journal.* The FBI comment reads: "Both sides criticized his ability to adequately portray life in Soviet Russia after such a short visit. It is noted that the articles criticized Soviet red tape and the Soviet government but were favorable to the Russian people." Book reviews from the Communist *Daily Worker* and the anti-Communist New Leader, both unfavorable, were placed in his file. Schizoid archives.

Because foreign publishers on both sides of the Iron Curtain wanted to translate his books, *their* interest was included in his file. In 1954, an Army Counterintelligence Corps report said that Verlag der Nation—described as a Communist-oriented publisher in Berlin's East Zone—was about to negotiate publishing rights with seven American authors, including Steinbeck. The military report on translation found its way into his file.

Whenever a name-check on Steinbeck was requested, all the previous accusations against him were passed along by the FBI with the familiar line: "Without clearance or nonclearance of the individual involved." A 1956 memorandum, stamped *Secret,* still declared, as if significant, that *The Grapes of Wrath* was a book favored by the Communists.

Even Steinbeck's infrequent book reviews were monitored. For example, he wrote a review of Harvey Matusow's *False Witness* that appeared in the Saturday Review in 1955. The FBI noted that in the review "Steinbeck speaks with 'harsh contempt' of the author as an 'anti-Communist hired informer.' " Also that he wrote, "The Matusow testimony to anyone who will listen places a bouquet of forget-me-nots on the grave of McCarthy."

In 1961, the year before Steinbeck received the Nobel Prize, an FBI interoffice memorandum made note of the contents of his novel, *The Winter of Our Discontent.* The memorandum headlined the fact that the FBI was mentioned in the book. The novel was set in the fictional town of New Baytown, New York, the name for Sag Harbor, the old whaling town on the South Fork of Long Island, where he resided at the time. "At the beginning of the book he describes various persons of the town, including Stonewall Jackson Smith, the chief of police, whom he describes as being of above-average intelligence for the town and who 'even took the FBI training at Washington, D.C.,' " the memorandum reads. The FBI found implicit criticism of the bureau in an observation about the novel's plot: "While Steinbeck does not belabor the fact that the chief of police is FBI trained, nevertheless a careful reader cannot fail to recall the reference in the initial introduction to the chief when his behavior concerning the indictments comes up."

The FBI passed along information to the CIA about Steinbeck in 1964. It reported that the year before Steinbeck had visited the Soviet Union and a headline in the *Daily Worker* in New York read: "Steinbeck in Moscow Impressed by Progress." The FBI threw in all the previous material, beginning with the 1930s, in its memorandum for the CIA. Why the CIA was interested in Steinbeck is not revealed.

In an internal memorandum, the FBI in 1965 reported that Steinbeck had been on the mailing list of the Japan Council Against Atomic and Hydrogen Bombs and "another reliable source has described this organization as Communist-infiltrated in Japan." Another "reliable source" reported that his literary agent, McIntosh & Otis, had been paid $188.70 on his behalf by the National Bank of Bulgaria. And still another "reliable source" reported that Steinbeck "had received $420 as an author's fee from the Soviet publication, Novyi Mir."

In 1956, the year Steinbeck died, the FBI provided a name-check on him to the White House. The purpose of this cannot be determined because, like much of the material in the Steinbeck dossier, the document is blacked out and stamped *Secret.*

THOMAS MANN

Thomas Mann, Germany's greatest twentieth-century author, was among those whose books were burned by the Nazis. A few years after receiving the Nobel Prize in 1929, he turned westward, first into voluntary exile in Switzerland in 1933 and then to the United States in 1938. His lectures and writings against Nazism and for democracy helped to alert the nation to the dangers of totalitarianism. He became an American citizen in 1944.

I was particularly interested in Mann because of his classic works—*The Magic Mountain, Buddenbrooks, Death in Venice,* the "Joseph" tetralogy. His *Stories of Three Decades* had become a well-thumbed book in our small personal library at home. All of his stories offered a different kind of literature from the American naturalistic novels we admired; his Old World themes and language seemed to be constructed like librettos—interwoven, tragic and inevitable.

I also had a more personal reason: his son, Klaus Mann, author of *Mephisto,* and I were friends and army correspondents together in wartime Italy. Klaus was far ahead of his colleagues in understanding the meaning of the dictatorial madness that had descended all over Western Europe. Although not Jewish, his family had scattered in voluntary exile, despising the Third Reich and their neighbors who had supported Hitlerism. Fortunately, after moving to Switzerland they came to America. His younger brother, Golo, also was serving in the American army. As the Allied armies swept into Germany, Klaus accompanied them, and without identifying himself discovered that his parents' abandoned old house in Munich had been used by the SS as a brothel. He found one young woman living there who thought that a previous owner had been "a writer or something" who had been sent to a concentration camp. Nothing pleased Corporal Klaus Mann more than to see the conquest of the Germans who had approved of Nazism and brought on the Holocaust. If we Americans of German stock cherish freedom and peace, Klaus said, we have to help in defending those supreme values, even if the aggressors happen to be our former countrymen.

Unknown to Klaus then—or in the few remaining years of his life (he died tragically in 1949)—his father was under surveillance in the United States just as he had been in Nazi Germany. Looking over Thomas Mann's dossier, I found it particularly ironic to discover that while Klaus and his brother were serving in American uniforms in a war theater, his distinguished father was being falsely Red-baited and watched by the FBI and Army Intelligence. And more than ironic: uninformed, wasteful and mean spirited. The entire Mann family had proved its opposition to the Nazis. I could not help wondering: Didn't the FBI have enough to do keeping an eye on the members of the pro-Nazi German-American Bund in the United States?

An internal memorandum in the novelist's dossier read: "In the case of Thomas Mann it should be noted that there are approximately eight hundred references in our files to this individual." Eight hundred pages! The effort and treasure that must have been expended to accumulate such a thick file on the internationally renowned author. I was able to obtain only about one hundred pages. One army-originated paper was provided to me after an appeal; a second paper was refused by the secretary of the army's Office of General

Counsel on grounds that disclosure would damage "national security." The army document I received showed that Mann was being tracked for his writings and indicated that there had been a mail-watch on him at his home at 740 Amalfi Drive, Pacific Palisades, California.

An FBI "summary" in the form of a memorandum revealed that Mann's name first appeared in the bureau's records as far back as 1927, two years before he received the Nobel Prize. It was noted that he was a member of the American Guild for German Cultural Freedom in New York City. This was reported to be a "racket." The words "culture" and "freedom" often have seemed to raise a red flag in the FBI.

About ten years later, when he was living in the United States, the file noted that Mann was a sponsor of the North American Committee to Aid Spanish Democracy, the group supporting the Republic against Franco's legions. Scores of American authors, including Ernest Hemingway, Sinclair Lewis and Lillian Hellman, belonged to the group. Like all organizations opposed to Franco, it was constantly watched by Hoover's men.

When Erika Mann read a letter from her father at a 1937 meeting of an American Artists Congress in New York, a report appeared in the Deutsches Volks Echo, which was described as a German-language Communist weekly. It was also noted that Thomas and his older brother, Heinrich Mann, were contributors to this publication. In the same year, the FBI recorded that "Dr. and Mrs. Mann were speakers at a meeting for the German-American League for Culture, and that about half of the audience were Communists or Communist sympathizers." The FBI did not explain how this esoteric distinction within an audience was determined.

Into the Mann record—from an unnamed source and with an undocumented interpretation—went an accusation that communism appeared in one of his books. The file reads:

"Information was received in August 1938 that a book, *Coming Victory of Democracy,* was a reproduction of the text of the lecture that was delivered by the German writer, Thomas Mann, during his lecture tour in the United States. It was said that the book was extremely Communist in its presentation of the case for Democracy and its continuance as a form of Government." How exquisitely Orwellian!

When Mann spoke at a mass meeting of the "Save Czechoslovakia Committee" in 1938, it was described as "strongly radical, and particularly strongly pro-USSR." Guilt-by-lapel-emblems was found in his audience: "It was also said that the lapel emblems of the 'Friends of the Abraham Lincoln Battalion and the American Relief Ship for Spain' were very much in evidence."

The FBI, to give it its due, did report that Mann was condemned by German propagandists in 1939. An article appeared in a German publication titled "The Disgusting Thomas and His Chaste Joseph," which was a violent attack on the author and his novel, *Joseph in Egypt.*

When Mann participated in the Third American Writers Congress at Carnegie Hall in 1939 other speakers included Louis Aragon, Heywood Broun, Vincent Sheean and Langston Hughes. This event was inscribed in his record because it was reported in the *Daily Worker;* the other newspapers that covered the event were not mentioned.

One of several blind pro-Communist accusations against him appeared in his file this way: "Information was received in October 1940 that among the persons mentioned in a pamphlet published by the 'League of Fair Play,' who were known to have Communist tendencies, was Erika Mann's father, Thomas Mann." An informant (several sentences blacked out) stated that "Mann was not a Communist or fellow traveler but has permitted himself to be 'used' several times in recent years."

Another document attacked a writers' organization and, ambiguously, Mann: "The New York Telegram for June 5, 1941, stated that the Fourth American Writers Congress was a Communist cultural front and had consistently followed the political deviations of the Soviet Union and the Communist party. It stated that most of the distinguished writers that backed the Writers Congress have resigned and lists among such distinguished writers Thomas Mann, formerly honorary president. The article stated that at present its sponsors consist largely of party members, writers for the party publications such as the 'New Masses,' and active Communist-front supporters."

In 1942, after America entered the war, Mann and another person (name censored) sponsored a "well-known" Polish author (censored) and his wife for visas so that they could remain in the United States. The Immigration Service looked upon the application favorably. But an angry response was filed by the FBI in a memorandum attacking Mann for his humane act of sponsorship.

A memorandum on the matter that went up to Hoover read: "The bureau had furnished information, from a number of sources, indicating the Communistic background and activities of the applicant and sponsor, Thomas Mann." The State Department's visa appeals board then turned down the (unnamed) applicant, repeating the FBI judgment: "A write-up furnished by this bureau contained approximately seven pages of references indicating the Communistic background and activities of sponsor Thomas Mann."

In 1945, the last year of the war, a letter written to Mann was intercepted by customs and turned up in his FBI file. The letter was from a former concentration camp survivor who had witnessed atrocities. In the letter was a list for future punishment of German war criminals who ran the camps. The letter writer had heard a Mann broadcast on concentration camps and considered him an important voice for justice. That mail intercept made me wonder if Klaus Mann's letters from Italy to his father and mother in California were also read first by the FBI.

After the war, whenever the Manns traveled to Europe, Thomas Mann was a marked man. The bureau in Los Angeles kept headquarters in Washington informed of Mann's foreign trips. The FBI then told its agents in the embassies and the legal counselors that Mann was present in their country. On the 150th anniversary of the death of Schiller, the FBI "liaison representative" in Heidelberg reported that Mann would deliver a speech. This, too, became cause for suspicion.

The Mann file included derogatory columns about him in the New Leader, the Freeman and other such publications. Again and again the Nobel laureate, now an American, was accused of being a Communist or "Communistic"—but no evidence to prove it can be found in his FBI file. His exile and anti-Nazism were evidently not taken into account in judging him. Furthermore, there is no evidence in his extensive dossier to show that, at least as a possible clue to his beliefs and ideals, any of Hoover's accusatory G-men had ever exposed themselves to a story written by Thomas Mann.

IV.

REVERED AUTHORS

Even in the Reagan era of officially sanctioned "disinformation," presented with thespian skill to the American press and public through Teleprompters, political pollsters and communications counselors, and in a time of officially maligned individuals and groups considered disloyal by White House subalterns below and above the stairs, it still comes as a surprise to discover that authors have been watched in Washington because of their beliefs and writings.

Whether surveillance still continues in the electronic era is difficult to prove—the FBI says it does not watch authors unless they are involved in criminal activities. But, to this day, files are maintained by the Federal Bureau of Investigation and other government agencies that point a finger of suspicion at well-known authors and artists as possible enemies of the United States. After decades of darkness—from J. Edgar Hoover's private blackmailing files to Joseph McCarthy's public accusations with senatorial immunity to Richard Nixon's "enemies' list"—the dossiers of these writers have not been expunged. They are inherited by children as unproven sins of their fathers for future zealots, in and out of government, to examine and use.

A number of major American novelists, playwrights, poets and artists, as well as respected foreign writers, appear in the files. In addition to Nobel laureates in literature, they range from Carl Sandburg and Theodore Dreiser to Thornton Wilder and Tennessee Williams, from Alexander Calder to Georgia O'Keefe, from Dorothy Parker to Aldous Huxley.

But the FBI watched more than seignorial figures in American and European literary and cultural life—figures who are read and studied on campuses, whose works are performed regularly in theaters, and seen in museums all over the country. Mr. Hoover's sleuths also kept track of a miscellany of authors in various fields of writing, including Thomas Wolfe, Archibald MacLeish, A.J. Liebling, Dashiell Hammett, Irwin Shaw, Truman Capote and Nelson Algren.

I particularly enjoyed reading my friend Algren's file because he had the last laugh posthumously; as a practical joker, he confused and ridiculed his watchdogs and caused them to pursue him dutifully up a blind alley. To this day the FBI does not know, or acknowledge, that he was having fun at the expense of their investigative warriors.

After examining the heavily censored documents in the files of writers of fact as well as of fiction, several conclusions can be drawn: Even though the FBI shadowed the lives and selected writings of authors as if they were criminals, the bureau had little or no inkling of the links between a writer's themes, dreams and personal life; the raw FBI files are riddled with errors, speculations and accusations from anonymous or blacked-out sources without supporting evidence; and—the ultimate judgment on their activities—all the investigations and recordkeeping, at an untold cost to the United

States in policing man-hours and money, did not result in a single criminal conviction. The list of targets is a Who's Who in the pantheon of American creative genuises.

CARL SANDBURG

Carl Sandburg, Chicago poet, Lincoln biographer, journalist and political activist, had an Army Intelligence file of six pages dating back to 1918 and an FBI file of twenty-three censored pages. Sandburg (1878–1967), who received Pulitzer prizes for both poetry and history, was given the Medal of Freedom by President Johnson at the White House. His multi-volume *Abraham Lincoln: The Prairie Years and the War Years* is surely the most popular presidential biography published in this century.

Although this writer knew Sandburg and had spent time with him wandering around the Lincoln landmarks in Illinois and at his home in Flat Rock, North Carolina, while writing a documentary film and editing his letters, it was hard to imagine that such a quintessentially American author would be the subject of a government dossier. Yet what he had said and written were considered dangerously liberal, or worse, by the Federals. In his early years he had been a Social Democratic party organizer and a supporter of Eugene V. Debs; later he was a Roosevelt New Dealer and close friend and campaigner in Illinois Governor Adlai E. Stevenson's try for the presidency. Now and then, he would feel free enough and angry enough to take a crack at such as Hoover and McCarthy as well as others who violated his libertarian views about those he called, "The People, Yes."

The first entry in his file that goes back to the First World War resulted from what today seems a comedy of errors. In

1918 Sandburg had served as a correspondent in Sweden for Newspaper Enterprise Association (NEA), the feature news syndicate. He was forty years old and a veteran of the Spanish-American War. On his passport application he advised his editor at NEA, Sam T. Hughes, to "tell them I have cooperated actively with the American Alliance for Labor and Democracy, which is the loyalty legion of the American Federation of Labor, and that the alliance gave wide circulation to my war poem, 'The Four Brothers.' " This was a patriotic poem about American unity with the European Allies against the German Hun.

Because he had been a Socialist organizer, Sandburg had wide connections here and abroad. On the way to Stockholm he stopped off in New York and saw John Reed and his wife, Louise Bryant. This association undoubtedly caused Sandburg to be watched by authorities. "While in New York I have kept away from the Socialist and IWW [Industrial Workers of the World] bunch," Sandburg wrote Hughes, "though I have had occasion twice to be thrown into the company of Jack Reed and both times got a lot of good pointers on how to travel, utilize aspirin and saccharin, and permits for supplies to be obtained from the Swedish embassy in Washington."

When he returned to New York all the notebooks, manuscripts and books that he had gathered in a neutral country were seized by customs, the Secret Service and military officials. Much of this research material for his articles referred to Finland and to Bolshevism in Russia. Included in his luggage was the raw material that he hoped to have translated and write about, including the Izvestia files on the Russian Soviet Congress earlier that year and Socialist and labor publications. All of which marked him.

Hughes protested the confiscation of Sandburg's papers to Secretary of War Newton D. Baker, calling it an act of censorship. The Secretary replied that Sandburg's luggage included "revolutionary literature," and added that he had also carried a ten thousand dollar draft on behalf of Finnish revolutionaries. Hughes responded by saying that those who had taken Sandburg's property did so because they thought his name was German even though his parents were of Scandinavian origin. He said that the authorities harassed Sandburg after they learned he had been a Socialist in his earlier days. The strong-willed NEA editor told Secretary Baker that he would instruct Sandburg to write exactly what he thought, regardless of censorship. Hughes wrote, "Isn't it fine for the government to treat such a man like a dog of a traitor?"

Eventually Sandburg's papers were returned, but neither he nor his editor ever forgave the attack on their journalistic integrity. Nor did Army Intelligence forgive or forget Sandburg. Nearly seventy years later and twenty years after his death, a file is maintained of the incriminating correspondence at Army Intelligence and Security Command Headquarters at Fort Meade, Maryland; and the FBI keeps a copy of this ancient dispute in its records. While Sandburg was writing and campaigning for causes and candidates he believed in, the file accusing him of being a courier for revolutionary literature was resurrected.

Sandburg's FBI record shows that, in 1941, an interoffice memorandum distributed among FBI officials noted that Sandburg (his name spelled Sandberg) had "manifested an unfriendly attitude" about the FBI at a luncheon given by March of Time filmmakers in Chicago.

Into the Sandburg file in 1947 went a clipping from the *Daily Worker,* the Communist newspaper, saying that a CBS documentary program had been written by Alan Lomax "with advice from Carl Sandburg." It was called "Dear Mr. Lincoln" and was based on letters to Lincoln found in the Robert T. Lincoln Collection in the Library of Congress.

A warning by Sandburg in the same year, also printed in

the *Daily Worker,* said that if the "hate Russia" campaign continued, it would lead to the most terrible war in history. In the same speech, Sandburg praised Secretary of State George C. Marshall for his calm patience in dealing with the Soviet Union.

An internal FBI memorandum in 1948 was filled with factual errors about Sandburg. The (censored) person who wrote the memorandum said Sandburg "was reported to be a well-known Communist in Chicago." It also said he owned a building in Chicago that was used as national headquarters for the Young Workers League of America. None of these statements was true.

A 1952 dossier on Sandburg, prepared by the FBI for the State Department, added more information collected by the bureau from its files. He was listed as a sponsor of the Veterans of the Abraham Lincoln Brigade in 1939. In 1942 he was listed in an advertisement in The Nation magazine as a speaker at a dinner sponsored by the Joint Anti-Fascist Refugee Committee; two years later he was a special guest at a concert in Chicago for the same organization. In 1945 he was listed as a sponsor of the Midwest division of the Independent Citizens Committee of the Arts, Sciences and Professions. All these organizations had once been cited as Communist fronts by the attorney general or the House Un-American Activities Committee.

A (censored) interoffice memorandum in 1954 added more information to the Sandburg file that had been omitted from his dossier. It said: "In a speech, 1942, Sandburg praised 'Russian courage' in World War II." At a rally in Chicago that year, Charles Chaplin and Carl Sandburg saluted "our Russian ally."

(In the eyes of the FBI and of superpatriotic elements in Washington—and their modern heirs, the neoconservative cold war writers and publications—to praise the Russians who were fighting the Germans on their invaded homeland during the war aroused suspicion. And this attitude existed even while the United States supplied the Soviet Union with war materiel, and Allied Force Headquarters on the western front coordinated air and ground actions with the Russians on the eastern front against the common Nazi and Fascist enemies.)

While many historians, poets and journalists offered words of praise for Sandburg's writings and statements, none could be found in his file. Instead the FBI included a column written by one of its favorite spear carriers, Westbrook Pegler, in Hearst's New York *Journal-American* of May 14, 1956. The Pegler column called Sandburg "a prosperous commercial biographer of Abraham Lincoln" and, in the same diatribe, ridiculed Albert Einstein. Coincidentally, in that same year Sandburg was campaigning for Governor Adlai Stevenson of Illinois for president against the incumbent, General Eisenhower.

In 1958, again without qualification, the FBI repeated all the derogatory information about Sandburg in his file while providing a name-check to the United States Information Agency. In the same year Sandburg was upgraded in the FBI records in an "Internal Security—C" (for Communist) matter involving another person (name and description blacked out). This individual had written a book and, the Sandburg file said, Sandburg "reportedly will write the introduction to [censored] new book." A clear example where a planned act of writing was considered worthy of suspicion and entry into Sandburg's "C" for Communist file.

In 1964, a *confidential* page appeared in his file, but it is totally blacked out except for the date, June 25, 1964, and the fact that he was born on January 6, 1878, in Galesburg, Illinois. And so when Sandburg was eighty-five years old and living quietly at home in Flat Rock, North Carolina, the FBI was still tracking him and making entries in his "C" for Communist dossier.

THEODORE DREISER

Theodore Dreiser (1871–1945) had 240 pages in his dossier, but the FBI withheld 42 pages from me—more than forty years after his death. The documents released are censored; those from Navy files are totally blacked out.

The influential novelist from Indiana who wrote *An American Tragedy, The Titan, The Financier* was active in defending the American workingman and attacking the excesses of big industry. Most of his views were out in the open—on the printed page and on the platform. He often put his name on the line for causes he believed in. His file shows that in 1928 he was a member of an international committee to save Sacco and Vanzetti, the anarchists executed by the State of Massachusetts. During the Depression he was active in his defense of mine workers who were striking for their safety and livelihood.

Dreiser's reasoning, it is true, was not always as farsighted as his powerful novels. Discussing his book *America is Worth Saving* in a radio interview ten months before Pearl Harbor, he absurdly equated the British Empire and Nazi Germany. This isolationist rhetoric, not uncommon in parts of the country at the time, may have helped cause the FBI to watch him more closely. But it was hardly the basis for their scrutiny. A censored memorandum shows that the word *espionage* appeared after his name, and his confidential file card is designated: *Communist.*

There was no question about their concern when, after America entered the war, an internal FBI memorandum in his file declared: "Subject is the well-known American novelist whose writings in recent years had a definitely pro-Russian slant." As in the instances of other writers, Dreiser's crime in the eyes of the FBI was that he was not inveighing against the United States' ally. Certain *idées fixes* about what was and was not a loyal American were not subject to such influences as a world war and who was fighting on whose side.

Dreiser's file also includes the compromising fact that—like many major American authors, including Ernest Hemingway and John Steinbeck—he attempted to save veterans of the Abraham Lincoln Brigade who had fought on the Loyalist side during the Spanish Civil War against efforts to deport them. He was also "one of many Communists and liberals" (the FBI routinely made no distinction between them) who contributed copies of their works to help members of the Newspaper Guild who were on strike in Chicago. His file reads: "Ardent propagandist for Soviet Union. Speaks at meetings and openly advocates Soviet form of government for U.S." Proof by documentation is not even hinted at.

One of the *confidential* FBI documents almost reads like a Dreiser novel; the bureau has always relished gathering material about marital and extramarital conduct. The FBI comments in this fashion on his private life:

"He separated from his wife at the age of thirty-one or thirty-two. . . . After the success of *An American Tragedy* his wife came to him and demanded money for a settlement, which he gave her. . . . [Unnamed mistress] has been living with him for ten years or longer. . . . Informant heard that she is a former Mack Sennett girl and has positively no literary acumen [as distinct, of course, from the director and his agents]. . . . He was indicted in 1931 in Bell County, Kentucky, for Criminal Syndicalism and Adultery. He had gone there to help striking miners and get material for a book. He went there with his mistress but left the state prior to the indictment. Basis for adultery was that he and his mistress were in the same room at the hotel for immoral purposes. Dreiser claimed impotency." All with a straight face. Good Americans are not allowed a sense of humor.

In a 1943 memorandum J. Edgar Hoover himself noted that the matter of Dreiser's mistress was brought to the attorney general, "who feels that the facts do not warrant investigation under the White Slave Traffic Act, particularly in the absence of commercialism." Hoover's effort to prosecute Dreiser on grounds of unmarried sex between two consenting adults came in the middle of World War II when, one would have thought, the FBI director had rather more important fish to catch.

Even just before the end of World War II Dreiser was still being spied upon. At the time he was living in Los Angeles at 1015 North Kings Road, and was the owner of a gray 1940 Plymouth sedan, license No. 10Q334. An FBI source reported that he would obtain information as to "any writing being done by Dreiser." Apparently the FBI had a source inside Dreiser's house who reported to an informant (her name blacked out) about him. The FBI agent wrote that Dreiser was doing "very little writing and what little work he does put out is not in great demand by publishers." In May of 1945, the FBI agent in Los Angeles rendered a chilling literary judgment on Dreiser: "A 'has-been' in the literary field." It is difficult to say whether this was good or bad for his security file. I suspect it was good, and that the road to Hoover's beneficence was to be rejected by one's publisher.

Dreiser, in fact, had not been a member of the Communist party during all the years that he was producing his great works. A few months before his death, however, a headline in the *Daily Worker* of July 30, 1945, reported: "Theodore Dreiser Joins Communist Party." Dreiser had requested membership because, he wrote, "The Communists have helped to deepen our understanding of the heritage of

American Freedom as a guide to action in the present." Six months later, he died.

Six years after his death, Dreiser was still in the FBI's *confidential* files. Nine years after his death a name-check on him was requested by the United States Information Agency. Either that agency did not know that he was dead, or someone wondered if his books should be displayed or removed as subversive reading matter from agency bookshelves overseas.

The final document in the material released to me is dated July 31, 1958. It is too blacked out to determine why it was made, except that the words "Faculty of Social Science" appear on it and also "International Publishers," a publishing house founded in 1925 that brought out Marxist literature. The page is stamped *Confidential.* So concludes the FBI's grand dossier on Dreiser, designated by the literary lights of the bureau a "has-been."

JOHN DOS PASSOS

John Dos Passos, author of the trilogy *U.S.A.*—one of the great American novels of the twentieth century—had about eighty-two pages in his dossier. These came heavily blacked out; my appeal some fifteen years after his death for more material and less censorship was denied.

The writings of Dos Passos (1896–1970) started out reformist and ended up conservative. The proletarian and freewheeling views found in his trilogy and in *Manhattan Transfer* were changed in the final years of his life; his novel *Midcentury* especially extolled an unfettered free-enterprise system.

The FBI file on Dos Passos said that he first sympathized

with the Soviet Union; that the anti-Fascist cause enlisted his interest during the Spanish Civil War; that he championed the rights of Kentucky coal miners. "In Russia he was immensely popular as a 'proletarian' writer," it was noted; "later his attitude became definitely anti-Communist." Despite this acknowledgment a 1951 document stamped *Secret* described him as a "fellow traveler and sympathizer." He was also listed as having a "connection with [Communist] front organizations." These reached all the way back to 1923, when a letterhead listed him as a member of the American Committee for Relief of Russian Children.

Once again, despite his later conservatism, the FBI made a little list of other Communist-"front" organizations he belonged to. These included the American Civil Liberties Union; International Union of Revolutionary Writers; Citizens National Committee for Sacco and Vanzetti; American Committee for the Foreign Born; American Friends of Spanish Democracy.

In the midst of the Depression, Dos Passos delivered a strong speech at the First American Writers Congress in 1935—and the FBI was present to monitor it. He spoke of "a country that is organized to build for socialism, instead of for the growth of the wealth and the power of a few bosses."

Carlo Tresca, the Italian anarchist, labor organizer and outspoken editor who was gunned down by an assassin on a Manhattan street corner in 1943—an unsolved murder that some of Tresca's friends said had been carried out on Mussolini's orders because of Tresca's anti-Fascist speeches and writings—became the subject of a pamphlet called "Who Killed Carlo Tresca?" Dos Passos wrote the foreword, in which he said that Tresca "died as a fighter for freedom."

On a page stamped *Secret* in 1951 the FBI summed up previous file material and concluded:

"Recommendation: A review of the above information reflects that although Dos Passos was probably a Communist [the FBI erred in this assumption] and subsequently a Trotskyite, he has in recent years become definitely anti-Communist. In view of this, it does not appear that an investigation of Dos Passos is warranted, and if you agree, no investigation will be instituted."

Nevertheless, when Dos Passos traveled outside the United States, the FBI tracked him. The Shanghai Municipal Police file on Dos Passos was sent to the FBI on June 13, 1951, and disseminated to supervisors in the bureau's security division. (The mysterious Shanghai material is omitted.) The FBI report is based on "a confidential source of known reliability [who] furnished the bureau with information contained in the files of the Shanghai Municipal Police." These files include a letter dating back to 1933 from Paris to someone (name censored) in Shanghai because Dos Passos was listed on an unidentified defense committee.

In keeping up with Dos Passos and his writings—at the same time that his conservative credentials were deemed impeccable—the FBI examined his 1952 novel, *The Chosen Country,* and ingeniously succeeded in discovering that it had been published by "Houghton Mifflin of Boston, Massachusetts." At about the same time an FBI informant (name blacked out) maintained a mail-watch and revealed to the bureau that Dos Passos received his mail at Spence's Point, Westmoreland Post Office, Westmoreland County, Virginia.

On June 3, 1952, two FBI agents interviewed Dos Passos at his home in Spence's Point and reported their findings directly to J. Edgar Hoover. Dos Passos provided the agents with a political biography that on June 10 they inscribed in his file: "Dos Passos informed that he was never a member of the Communist party, although he related that he had close association with the Communist party at various times." While naming names, he prefaced his remarks by saying that since he was never a party member, the names he gave them were "based entirely upon his personal belief due to his dealings with the Communist party."

Dos Passos then mentioned John Reed, Max Eastman, Earl Browder and other obvious names. He said that he had accompanied Theodore Dreiser to the Harlan, Kentucky, coal miners' strike and "got the impression that the National Miners Union was controlled by the Communist party." He also said that the Communist party was "interested in the Group Theatre" in New York. (Despite Dos Passos' generalization, the Group Theatre nurtured many of the best dramatists, actors and directors during the Depression era and left a lasting and beneficial mark on the American stage and screen.)

Dos Passos also said—in the course of this McCarthy-period interview—that during the Spanish Civil War he had tried to keep Communists out of the American Friends of Spanish Democracy. In 1937 he went to Spain with Hemingway to make a film, "Spain in Flames," but his name did not appear on it because the Communists were "down" on him. Later he became interested in seeking a refuge for Leon Trotsky because "Trotsky was getting a raw deal." The interview concluded with the FBI observation that Dos Passos was "cooperative but hazy concerning details." He "offered further cooperation at any time it was necessary to contact him" to give information and then mentioned additional names (blacked out).

Quite by accident—and regardless of his cooperation with the FBI agents in furnishing names to them privately—in 1960 Dos Passos discovered that he was still the subject of federal scrutiny. A Treasury Department agent visited the Washington *Daily News* and asked to see his file in the newspaper's morgue. An enterprising reporter, Joseph Cloud, who revealed the facts of the inquiry in the newspaper, then questioned the FBI agent, who said his mission was very "hush hush" and that he was trying to find out if Dos Passos had "recently changed his political ideology."

Dos Passos received a rude awakening. Asked if he knew that the government was interested in his ideology, he replied in the newspaper on April 6, 1960: "I have no idea why. The FBI might be interested in some of the many Communists I've known—but the Treasury—I just can't figure it out. It does sound as if the federal government now has 'Thought Police.' What rights does the government have to investigate the political opinions of any private citizen? And if they want to know mine, why the hell don't they ask me?"

In this fashion Dos Passos became one of the few authors to learn that he was under investigation for his beliefs. What he did not discover was that the FBI had a thick file on his life and writings.

THOMAS WOLFE

In the case of Thomas Wolfe (1900–1938), I was able to obtain forty-two pages but they were almost totally blacked out by the FBI. An additional eighty-one pages existed in his file, but my appeal to obtain them, even if censored, was denied. The inaccuracy of recordkeeping on Wolfe and undoubtedly other authors and artists can be measured by the fact that a request by David Herbert Donald, the well-known historian who wrote a major biography of Wolfe in 1987, resulted in a statement by the FBI that no file on Wolfe existed.

Judged by his four autobiographical novels—*Look Homeward, Angel, Of Time and the River, The Web and the Rock* and *You Can't Go Home Again*—it was difficult, indeed, to imagine Wolfe as an enemy of the state. It was known from biographical writings that his prewar travels in Nazi Germany came to the attention of the authorities because he was admired by some Germans who knew of his writings—and his great ego caused him to admire them in return. Eventually, however, he was sickened by the Nazi brutalities and lack of freedom and wrote against Hitlerism. But none of this background can be found in his vetted files.

Strangely, seven years after his death; and, again, nine years after his death; and yet again, in 1947, nineteen years after his death, his name turned up in a totally censored and incomprehensible *secret* file labeled "Espionage" and "Internal Security." From the fragmentary words in the blacked-out documents, it can be surmised that Wolfe's writings were suspect because they appeared on reading lists of schools said to be under Communist influence.

Even after Wolfe's death, his file continued to be maintained because his novels had become a talisman of suspicion. For example, in a 1945 report by the FBI office in Kansas City there appears a list of books that begins: "The following are the readings assigned by [name censored]." The suspect list included John Hersey's *A Bell for Adano,* Stephen Vincent Benet's *Western Star,* Howard Fast's *Freedom Road,* Edith Wharton's *Age of Innocence,* Sinclair Lewis's *Babbitt,* Ernest Hemingway's *Short Stories,* John Steinbeck's *The Grapes of Wrath,* Richard Wright's *Uncle Tom's Children* and Thomas Wolfe's *You Can't Go Home Again.*

In 1947, a *security matter* report by the FBI Boston office noted that "Communist Party, USA, Pamphlets and Publications" were sold at the Progressive Bookshop, 8 Beach Street, Boston. A flyer there was entitled "Give Books for Christmas." Among the books warranting a security check were Mark Twain's *Life on the Mississippi,* Howard Fast's *The American,* Dorothy Baker's *Young Man With a Horn,* Jack London's *South Sea Tales,* Maxim Gorky's *Last Plays,* and Thomas Wolfe's *Of Time and the River.*

David Blumgart, CBS News

Carl Sandburg had an Army intelligence file of six pages, dating back to 1918, and an FBI file of twenty-three pages. The poet and Lincoln biographer was described in one document as "a well-known Communist in Chicago." He is shown here with Herbert Mitgang, who wrote the documentary "Sandburg: The Prairie Years," during the filming in New Salem Village, Illinois.

In 1935, after *Of Time and the River* was published, Thomas Wolfe toured Europe. In Berlin, where this photograph was taken, he was lionized as a great American author. His heavily censored FBI file failed to reveal his shifting political views about Nazi Germany, which at first were characterized by a streak of anti-Semitism. Eventually, he woke up to the nature of the totalitarian state.

Thomas Wolfe Collection, Pack Memorial Public Library, Asheville, N.C.

John Dos Passos and Theodore Dreiser. Both American novelists investigated conditions in the coalfields of Southeastern Kentucky in 1931. The FBI duly noted their participation in its dossiers. Dreiser's file contained 240 pages, but 42 pages were withheld more than forty years after his death. The Dos Passos file contained 82 heavily blacked-out pages.

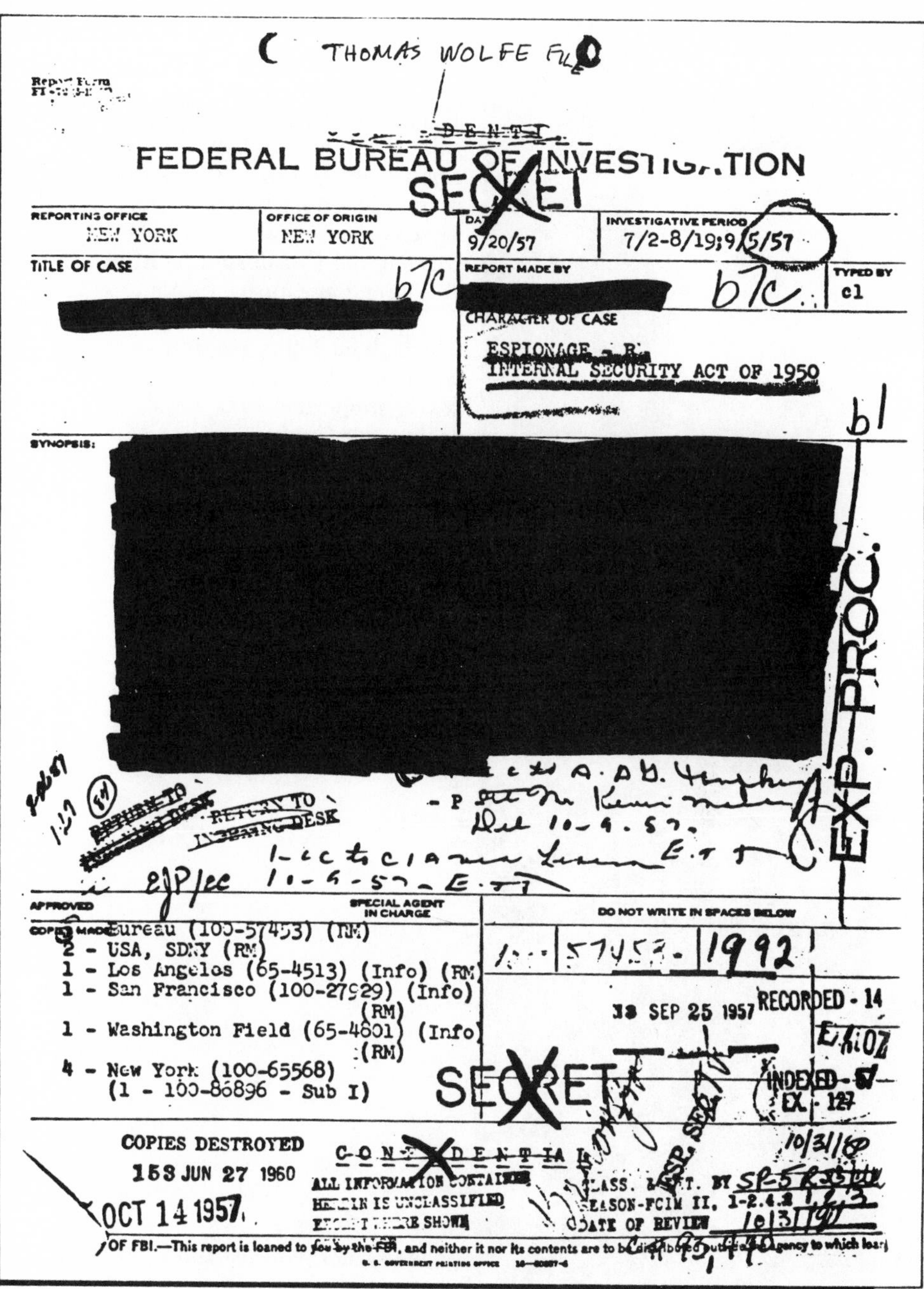
THOMAS WOLFE FILE

FEDERAL BUREAU OF INVESTIGATION

SECRET

REPORTING OFFICE	OFFICE OF ORIGIN	DATE	INVESTIGATIVE PERIOD
NEW YORK	NEW YORK	9/20/57	7/2-8/19;9/5/57

TITLE OF CASE	REPORT MADE BY	TYPED BY
[redacted] b7C	[redacted] b7C	cl

CHARACTER OF CASE

ESPIONAGE - R
INTERNAL SECURITY ACT OF 1950

b1

SYNOPSIS: [redacted]

EXP. PROC.

RETURN TO DESK

APPROVED — SPECIAL AGENT IN CHARGE — DO NOT WRITE IN SPACES BELOW

COPIES MADE:
3 - Bureau (100-57453) (RM)
2 - USA, SDNY (RM)
1 - Los Angeles (65-4513) (Info) (RM)
1 - San Francisco (100-27929) (Info) (RM)
1 - Washington Field (65-4601) (Info) (RM)
4 - New York (100-65568)
(1 - 100-86896 - Sub I)

100-57453-1992

38 SEP 25 1957 RECORDED - 14

SECRET

INDEXED - 57 EX. - 127

COPIES DESTROYED
153 JUN 27 1960

OCT 14 1957

CONFIDENTIAL

ALL INFORMATION CONTAINED HEREIN IS UNCLASSIFIED EXCEPT WHERE SHOWN

CLASS. & EXT. BY SP-5
REASON-FCIM II, 1-2.4.2
DATE OF REVIEW 10/3/90

OF FBI.—This report is loaned to you by the FBI, and neither it nor its contents are to be distributed outside the agency to which loaned.

U. S. GOVERNMENT PRINTING OFFICE

A page from Thomas Wolfe's "Secret" file. The character of the case is marked "Espionage." The reason the FBI gives for censoring certain material is that it contains information exempt "in the interest of the national defense or foreign policy." The author obtained the Wolfe file after appeals. In David Herbert Donald's 1987 biography of Wolfe, *Look Homeward*, the FBI noted that no file existed.

Dorothy Parker—poet, short story writer and Hollywood scenarist—was the wittiest member of the Algonquin Round Table. There were no fewer than 1,000 pages in the FBI dossier on Miss Parker and her husband, Alan Campbell, also a film writer, of which about 100 pages were withheld. Miss Parker was a strong supporter of the Loyalists against the Fascists during and after the Spanish Civil War, a fact that did not endear her to the FBI.

Random House

John O'Hara, novelist and short story writer, had ninety-one pages in his file. One of its main revelations was that he tried to become an operative for the Central Intelligence Agency but was turned down after a display of drunkenness and unreliability. The puzzling file indicates that his political views and affiliations with writers' groups were ambivalent.

Nearly a half-century after Thomas Wolfe's death, his dossier continued to be heavily censored and his books, and those of other celebrated novelists, were listed as a *security matter.*

DOROTHY PARKER

No proof exists that Dorothy Rothschild Parker (1893–1967) was or was not a member of the Communist party, but her voluminous dossier shows that the FBI treated this wit of the famed Algonquin Round Table as a major threat to the security of the United States. What there is no question about, however, is that her writing was a threat to the pompous, the cruel and the celebrated, from Manhattan to Beverly Hills. Her light verse, literary and dramatic criticism, sketches and short stories—including the classic, "Big Blonde"—appeared in the New Yorker and the original Vanity Fair and are still read with admiration. Parker was credited with many of the bon mots delivered with malicious intent at the Algonquin Round Table in the twenties. Among her books are *Enough Rope, Not So Deep as a Well, Laments for the Living* and *Here Lies.* She also wrote screenplays in collaboration with her husband, Alan Campbell, and, with Arnaud d'Usseau, a play called *Ladies of the Corridor,* about the lonely lives of widows living in a New York hotel.

The FBI released about nine hundred pages on Parker and Campbell, much of it censored; another hundred pages were withheld in their entirety. At the end of 1987 Marion Meade, Parker's biographer, was informed that additional material was still being processed. Knowledge of so much devoted attention by the federal gendarmerie, during much of her adult life, might well have inspired Miss Parker to produce not a bomb-throwing polemic but a ridiculing quatrain.

Like a number of her contemporaries in the Anglo-American literary world, the diminutive Miss Parker was politically involved in the public issues of her time. She marched in the demonstrations against the death penalty for Sacco and Vanzetti, the Italian anarchists executed by the State of Massachusetts, and she reported on the Loyalist side during the Spanish Civil War. To the FBI, this made her a dangerous person who had to be watched. One of the documents in her file is based upon what one FBI informer called his "mental list" of Communist party members. The informer claimed to have the names of four hundred party members in his head, among them Miss Parker.

She remained active in causes she believed in all of her life. So did a number of the most respected authors and dramatists in the country at the same time that they were earning a living by their pens and typewriters. Not all of her activities were political; most were concerned with civil, human and legal rights. Her record reveals that the FBI listed her as a member of such organizations that the attorney general or the California legislative Red-hunting committee considered Communist dominated as the Hollywood Anti-Nazi League, Friends of the Abraham Lincoln Brigade, Hollywood League for Democratic Action, League of Women Shoppers, Motion Picture Artists Committee, United American Spanish Aid Committee, Spanish Refugee Appeal, Writers and Artists Committee for Medical Aid to Spain, American Committee for the Protection of the Foreign Born, American Labor Party, Consumers Union, Civil Rights Congress, Progressive Citizens of America, Southern Conference for Human Welfare, American Committee for Soviet Relations, Joint Anti-Fascist Refugee Committee.

These and other organizations were monitored by the FBI. When Dorothy Parker served as chairperson of a luncheon on behalf of the Southern Conference for Human Welfare, to aid black education and rights, Mrs. Franklin D. Roosevelt was the guest of honor. Because of withheld material, it is not clear whether New York City's Police Department Alien Squad (better known as the Red Squad) or the FBI itself was on hand to eavesdrop on what Eleanor Roosevelt and Dorothy Parker said publicly.

Parker's file (in it she is sometimes called an "authoress") opens in the 1930s, when "an anonymous outside source" advised that she had contributed to the "Communist movement." She was watched all of her life; every address where she lived is recorded, from private buildings to hotels. When she stayed for a time in Cuernavaca, FBI sources in Mexico reported that she was "a very able authoress and also a valuable element in the idealistic fight on behalf of communism." Among the pages stamped *Secret* in her dossier is an article from Time magazine, January 6, 1941, on "The Revolt of the Intellectuals." It states that she was an ally of the Communists during the Spanish Civil War but not a Communist herself and "a fellow traveler who wanted to fight Fascism."

The army and navy also kept an eye on Miss Parker. In 1939, the Office of Naval Intelligence furnished the FBI a list of officers of the Hollywood League for Democratic Action, the successor organization to the Hollywood Anti-Nazi League, mentioning that she was on its executive board. Apparently Naval Intelligence was busier in Hollywood than at Pearl Harbor two years later. In 1940, the army's G-2 section reported on her to the bureau, describing her as a Communist party member (source not mentioned) and a writer for New Masses. Because of the censored documents, it is not known why military intelligence agencies became involved in domestic surveillance when the United States was not yet at war.

Her activities on behalf of the Joint Anti-Fascist Refugee Committee during World War II caused the FBI to use what her file describes as "technical surveillance"—that is, a telephonic or electronic device—at fundraising dinners at New York hotels on behalf of the victims of Franco's regime living in France and elsewhere. When returning American veterans were honored by the committee, the FBI made "a confidential search of the records of the Joint Anti-Fascist Committee and revealed that Dorothy Parker was to make a posthumous award to Captain Herman Bottcher, who had fought in the Abraham Lincoln Brigade in Spain and who was killed in action in New Guinea." Miss Parker was recorded as saying that she was proud to be associated with those who had worked to aid refugees from Franco Spain since 1937. Whenever she spoke for the organization at public events, before, during and after the Second World War, informants were present to listen and take down her words.

When a luncheon was given by the American book publishing industry to commemorate Children's Book Week in 1945, it was surreptitiously attended by special agents of the FBI, according to another page stamped *Secret* in her file. Among the participants was the women's committee of the National Council of American-Soviet Friendship. Speaking at the luncheon, Miss Parker is quoted by the FBI's agents: "We hold out our hands to our friends, our allies, our sisters and brothers, the people of the Soviet Union. There is no better way to reach the people of the Soviet Union than by books." She then presented the wife of the Soviet Consul in New York with a package of books chosen by American children.

The Alien (or Red) Squad of New York City's police department also watched her and passed on this information to the FBI: "Dorothy Parker was one of a committee which was active in a behind-the-scenes movement to place several alleged Communists on the staff of the newspaper *PM* in 1940. [Name blacked out] said that in November of 1938 Dashiell Hammett established a suite in the Hotel Plaza in New York City. While there he acted as the personnel director for Research, Inc. He interviewed applicants for a new kind of paper to appear on June 18, 1940, known as *PM.* He consulted Dorothy Parker among others. [Censored] Dorothy Parker as a contributor to New Masses and as a sponsor of several Communist-controlled committees."

With respect to the pioneering newspaper *PM*—which did not take advertisements and depended upon its readers for revenue—it is necessary to note here that the FBI kept its own file on the paper and its staff. In fact, the tabloid was founded in 1940 under the editorship of Ralph Ingersoll. It was purchased in 1945 by Marshall Field and resold to Bartley Crum and Joseph Barnes in 1948, when its name was changed to the New York *Star.* The paper ceased publishing in 1949. Miss Parker is not listed among the staff members. In front of me are documents from *PM*'s heavily censored file maintained by the New York Special Agent in Charge (name blacked out) at the request of bureau headquarters in Washington. The category for "The Newspaper, *PM,* Incorporated" is the ubiquitous "Internal Security—C" (Communist). The FBI documents list all the members of the editorial staff—blacked out, except for the name of a single individual requesting the file. There are three exceptions in which the names are not omitted: Dashiell Hammett, Lillian Hellman and Marshall Field. Its news departmentalization and horizontal typography made it the most readable daily in the country; the paper's appearance has since been followed by *Newsday* in metropolitan New York and other newspapers.

PM was bolder and more liberal in its editorial policies than the traditional morning and evening newspapers in New York City. But to label the newspaper as a matter of "Internal Security—C" was an inaccurate reach and a clear violation of the spirit of the First Amendment by both New York City's Red Squad and Washington's Federal sleuths. It was another case demonstrating that J. Edgar Hoover's FBI had its own political agenda and viewpoint.

In 1950, Hoover alerted his New York SAC (Special Agent in Charge) to look into the records to see if Dorothy Rothschild Parker warranted a full investigation because she had been named by (censored) to be a "concealed Communist." The SAC in New York reported that its informer (name blacked out) said that Dorothy Parker was a "concealed Communist," meaning "one who does not hold himself out as a Communist and who would deny membership in the party." She was described by the informer as "the chief co-worker for the party with Donald Ogden Stewart in influencing writers in Hollywood and in the party writers-unit there." The informant came up with such damning intelligence as that she was a writer "of note" and that her publisher was the Viking Press. Separately, the SAC in Philadelphia (because she had once lived in New Hope) reported her as a "Security Matter—C." She had once been visited by Lillian Hellman, "a dedicated Communist." The agent wrote to Hoover: "While she was living in Bucks County she was considered by people [unnamed] there to be the 'queen of the Communists.' "

In 1951, the SAC in Los Angeles reported that when Miss Parker had been interviewed by one of his agents she described herself as "unemployed." Clearly grounds for designation of security risk. At the same time, she denied membership in the Communist party, that she had ever been contacted by any of its members to join or that she had ever donated to the party. She confessed that she "formerly was active in the Screen Writers Guild, the Joint Anti-Fascist Refugee Committee, Hollywood Anti-Nazi League" and similar groups. She said she knew Lillian Hellman, Dashiell Hammett, Donald Ogden Stewart and Ella Winter, but had never sat in a meeting with any of them. The agent interviewing her also came away with this vital information: Miss Parker was five feet four inches tall, weighed 125 pounds, had a neat appearance, and appeared to be "a very nervous type of person." One was well-advised to tranquilize or become a Security Matter—C.

In that same year Walter Winchell, the Hearst gossip columnist, informed his good friend, J. Edgar Hoover, that "Dorothy Parker, the poet and wit, led many pro-Russian groups," that they were once good friends but she became "a mad fanatic of the Commy party line" who once tried to get his radio program off the air. Winchell signed himself "W.W. (Walter)." In 1952, still on the case, Winchell sent Hoover a copy of an appeal by Dorothy Parker on behalf of the Joint Anti-Fascist Refugee Committee. She was listed as chairman, with Pablo Picasso as honorary chairman.

Four years later in 1955 the SAC in New York sent a memorandum for the personal attention of Hoover regarding the case of Dorothy Rothschild Parker, "Security Matter—C," in which he wrote that she had been associated with thirty-three cited Communist-front groups between 1939 and 1950 but that "no reliable evidence of CP membership has been received." The SAC then said that although the record reflected "CP-front activity in the past three years, and the subject could technically qualify for inclusion in the Security Index, it is not felt that she is dangerous enough to warrant her inclusion in same." He then recommended that she be removed from the Security Index.

And so, after at least a thousand pages of documents about her had been compiled by agents in New York, Pennsylvania, Los Angeles, Washington and Mexico for a quarter of a century, Miss Parker finally stopped being an official threat to the survival of the Republic.

JOHN O'HARA

Re: Request for Investigation.

From: Central Intelligence Agency to Federal Bureau of Investigation.

Subject: John O'Hara. Other names used: "Franey Delaney."

Remarks: "Limited investigation . . . in 1943 disclosed that in the past Subject was inclined to drink to excess; that he was hot-tempered and temperamental, which necessitated his transfer from one office to another because of personal friction."

Those "Remarks" made in 1949, when O'Hara was applying for a job in the CIA, followed him throughout his highly revealing, pretentiously sad, paper trail. The "Franey Delaney" referred to a pseudonym he used in 1930 while writing a radio column for the New York *Morning Telegraph,* the race-track newspaper that opened its pages to several fine writers, Djuna Barnes among them.

Perhaps the most curious case of ambivalence that I came across involving the Freedom of Information Act concerned John O'Hara (1905–1970), author of *Appointment in Samarra, Butterfield 8* and *Pal Joey,* which became the basis for the Broadway musical.

At first his file was denied to me in its entirety. After a few appeals and a wait of nearly a year and a half I finally received ninety out of ninety-one pages from the FBI in mid-November 1987, with the possibility of still more documents coming from the CIA. The FBI's Records Management Division deserves a kind word, in this case, for diligently following up my efforts through channels and between agencies. The reversal also made me wonder: In the dying second term of the Reagan-Meese administration, was the bureaucracy (that would be around afterward) cleaning up its act? Originally, I had received a letter in response to my appeal saying: "After careful consideration, it has been determined that all material concerning Mr. O'Hara is exempt from release pursuant to subsection (b)(1) of the Freedom of Information Act. This subsection allows for the withholding of information which is currently and properly classified in accordance with Executive Order 12356."

The Executive Order, which hobbled the Freedom of Information law, was signed by President Reagan on April 2, 1982. It superseded a 1978 order by President Carter that had encouraged agencies toward more open government—the original intent of the legislation. The particular subsection (b)(1) of United States Code 552, used for the denial of all O'Hara material, reads: "Information which is currently and properly classified pursuant to Executive Order 12356 in the interest of the national defense or foreign policy, for example, information involving intelligence sources or methods."

In appealing, I pointed out that nothing that I could find in O'Hara's stories or journalism seemed to endanger "the national defense or foreign policy." In September 1986, Richard L. Huff, codirector of the FBI's Office of Information and Privacy, affirmed the initial decision and continued to deny any access to the file. And then, together with the ninety pages, came an explanation from the FBI saying that the O'Hara file was properly classified "at the time of our denial." However, because of my renewed request the CIA had agreed to declassify some of the material in its O'Hara file and pass it along through the FBI. The file arrived in the usual censored form; but at least it showed that even intelligence agencies can occasionally change their minds, never mind the reason.

The O'Hara dossier reads like a short story by O'Hara himself. The squire of Pottsville, Pennsylvania, and Quoque,

Long Island, was his own best character. It is authentic because he was filling out factual forms on himself rather than parodying the fictional lives of real people. In 1942, he tried to get a navy commission, writing to his friends James Forrestal and Robert A. Lovett, both high-ranking civilian officials in wartime Washington, to help him. He was rejected by both the navy and the army. Instead he served as chief story editor in the motion-picture division of the Office of Coordinator of Inter-American Affairs but resigned this one-dollar-a-year post after a few months. In 1943 he was accepted for Office of Strategic Services (OSS) training but resigned for health reasons. In 1949 he and his important friends made an effort to get him some kind of job in intelligence in Washington. It turned out to be with the CIA.

When O'Hara applied for the CIA job he put down as references Harold W. Ross, founding editor of the New Yorker, Herbert Bayard Swope, former editor of *The World*, and W. Averell Harriman, ambassador to France and future Governor of New York. His credit references included Tiffany and Brooks Brothers in New York and Brock & Company of Los Angeles. He also listed membership in six social clubs and noted that he had been a member of the Authors Guild from 1934–1939. Although "no longer active participant in sport," his interests included all the major sports plus "rifle shooting and pool." As for the use of intoxicants, he responded: "Moderately."

A puzzling entry from the New York FBI office to Washington, censored because it involved the name or names of informants, obviously referred to the New Yorker magazine. It went: "[Blacked out] for which applicant has written many short stories. Bureau requested to advise if investigation should be conducted [blacked out] in view of previous bureau instructions regarding contacts at that magazine." The implication of the message was to proceed gingerly when speaking to "contacts" at the New Yorker. Washington responded that the New York office should have "a mature, experienced and well-qualified agent interview [name censored]" but that "no specific inquiry concerning the applicant's writings should be made."

Several FBI offices weighed in with reports on O'Hara. Baltimore said that he was a loyal American, trustworthy, of good character and a good family man. His excessive drinking was now "very temperate." Los Angeles said that there was nothing unfavorable about his loyalty and patriotism. However, a censored source said he drank "heavily" and was not reliable. Another censored source in Los Angeles, a neighbor who admitted that she did not know his name, said that "he had the reputation of writing 'sex' stories concerning Hollywood, and he was seen to entertain girls in his apartment and understood he was getting material for his books." A censored item from the Washington field office said that he drank to excess, went on sprees and caroused with men and women friends, had an "unpleasant disposition, hard to get along with." Philadelphia reached far back to his employment on the Pottsville *Journal* in 1924–25 and reported that he had been "dismissed because of habitual tardiness," but he was regarded as "a very good writer."

One of O'Hara's references, name deleted, delved into his political thinking. He reported that "while many of the literary people are liberal or even left of liberal, O'Hara never was inclined that way. O'Hara would not be mentally intrigued by such asinine concepts as Communism and [censored] argued against Communism with his friends in the literary field."

Since O'Hara had listed membership in the Authors Guild of the Authors League of America, the FBI checked the organization—as it had been doing for some time through an informant in the League. "Confidential Informant T-1, of known reliability," the report said, "advised that the Authors

League of America is Communist infiltrated and that some of its members are known to belong to the Communist party; however, according to Confidential Informant T-1, membership in the Authors League of America is not in itself indicative of Communist party sympathies."

In an apparent reference to the Screen Writers Guild, another unnamed source advised that "both he and O'Hara were active in trying to throw out the leftist wing of the Writers Guild, and feeling that they were unsuccessful, resigned from the Guild and set up their own association." This blind item is not substantiated in the file. A Hollywood source noted that, in 1939, together with many other prominent writers, O'Hara had been on the executive board of the Hollywood branch of the League of American Writers, an organization listed as Communist-dominated by the House Committee on Un-American Activities. O'Hara is mentioned as being with the "anti-Communist" element in the Hollywood branch. He omitted mentioning the League of American Writers on his job-application form.

In any event, O'Hara was turned down by the CIA.

V.

SLEUTHING THE STORYTELLERS

NELSON ALGREN

Nelson Algren (1909–1981), winner of the first National Book Award for his 1949 novel, *The Man With the Golden Arm,* kept the FBI, Army Intelligence, Navy Intelligence and the State Department hopping during his lifetime.

His FBI file contained 546 pages. I received 461 censored pages and was denied 115 pages. My appeal for the denied pages initially was turned down by Richard L. Huff, codirector of the Office of Information and Privacy, Office of Legal Policy, Department of Justice, but later 30 additional pages were provided after being cleared with other government agencies. Sometimes one can pick up fragments of information indirectly from different sections of the FBI. In Algren's case I learned from my appeal that the author was the subject of one FBI file in Washington and a second in its Chicago field office. Both were labeled "Security Matter—Communist." In addition, he was included in the records of the "Criminal Division"—although, as his extensive dossier shows, he committed no crime.

After a wait of more than three years, the State Department independently provided five additional pages that exposed its policing rather than diplomatic activities. The reason for the secrecy—though not for such a long delay—was that the State Department controlled passports and had an application from Algren in 1965, and again in 1968, to travel abroad.

State informed its embassies in Mexico, Paris and Moscow that Algren was on the way and "to furnish the department with any pertinent information coming to their attention regarding Algren's activities." The embassies were also warned that he had a record of "Communist party front activity" from 1941 to 1952. (It is puzzling to know how the State Department concluded that he carried on such "activity" while serving as an army litter bearer in wartime Europe.) When Algren went to Asia during the Vietnam War in 1968, it was noted that the purpose of his trip was an "assignment from Atlantic Monthly."

Algren, a struggling writer for most of his life, was more honored in Europe for his muscular prose and daring subject matter than in the United States. He was greatly admired by fellow writers, including Ernest Hemingway and Studs Terkel (who dedicated his great oral history, *American Dreams: Lost and Found,* to Algren), as an American original who exposed the underside of the American dream in his articles, short stories and novels. The American Centre of the International Association of Poets, Playwrights, Editors, Essayists and Novelists (PEN) gives an annual award in his name to a writer in need of financial assistance to complete a novel or short-story collection. In the last year of his life, Algren was elected a member of the American Academy and Institute of Arts and Letters.

To the FBI, however, he was a "dangerous" American: the subject of an Internal Security file. He was included within its "Program for Apprehension and Detention of Persons Considered Potentially Dangerous to the National Defense and Public Safety of the United States."

In 1942 J. Edgar Hoover himself (the letter is in Algren's file) wrote to the president of the Polish-American Council in Chicago and advised him that its resolution condemning Algren's novel, *Never Come Morning,* would be made "a matter of record in the files of this bureau." The organization did not like Algren's Polish characters. (There is no record that the chief had read the novel or that it had been assessed by any other "literary critic" in the FBI.)

Algren was pursued in uniform during World War II, even while serving in the European Theatre of Operations. Private Algren was first tracked to the 460th Medical Collection Company at Camp Maxey, Texas. Oddly, the FBI lost him and had to rely on "former neighbors" to discover that he was in the army.

Five years after his honorable service in World War II the Chicago FBI office told the New York and St. Louis FBI offices to check his army record and find his "whereabouts." By this time he was a well-known writer around Chicago and New York. When he was found, his correspondence was watched through a "mail cover" in Chicago that noted the name and address of anyone who wrote to him. Copies were made of his signature and how he signed his name. FBI agents in at least five cities followed his movements.

Algren was unafraid to lend his name to causes he believed in and injustices he deplored. Every petition he signed and every time his name appeared in the press—and it appeared often as a book writer and occasional book reviewer for several newspapers and magazines—clippings of what he had to say or what was said about him went into his file. Writ large was his defense of the "Hollywood Ten," the blacklisted screenwriters and directors, and membership on a national committee to secure justice for Ethel and Julius Rosenberg, accused of divulging atomic secrets and executed by the United States in peacetime.

Unnamed informants monitored whatever Algren wrote as a free-lance journalist and novelist and passed along the material to the FBI. "Informant reported Algren wrote left-wing article for magazine Holiday," one entry read. (Holiday was a nonpolitical travel magazine that introduced many novelists to travel writing.) Another informant described him as the "Communist author" of *The Man With the Golden Arm* and *Chicago: City on the Make.* A new accusatory phrase—"Communist tendencies"—appeared in his file. (The *degree* of such tendencies was never explained by the FBI's Chicago field office.)

Algren was also on the FBI's SI—"Security Index." When he obtained a passport and stated that he was not a Communist, the FBI considered "possible prosecution of him for execution of non-Communist affidavit for State Department." But the matter was dropped for "lack of proof"—a phrase that characterizes many of the accusations by unnamed informants in the FBI dossiers, not only against Algren but others accused of Communist party membership, sympathies or "tendencies."

In 1949 friends gave Algren a farewell party before he embarked for Europe. The party was infiltrated by the FBI. When he went to Spain in 1960 the FBI cabled the American legation in Madrid, gave them the name of his hotel and asked the foreign-service officers to cable Washington and tell them what he was up to. But Algren was denied a passport in 1952 "because of allegations of Communist party activity." Responding, Algren politely but (to those who recognized his style) sarcastically wrote to Mrs. Ruth B. Shipley, director of the State Department's Passport Office:

"Dear Madam: Thank you for advising me of the State Department's tentative disapproval of my application. May I take the liberty of advising the department in turn that Applicant is not a member of the Communist party nor has he recently terminated such membership. The conclusion that his actions are in furtherance and under the discipline of the Communist party is therefore a falsehood. Applicant is not, formally nor informally, in support of the Communist movement. The conclusion that his actions are the result of direction, domination, and control by the Communist movement is therefore a falsehood. Applicant's motives in applying for passport facilities is neither to further the Communist movement nor to violate the laws of the United States, but to attend interests associated solely with his livelihood. The conclusion that Applicant constitutes a peril to the United States is a gratuitous insult which works a personal hardship upon the Applicant and is a falsehood. Cordially yours, Nelson Algren."

(During the Eisenhower administration, the same Mrs. Shipley was busy denying passports to applicants in the arts and other fields. In 1953 Arthur Miller was invited by the Belgian-American Association to attend the premiere of his play, *The Crucible,* in Brussels. The playwright's attorney in Washington was informed by Mrs. Shipley that his passport would not be renewed because his going abroad was "not in the national interest." So Miller could not attend a performance of his own drama after he had accepted the invitation from the business association. In his autobiography, *Timebends,* Miller writes: "Mrs. Shipley doubtless had my dossier, of which she doubtless distinctly disapproved, with its lump of left-wing entries, petitions I had signed and meetings I had attended.")

All through Algren's dossier the FBI maintained that he was a security risk and a Communist but without accompanying evidence. Nevertheless, Algren wrote to the Passport Office in 1956: "I wish to affirm and take oath that I am not at present a member of the Communist party nor have been a member of that party in the past." Again, he was denied a passport.

In 1958 he was issued a passport for six months of travel in France. He gave as his occupation: Novelist. The next year the legal attaché at the American Embassy in Paris filed a report to the FBI on Algren—at the time that Algren was being celebrated in the French press as one of America's most important authors. What the Embassy reported is censored in his file. In 1960 the American Embassy in Madrid tailed Algren, reporting that he was stopping at the Hotel Colon in Seville. His whereabouts were also reported to Washington and the FBI office in Indianapolis.

J. Edgar Hoover himself thought Algren important enough to write a personal letter to the director of the State Department's Bureau of Intelligence in 1966, telling him that Algren was either traveling abroad or planning to. In addition, Hoover asked the Central Intelligence Agency to provide any information they could find out about Algren while he was traveling in Europe. Details of the letter by the chief were blacked out a few years after Algren's death—and remain so in the material provided to me.

In 1955 an FBI informant managed to see the books that Algren had stored in a box in the basement of his building. The unnamed informant reported that the titles included "Communist books." Among the suspicious authors were Marx, Engels and H. G. Wells—guilt by association with books.

In the summer of 1955 Algren taught creative writing at the University of Montana. The FBI asked the school administrators to report on him and provide copies of his signature. The FBI laboratory then compared his handwriting with samples made some twenty years earlier. It also requested specimens of his handwriting from the University of Illinois, from which Algren had graduated in 1931 with a degree in journalism.

In 1956 the FBI's Chicago office thought it vital enough intelligence to tell the FBI's New York office that Algren's publisher, Farrar, Straus & Cudahy, was giving him a party at Brentano's and other bookstores in Chicago. Guilt by party if not by Party?

Ever on the alert to protect the Republic from its enemies, foreign and domestic, in 1957 the FBI made note of Algren's wardrobe. "He showed up at a luncheon of fellow author Studs Terkel wearing a gray workshirt, no tie and baggy suit with a long tear down the back," according to an FBI informant. "While saluting Terkel's *Division Street: America,* Algren made his ever-ready damn-the-capitalists speech. Algren was alone."

There is a fine irony in the FBI file on Nelson Algren: how he fooled the special agents (and kidded his friends) with an alias that was really an inside joke. The bureau was obviously ignorant about anything that involved his writings and literary friendships. Algren had an acerbic sense of humor. One of his favorite homemade pieces of advice went: "Never eat at a place called Mom's, never play cards with a man named Doc, never go to bed with a woman whose troubles are greater than your own."

After his affair with Simone de Beauvoir, the French author and longtime companion of Jean-Paul Sartre, Algren used the name Simon de Beauvoir as his telephone listing. The 1954 telephone directory for Gary, Indiana, lists "de Beauvoir, Simon 6228 Forest. . . . Gary 8-2463." There is no listing for Nelson Algren in the directory.

The FBI apparently had never heard of Simone de Beauvoir. A memorandum in Algren's file notes that "Nelson

Algren Abraham"—the name on his army service record—used several aliases, including "Simon Beauvoir, Simon de Beauvoir and Simone de Beauvoir." The file accurately said that he received telephone service at 6228 Forest Avenue, in Gary, across the state line from Chicago.

Hoping to obtain additional pages and information from Algren's censored file, I pointed out in my letter of appeal that Simone de Beauvoir was the well-known French author and that she had written about their affair. I thought that the FBI might be interested in a fact that had eluded their various agents and recordkeepers: that the alias was literary, not criminal. But the humorless bureau neither acknowledged that it had been fooled nor responded to my letter. It would have been too much to expect that Hoover or his sleuths were aware of Mlle. de Beauvoir's book, *The Mandarins,* or of Existentialism, or, it would seem, of any *ism* other than communism.

DASHIELL HAMMETT

Dashiell Hammett (1894–1961) was respected by professionals in the field of the detective novel as a true original. The author of *The Thin Man* introduced a new kind of character, the cynical private operative Sam Spade, in *The Maltese Falcon.* His dialogue and style were admired by André Gide, Hemingway and writers, readers and filmgoers all over the world. By now Hammett's career, and his troubles with the government, are literary history.

His heavily censored file contained 356 pages. Like Nelson Algren, Hammett was tracked by the FBI and Army Intelligence while he was serving as an enlisted man outside the United States during World War II. And, like Algren, Hammett was outspoken about political injustices—and considered to be an ally of the Communists by the FBI. In 1951 he was sentenced to six months in jail—not for a crime but for contempt because he refused to name persons who had contributed to the Civil Rights Congress bail fund, of which he was a trustee. After three months he was released for good behavior. During the McCarthy era, he was blacklisted from work in films and some libraries removed his books from their shelves.

His file began in 1941 when "an unknown outside source" informed the FBI that "Dashiell Hammett is wearing himself thin trying to prevent the Communist party being ruled off the ballot in New York. He is passing himself off as a political independent but in October he deluged New York unions with telegrams urging support of Earl Browder in the November Presidential elections." Thereafter, the FBI added his photographs to its file. A note said that he is a "Communist sympathizer connected with the staff of the newspaper *PM* in New York."

Hammett served in World War I and enlisted at the age of forty-eight as an army private in World War II, calling his acceptance for military duty the happiest day of his life. When he joined the army in 1942, J. Edgar Hoover sent a message to the chief of military intelligence in Washington, noting that Hammett was president of the League of American Writers, "a Communist-front organization." Thereafter, "confidential informants" (names blacked out) kept track of Private Hammett in this country and in the Aleutian Islands.

According to the file, neither the army nor the FBI seemed to be able to confirm that he was in uniform, or where he served. In 1944 an FBI memorandum said that in the event the subject was not in the army, "present a case against the subject for impersonation." When the FBI finally found Corporal Hammett, they discovered that he indeed was himself and not an impersonator. He was a revered figure among his younger army colleagues, editing the Aleutians' newspaper in the Alaskan theatre of war. The files reveal that "a casual surveillance" was maintained on him there.

After he was honorably discharged the FBI reopened his case in its Los Angeles office. An informant who had spied on Hammett in uniform reported that "during his service there was no evidence of Communist activity nor had he given any indication of doubt concerning his loyalty to the United States. While in the army, however, he did correspond quite regularly with Lillian Hellman, the well-known playwright."

Because he had served as a president of the League of American Writers, Hammett was designated a "key figure" by the FBI after the war. An FBI memorandum goes: "Subject was being watched while residing with Lillian Hellman at Hardscrabble Farm, Pleasantville, New York. House not visible from the road. Completely surrounded by trees. Subject not active in any village meetings." Later, FBI informants noted that he also lived with Miss Hellman at 63 East 82nd Street, New York. (Guilt by cohabitation?)

All during the postwar years, every move Hammett made was tracked by FBI informants (names blacked out). He was a member of the Duncan-Paris Post of the American Legion in New York, made up of alumni of Yank magazine, *Stars and Stripes* and other army papers who were trying to reform the legion from within, which resulted in the post being kicked out by the old guard. As president of the Civil Rights Congress, he protested police brutality against blacks. He spoke at a reunion of the Abraham Lincoln Brigade. He and Dorothy Parker, the New Yorker writer and Hollywood scenarist, served on a committee to restore liberal commentators to the radio networks.

All this was added to his file as he was being watched by FBI agents. The Hammett file reveals that the FBI had informants in many organizations. The Hearst press in New York (the *Journal-American* and *Daily Mirror,* both defunct) and the Scripps-Howard *World-Telegram* (also defunct) reported Hammett's activities, indicating that they were being fed information because they were friendly newspapers. Among magazines, the New Leader, which also reported on Hammett, is described in the file as "strongly anti-Communist in its policies." (The name of the informant or writer on the magazine's staff is blacked out.) He was also a target of "Red Channels," a blackmailing newsletter used against television and radio networks to "clear" names of Communist taint, to which the networks and sponsors succumbed.

In 1953 Hammett appeared before Senator McCarthy's committee and was examined by Roy M. Cohn, its counsel, about some of the books he had written. He was asked if royalties he had received as a result of purchases by the State Department for its United States Information Service libraries abroad were sent to the Communist party. Hammett pleaded the Fifth Amendment. Messrs. McCarthy and Cohn were, of course, trying to use Hammett to attack the targeted State Department.

In 1955, his FBI file shows, Hammett testified at a public hearing in New York State on charitable organizations: "Communism to me is not a dirty word. When you are working for the advance of mankind, it never occurs to me whether a guy is a Communist."

After Hammett's death on January 10, 1961, the FBI literally tried to hound him to his grave at Arlington National Cemetery. A memorandum proposed that Hoover's assistant director, Cartha "Deke" DeLoach, use "one or more of his press contacts" to call attention to the fact that "a member of an organization that believes in the violent overthrow of government by force" should not be given "a hero's burial among those who gave their lives to support this government."

Hammett had served in America's two world wars and expressed a wish to be buried in Arlington. Nothing came of the FBI memorandum; its long pursuit of Hammett was no longer necessary.

IRWIN SHAW

Irwin Shaw (1913–1984), novelist, short-story writer, playwright and scenarist, had twenty-seven censored pages in his FBI file. Some of the material was blacked out "in the interest of national defense or foreign policy." Former Private Shaw—the rank he held when we first met in wartime Algiers—would have been delighted to learn that the FBI listed him as "Colonel Shaw" during World War II and might well have asked for back pay. Apparently the FBI did not communicate too well with the War Department. Other imaginary and inaccurate material appears in his dossier.

Coming almost directly off the football field of Brooklyn College to the New York theater, Shaw first rose to prominence in 1936 with his antiwar play, *Bury the Dead.* It was followed three years later with *The Gentle People,* a parable against Fascism. His short stories, including such classics as "Sailor Off the Bremen" and "The Girls in Their Summer Dresses," appeared regularly in the New Yorker. During the war he turned out military scripts and occasionally contributed to *Stars and Stripes,* the army newspaper. After writing his widely praised and highly successful war novel, *The Young Lions,* Shaw took on the blacklisting commercial television networks in his 1951 novel, *The Troubled Air.*

While Irwin Shaw was in the Mediterranean Theatre of Operations before moving on with the signal corps to England and France, J. Edgar Hoover personally sent a memorandum—"Confidential, by Special Messenger"—to the assistant chief of staff, G-2, in the War Department, Washington. Its "Subject" was both Irwin Shaw and *Stars and Stripes.* The memorandum alerted Army Intelligence to Shaw's background, branding him a "Communist sympathizer." It mistakenly said that Shaw was a writer for *Stars and Stripes.*

Shaw was not, but he would have liked to have been on the paper. After the end of the Tunisian campaign he had made the long drive from Cairo to Algiers, in that springtime of victory in North Africa achieved by the British and American ground forces. Shaw then contributed a few pieces to the paper. One was a semifictional article about all the funny things that would happen the day the war ended. Hanging out with the *Stars and Stripes* editors and writers in their quarters on the Boulevard Baudin—up from the Algiers waterfront that occasionally was bombed by the Luftwaffe taking off from the Balearic Islands, part of Franco Spain's so-called neutral territory in the Mediterranean—Private Shaw expressed a wish to join the staff. An effort was made to have him do so; those already on *Stars and Stripes* hoped that he would join us. But, somehow, it never happened. After all this time, the reason why becomes evident in his FBI file: Wherever Shaw was assigned, Hoover's letter to G-2 was flagged on his service papers.

Those papers are not included in Shaw's FBI file. But a copy of the derogatory directive, which I obtained from another source who was hounded by the army while in uniform (Emil de Antonio, the brilliant documentarian whose films include "Point of Order," on the Army-McCarthy hearings, and "Millhouse: A White Comedy," an ironic biography of Richard M. Nixon), reveals how the War Department handled soldiers it considered radicals even while they were serving in combat zones. Among others so stigmatized were, of course, Dashiell Hammett and Nelson Algren.

The wartime *confidential* directive—headed "Disposition of Subversive and Disaffected Military Personnel"—was signed by Major General J. A. Ulio, the adjutant general in Washington. It defined "subversive personnel" as those who had engaged in "subversive activity of any sort" while in the army. It defined "disaffected personnel" as those "who lack affection for or loyalty to the government and Constitution of the United States." When the facts proved that an enlisted man was "disaffected," he could not be transferred to an outfit where he might "seriously hurt the war effort." In no case could a "disaffected" soldier be assigned to security and intelligence duties, radar jobs, or secret or confidential cryptographic systems or equipment. It was up to a theater commander to decide if a job on *Stars and Stripes,* for example, was considered too sensitive for someone burdened with a radical past in his army file. Since "loyalty" was such a subjective matter of judgment, it was not defined by the adjutant general in his directive.

Almost from the beginning of his playwrighting career, Shaw had come under suspicion. Hoover's letter contained these statements about him, including interpretations of the themes of his theater work:

"With respect to the play, *Bury the Dead,* [name censored] has advised that this was Shaw's most outstanding revolutionary play and that it followed the antiwar Communist party line of the period 1933–1936. [Name blacked out] said that this play was produced in all Communist-controlled 'Little Theatres' and other places, such as union halls and radical meeting places. This play is said to have been supported by all propaganda agencies of the Communist party and can still be purchased in Communist bookstores."

Hoover's letter went on: "Shaw was a member of the League of American Writers and was described by the informant as having been unusually active in the affairs of Com-

Stephen Deutch/Hill and Wang

Nelson Algren won the first National Book Award in 1949 for his novel *The Man With the Golden Arm.* He struggled at the same time that he was acclaimed as an influential writer. The FBI was in hot pursuit of Algren during most of his career; they did not like his themes or political views on civil and constitutional liberties. Algren's heavily censored file contained more than 500 pages.

Reuters

Dashiell Hammett's heavily blacked-out file contained 356 pages. A veteran of both World Wars, he was outspoken against what he regarded as political injustices. The author of *The Thin Man* and *The Maltese Falcon* was sentenced to a jail term for contempt because he refused to name persons who had contributed to the Civil Rights Congress, of which he was a trustee. He is shown here testifying in 1953 before Senator Joseph McCarthy's committee.

Delacorte Press

Irwin Shaw, novelist, short story writer and playwright, had twenty-seven pages in his FBI dossier. A memorandum from J. Edgar Hoover to the War Department while Private Shaw was in the Army branded him a "Communist sympathizer." Wherever he was assigned, the Hoover memorandum was flagged on his service record. Nevertheless, he continued to serve in combat zones and absorbed enough of war to write *The Young Lions*.

munist fronts in Los Angeles, California, since 1937. [Censored] stated that Shaw wrote plays for such groups as 'Contemporary Theatre,' 'New Theatre League,' 'Rebel Players' and 'League of Workers Theatres,' all of which groups, according to informant, were Communist inspired and controlled and at one time affiliated with the International Union of Revolutionary Theatres, set up in Moscow, Russia, in 1932." (Moscow, Russia! Compare Paris, France; London, England, and other secret geography lessons.)

Among the organizations Shaw belonged to, according to Hoover's letter, were the League of American Writers, the Western Writers Congress, the New Theatre School in New York, the Los Angeles Contemporary Theatre and (censored) active in the Hollywood Anti-Nazi League. All were labeled as Communist dominated. The letter concludes that "[words blacked out] it is well known in Hollywood Communist circles that Shaw is a faithful sympathizer and a follower of the Communist party line and, further, that his efforts are always at the disposal of the Communist party."

After the war and into the early 1960s, Shaw's record continued to grow in the FBI files. When the short-lived magazine, Salute, was started in 1946 by a group of former editors and writers for Yank, the army weekly, and *Stars and Stripes,* it was called a "shrewdly camouflaged publication" that criticized the military and "follows the Communist party line to the letter." It was noted that Shaw wrote for Salute and that his name appeared on the masthead.

In 1956 and again in 1961 the United States Information Agency requested information about Shaw for its People-to-People program. The FBI fed the USIA most of its file material and also referred the agency to the House Committee on Un-American Activities. Shaw's honorable military service record is not included in the file material.

Shaw's career included another item that might have been

considered favorable—compared to the slanderous comments about him by unnamed informants and the critical judgments about the content of his plays. He had publicly denied permission to Soviet theater authorities in the sixties to put on a production of *Bury the Dead,* saying that he did not want the play to be used for propaganda purposes against the United States. Whether this omission was deliberate or another of the FBI's errors of fact is not known.

What Shaw's dossier does illustrate is that the FBI's files on authors and playwrights and essayists and poets are tilted in the direction of unfettered suspicion as opposed to free expression.

TRUMAN CAPOTE

Surprisingly, Truman Capote (1924–1984), who was far more of a social than political activist, had 185 pages in his FBI file. Only 110 pages were released to me; one document in a CIA file concerning him was denied. The FBI said that Capote had "never been the subject of an FBI investigation." However, he was identified in numerous files relating to other individuals and organizations. Despite the official statement that he was not investigated, a document stamped *Secret* (crossed out now, after his file was released to me in censored form) reads:

"Investigation is presently being conducted to determine whether [blacked out] present activities warrant his being placed on the Security Index." Since so many pages in his file were withheld, it is not known if Capote was indeed listed as a security risk.

Capote, author of *Breakfast at Tiffany's* and *In Cold Blood,* also wrote *The Muses are Heard,* an account of his travels in the Soviet Union with the black cast of *Porgy and Bess.* Some of his writings were serialized in the New Yorker. The FBI was particularly watchful of him when he accompanied the theatrical troupe to Russia.

An FBI source (name blacked out) reports on the 1956 book, *The Muses are Heard,* and describes it as a "novel." (It was, of course, reportage.) As if revealing something insidious, the source quotes from page fifty-seven of "this novel"—which could have been read in the magazine or found in a bookstore without depending on an informant—to convey its dangerous nature:

> Joachim, an overly avid photographer, had broken the rules by getting off the train, then compounded that error by attempting to take pictures. Now he was racing zigzag across the tracks, narrowly avoiding the wrathful swipe of a woman worker's shovel, barely eluding the grasp of a guard.
>
> Joachim, however, turned out to be a resourceful young man. Slipping past his pursuers, he hurled himself onto the train, rushed into a compartment, threw his coat, his camera and his cap under the seat, and to further alter his appearance, whipped off his hornrimmed glasses. Seconds later, when the angry Soviets came abroad, he calmly assumed his role of company interpreter and helped them hunt the culprit, a search which included every compartment.

Explaining the reason for some of the censored material, the FBI said: "Information has been deleted which originated with the United States Senate, Subcommittee to Investigate the Administration of the Internal Security Act and other

Internal Security laws of the Committee on the Judiciary, Fair Play for Cuba Committee, January 6, 1961, in executive session. This information is exempt from disclosure since it is considered to be outside the purview of the Freedom of Information-Privacy Acts."

An FBI document on the Fair Play for Cuba Committee, dated November 21, 1960, includes Capote's name plus others—Simone de Beauvoir, Jean-Paul Sartre, I.F. Stone, Norman Mailer, Kenneth Tynan, C. Wright Mills and James Baldwin. An FBI memorandum notes that J. Edgar Hoover requested "summaries" on the Fair Play for Cuba signers. A *confidential* document in his file reads: "Truman Capote, says Cabreba Infante, supports the revolution."

In the FBI summary, Capote is described in these words: "A close friend of publisher Bennett Cerf, a nationally known author and writer for the New Yorker magazine." (Not to mention star panelist on television's "What's My Line?")

A final entry in Capote's released file is dated May 23, 1968, from Los Angeles. It reveals that an informant was tracking someone who was known to Capote. This somewhat mysterious entry goes: "He was advised by Capote that [name censored] is staying in some friend's home in Palm Springs while he is rewriting some portions of his book [title censored]. Capote could not recall the name of the street but said it was some "Circle" approximately one mile from downtown Palm Springs." The FBI memorandum mentioned the Palm Springs Spa Motel.

Capote was gifted, but the nature of his gifts hardly made him deserving of so lofty a political tag as "Security Risk" and thus a potential threat to the United States. For the FBI to follow him, have his documents stamped *Secret* and *Confidential,* and study his writings is an especially ludicrous example of the length to which its surveillance of authors has gone.

A.J. LIEBLING

In the dossier, his name is given as Abbott Joseph Liebling (1904–1963). To those who followed his perceptive articles and commentary, his signature, A.J. Liebling, stood for graceful writing and fierce integrity. Yet before and after World War II he became one of the Usual Suspects. His censored FBI file contains eighteen pages.

In his "Wayward Press" column in the New Yorker, Liebling pursued and refined the idea that newspapers and magazines should not be above criticism and ought to improve themselves (a belief that, one would imagine, the chief could endorse). Between 1940 and 1945 he was a highly respected war correspondent; one of his books was *The Road Back to Paris.* This writer recalls seeing Liebling in Algiers in 1943, hanging out of his uniform, his overseas cap askew, hardly the picture of the dashing correspondent. Yet Liebling was considerably more impressive than most of the other correspondents, a man fluent in French who understood the complexities of Free French politics and North African colonialism. He set a standard of writing and courage that is still admired by journalists.

His file reveals that an unnamed informant had access to internal editorial information at the magazine and passed it along to the FBI. A 1937 entry in the Liebling file, which appears later in a 1950 FBI memorandum, discloses some of his personal history and writings:

"[Name and affiliation blacked out] advised that Jack Alexander was writing a special feature article for the New Yorker on the director [that is, J. Edgar Hoover]." The entry continues: "[Name blacked out] Liebling was Alexander's research assistant."

Liebling first came to the attention of the FBI because he took a crack at J. Edgar Hoover in a newspaper piece.

Forever after he was considered hostile to the bureau. Making fun of the publicity-minded director was considered—if not a high crime worthy of being adjudged a security risk—at the least an unpatriotic misdemeanor. In either case, it meant having one's writings watched and one's file grow thicker.

His entry reads: "On January 16, 1937, the New York *World Telegram* carried an article entitled 'A Tough Detail,' by A.J. Liebling. It was written in fictional form with the leading character named Patrolman McGimlet. In a satirical manner Liebling described an alleged raid conducted in New York by the bureau and portrayed the director as 'A. Edwin Doover.' The story described an apartment house that was illuminated with floodlights, with a front roped off and agents with cameras and sound equipment. A character portrayed as a cab driver was quoted: 'Looks like a Minsky burlesque opening.' The entire article was an apparent nasty dig at the director and the bureau."

In 1950, one war and thirteen years later, the FBI put together a report on Abbott Joseph Liebling. It summarized his personal history: "Born, Oct. 18, 1904; student at Dartmouth and received degree in literature from Columbia in 1925; student at the Sorbonne, 1926–27; married Ann Beatrice McGinn on July 28, 1934." Thereafter, the file continues, he worked on newspapers in Providence and New York before joining the New Yorker in 1935. It is noted that he was a correspondent for the magazine from October 1939 until the end of 1945 in England, North Africa and France; but this major part of his wartime writing-life overseas is ignored by the FBI.

The remainder of his file deals with his associations with others. The FBI took the trouble—and had the inside connections—to report that Richard Owen Boyer had ordered his publisher, Little, Brown & Company, to send a copy of his history of the National Maritime Union, *The Dark Ship,* to

Liebling for publicity purposes. (This may be one of the rare cases when getting a free copy of a book subjected the receiver to guilt by association with the author.) Referring to Boyer, the FBI report says: "[Name censored] it is alleged that he writes articles in which he admits that he is a Communist."

Liebling's association with Howard Fast, author of *Citizen Tom Paine* and *Freedom Road,* was also noted. Fast is described as a columnist for the *Daily Worker.* In 1947 Liebling was listed as one of the sponsors of a meeting to protest the action of the House Un-American Activities Committee against Fast.

Criticism of Liebling as a journalist and author appeared in his file whenever he reported about the Whittaker Chambers–Alger Hiss case. In the magazine Plain Talk, Ralph De Toledano, a Red-hunter, wrote: "A.J. Liebling, a careless journalist of the New Yorker smart set, also rushes into print with a misleading article which disregards the Chambers evidence but makes sure to call him a 'dead beat.' "

In Liebling's FBI file, the New Yorker itself is criticized by Peter Minot in the October 1949 issue of Plain Talk, in an article entitled, "The Wayward New Yorker." The magazine is reprimanded for "its pro-Communist activities in reporting." In November 1949 the same writer in Plain Talk writes about "The Wayward Mr. Liebling." It calls him "a kind of assistant counsel and private detective for the defense" in the Hiss trial. The New York FBI office then advised the Washington headquarters that Thomas J. Murphy, assistant United States attorney, had "speculated" that the Hiss lawyers had "probably" engaged Liebling to work for them at the same time that he reported for the New Yorker. This wild and of course unproved speculation became a part of Liebling's permanent file.

"An individual named Liebling," said an internal FBI office

memorandum, wrote "an unfavorable article" about Senator Pat McCarran in the New Yorker on March 27, 1954. This article dealt with Nevada and gambling in Las Vegas under the title, "Our Far-Flung Correspondents." Someone in the bureau, after checking the article, said that it was written in "a somewhat humorous, caustic vein."

Nevertheless, a detailed FBI memorandum on Liebling did not recognize his humor. The memorandum was sent to the State Department in 1964. It maintained that "No investigation has been conducted by this bureau concerning Abbott Joseph Liebling. The information set forth herein is strictly confidential and must not be disseminated outside of your agency. This is the result of a request for an FBI file-check only and is not to be considered as a clearance."

Ideally, Abbott Joseph Liebling's FBI dossier should have been written—with wayward ridicule exposing its farfetched accusations—by A.J. Liebling.

VI.

TROUBLEMAKING PLAYRIGHTS

America's leading twentieth-century playwrights were watched by the federal government—sometimes for what they said, sometimes for what they wrote, often for both. Like scores of novelists, dramatists came under particular scrutiny by narrow-minded officials because their works were considered dangerous and un-American. But neither the House Committee on Un-American Activities, the Senate Internal Security Committee nor the FBI ever could define who or what was "Un-American."

Arthur Miller, whose plays are regularly performed in many countries, served as an international president of PEN and has regularly fought in defense of freedom to write, here and abroad, refers several times in his autobiography to having a "dossier." His appearance before the House Committee on Un-American Activities in 1956 assured that he would have a file; the FBI exchanged material with the Red-hunting congressional committees. Miller told me, "The Committee did question me about my work, including a satire of the Committee written many years earlier, which they took exception to." Speaking before the Newspaper Guild, he once attacked Secretary of State John Foster Dulles for refusing to allow journalists to report from China. "I had no doubt such speeches of mine," Miller said, "were simply going into J. Edgar Hoover's dossier on me."

Of course, not every dramatist was pursued for this book, but those whose records follow help to reveal that the American theater was not immune from scrutiny for subversive themes by government committees and agencies. These Red-hunters, with no awareness of the creative process and little knowledge of American history, somehow believed that they alone knew the meaning of Americanism and something they invented called "Un-Americanism."

THORNTON WILDER

Thornton Wilder (1897–1975) had ninety-eight pages in his heavily censored FBI file; six pages were withheld. Playwright, novelist, teacher, activist in literary affairs, he was one of the most erudite authors in the country. His 1927 novel, *The Bridge of San Luis Rey,* was a philosophical story of fate set in South America's past, and his 1948 *The Ides of March,* a novel about Julius Caesar. His best-known dramas are *Our Town* (1938), an American pastoral, and *The Skin of Our Teeth* (1942), a morality play on marriage and its escapades.

Variously, his FBI categories included "Espionage" and "Internal Security." One of the interesting documents reveals that an "FBI Watch" was kept on him as a "Suspect" while he was serving overseas as an air corps intelligence officer. His personal mail was checked and censored. FBI offices tracked him in Boston, Detroit, Newark and New York. The bureau was particularly concerned with his associations and affiliations—especially (an old refrain) with writers' organizations that took stands on such issues as aid for the Spanish Loyalists against *Generalissimo* Franco's Fascists and activities against Nazi Germany. Like Robert Sherwood, his contemporary in the theater, he came under suspicion because he willingly put his name on causes he believed sacred to freedom and, therefore, literature.

In 1938 Wilder was reported to be in a group of thirty-eight American authors who petitioned President Roosevelt to "sever trade relations with Nazi Germany and declare an embargo on all Nazi German goods." There was nothing furtive about this action, yet it wound up in his FBI file.

In 1940, the FBI hit a dead end in attempting to link Wilder to a supposed matter of espionage for Germany at an Austrian refugee camp in New Hampshire. In addition to the license numbers of his two cars, and the fact that he owned a house in Hamden, Connecticut, the FBI reported that he was "on the Republican voting list" but "boosted for President Roosevelt" in the 1936 election. The best—worst—they could come up with was that he spent a great deal of time at a writers' camp in Vermont. In the end, the FBI had to conclude that there was "no information received which would link subject Wilder with any espionage or subversive activities."

The record, however, rolled on. A hostile article in the Washington *Times Herald* in 1942 stated that the War Writers' Board included Thornton Wilder on its advisory council. The article said that the board, "which functions under the direction of the Office of Civilian Defense, and uses the government's mailing frank of the 'Executive Office of the President,' is participating 'unofficially' in the campaign of the Communists and other totalitarians." Furthermore "Rex Stout, writer of murder mystery stories," who had a record as "a Communist fellow traveler and is one of the prize exhibits of the Dies Committee on Un-American Activities," was chairman of the War Writers' Board.

This smear, which found its way into Wilder's file, totally misrepresented the War Writers' Board, which included many prominent volunteers from the Authors and Dramatist guilds who contributed their writing skills to aid the war effort.

A detailed report in 1954, stamped *Confidential,* presuming to summarize Wilder's life and career, came under the FBI's familiar euphemism to cover its bureaucratic backside: "No investigation has been conducted by the bureau of Thornton Wilder." This, of course, was a matter of degree: for a so-called noninvestigation, the FBI had clearly devoted many man-hours to produce its material about the dramatist.

The Wilder report noted that he had been educated at Yale and Princeton; taught at the University of Chicago; served in World War I as a corporal and in World War II as a lieutenant colonel in Air Corps Intelligence; that he was a bachelor and a Democrat, and that he had won three Pulitzer prizes—for *The Bridge of San Luis Rey, Our Town* and *The Skin of Our Teeth.* As if service in both wars was insufficient as a test of his patriotism, the file recorded that he had been affiliated with "Cited Organizations." The report went back to 1933. A number of the sources of information are blacked out, indicating that the FBI had plants inside these organizations—including writers' organizations—who provided mimeographed or typewritten copies of their activities.

Wilder was also listed as a member of the National Committee of the American Committee for Struggle Against War, a mouthful organization cited by the House Committee on Un-American Activities in 1933 as a Communist front under the auspices of the Communist International. A circular in 1935 further named Wilder as a member of the American Committee of the American League Against War and Fascism, "an organization designated by the attorney general pursuant to Executive Order 10450."

Wilder was included in a typewritten report (the source's name is blacked out) as a participant or sponsor of the Second National Congress of the League of American Writers held in New York in 1937. In a pamphlet entitled "Writers Take Sides," published by the league in 1938, Wilder is quoted as saying: "I am unreservedly for the legal government and Loyalist party in Spain." (In 1937 a number of leading British and Irish writers, among them W.H. Auden, Samuel Beckett, Ford Madox Ford, Aldous Huxley, V.S. Pritchett, Herbert Read and Stephen Spender, had put out an anti-Franco pamphlet called "Authors Take Sides on the Spanish War.") The League of American Writers was placed on the attorney general's list.

He was named as a national sponsor of the American Committee for the Protection of the Foreign Born in 1940 and 1941—an organization also cited by the attorney general. A mimeographed sheet of the National Committee for People's Rights, obtained by the FBI in 1941, listed Wilder as one of the members of the organization who lived in or near New York City and was eligible for election to its executive committee. It was cited by the House Committee on Un-American Activities as a Communist front that succeeded the National Committee for the Defense of Political Prisoners. A totally blacked-out paragraph in his file, undated, is followed by: "The National Council of American Soviet Friendship has been designated by the attorney general pursuant to Executive Order 10450."

All through the McCarthy years, and afterward, former Lieutenant Colonel Thornton Wilder was the subject of attention for anything he dared to sign, including statements in defense of freedom to write by other writers.

In 1948 Wilder was one of the signers of a letter to the Speaker of the House of Representatives protesting "the methods employed by the Committee on Un-American Activities, under the chairmanship of Representative J. Parnell Thomas, in the examination of certain writers summoned to appear before it. This letter was sponsored by members of the National Institute of Arts and Letters, an honorary organization of American writers, artists and musicians. The National Institute of Arts and Letters has been cited by the California Committee on Un-American Activities as a Communist front."

The California committee was, if possible, more careless than the Congressional Un-American Activities Committee. The National Institute of Arts and Letters, combined with its senior body, the American Academy, is limited to 250 members. It is the most distinguished arts group in the United States.

Whenever a name-check was requested on Wilder by other government agencies—including the White House, State Department and Central Intelligence Agency—all the accusations in his raw files were repeated and supplied without comment by the FBI. Its typical boilerplate language denied any responsibility "for clearance or nonclearance of the individual involved." As late as 1970 such FBI information was passed along to other agencies.

But Wilder, not his watchdogs, continues to have the last word through the performances of his plays. *Our Town,* often regarded as dramatizing the essence of the American experience, is repeatedly staged all over the United States. Its ideas portray Wilder far more accurately than the falsehoods in his file.

ROBERT SHERWOOD

In the FBI file on Robert Sherwood (1896–1955) there were eighty FBI pages, some totally blacked out; in addition, nine pages released were attributed to the White House. Sherwood's file indicates that at the same time that he was writing speeches for his friend, President Franklin D. Roosevelt, and serving as director of overseas operations in the Office of War Information, he was under suspicion. J. Edgar Hoover repeatedly passed on material branding Robert Emmet Sherwood, friend of the president, a Communist.

The playwright *(Idiot's Delight, The Petrified Forest, Abe Lincoln in Illinois)*, screenwriter (*Best Years of Our Lives*), and biographer *(Roosevelt and Hopkins)* was active during the rise of fascism and nazism, trying to convince Americans of the danger of totalitarianism.

All of which earned him, during the early part of the war in 1942, a ranking as an "Internal Security—C" case. After the war, during the Eisenhower presidency, and right up to the year of his death, Sherwood was watched by the FBI. He was critical of Secretary of State John Foster Dulles' brinkmanship policies in the name of national security, and defended the rights of authors—including the blacklisted "Hollywood Ten."

Again and again in the Sherwood file reference is made to his activism in the theater, his leadership in dramatists' organizations and the subjects and themes of his plays. The man as well as his writings were scrutinized. Parts of his FBI file read like a listing of credits in the Playbill. He was a member of the Playwrights' Company, a group of outstanding dramatists founded in 1938 that also included S.N. Behrman, Elmer Rice, Maxwell Anderson and Sidney Howard. An internal memorandum prepared for Hoover in 1941 lists Sherwood's plays, beginning with *The Road to Rome* in 1927, and the memorandum provides the earthshaking intelligence that in 1936 he was Secretary of the Dramatists Guild.

Together with other American authors, his name appeared on a letter written to President Roosevelt in 1938: "We feel that it is deeply immoral for the American people to continue having economic relations with a government that avowedly uses mass murder to solve its economic problems. We ask you to sever trade relations with Nazi Germany, to declare an embargo on all Nazi Germany goods."

In the same year of 1938 Sherwood was a member of the National Council on Freedom from Censorship, which according to the House Committee on Un-American Activities was affiliated with the American Civil Liberties Union—"a Communist-front organization." Three years before, Sherwood had helped to develop the New Theatre School "to write and produce agitational and propaganda plays." This school was an offspring of the New Theatre League—"the mainspring of the Agitprop theatre movement. The New Theatre League was cited as a Communist front by the special committee on Un-American Activities on March 29, 1944." (By such criteria, Sherwood's play, *Abe Lincoln in Illinois,* could be deemed Communistic agitation and propaganda because of its association with the playwright. Absurdity is the mother of absurdity.)

Also in his file is a 1941 report by the American Legion saying that it was "considerably aroused" over plays and broadcasts put on by the Free Company. The legion called them "un-American, Communistic and operating under the guise of appearing for free speech but actually campaigning for the light of communism and other subversive elements." Sherwood was listed as chairman of the writers' division of this group.

One censored page, undated but possibly 1941 or 1942,

says: "On [blacked out] information was received from a confidential source that Robert Sherwood was a member of the Communist party. The informant further advised that all plays going into army camps must be approved by the National Theatre Conference. Sherwood and one [censored], a Communist party member, were the two men who approved the plays for the National Theatre Conference. The informant further advised that [censored] who was recently president of the National Theatre Conference [censored] and Sherwood were all tied up with the old 'Chekov [sic] Conference' held at Moscow, Russia, for the purpose of discussing the theater for spreading Communist propaganda throughout the world."

In 1950 Sherwood was one of the signers of a telegram sent to Associate Justice Robert H. Jackson of the Supreme Court, including many persons in the theatrical arts, requesting the court to reverse the contempt citation against the "Hollywood Ten" for refusing to answer questions about possible Communist party membership.

In 1952, at the beginning of the Eisenhower presidency and McCarthyism, Sherwood's file reads: "Various sources have stated that Sherwood is a Communist, appears to favor Socialist organizations, etc., and was believed to be a member of the National Council of the Arts, Sciences and Professions. None of this type data is being set out in the blind memorandum due to lack of substantiating evidence and the fact that these allegations were furnished by highly confidential sources."

As seen repeatedly, the FBI records—in the case of Sherwood and other writers—could be flagrantly contradictory to be self-protective. Although the FBI maintained that "no investigation has been conducted by this bureau on Sherwood," an internal memorandum, dated January 30, 1942, reads: "However, there is considerable derogatory information in the files relative to Robert E. Sherwood and your attention is particularly directed to Serial 5 of File 100-9568, which is the main file on Robert E. Sherwood." Another internal memorandum dated December 12, 1942, confirms the existence of such a file with the same number: New York File 100-9568, titled Robert Emmet Sherwood, and categorized as a Communist Internal Security file. All the slanderous comments about Sherwood are carried in his "main file." The FBI passed these along, without qualification, to other government branches, including the White House.

In a 1952 speech to the Anti-Defamation League—reported in his FBI file—Sherwood called the Eisenhower administration's internal security program a "heartless, soulless, callous tyranny." He said, "I think that we, the American people, the taxpayers who pay the salaries of Secretary of State John Foster Dulles and State Department Security Chief Scott McLeod would like to know just when did we resolve that the rights of the individual American citizens should be subordinated and indeed destroyed by some undocumented interpretation of what some official tells us is national security."

He was still being tracked by the FBI for his views in 1955. When he spoke before the Anti-Defamation League in New York, an internal FBI memorandum noted that all three speakers—Sherwood, Dore Schary and Henry Schultz—had "bureau files." Said Sherwood, "If our national security is to be rated above the security, the civil liberties, the dignity of every individual American, then our national security is not worth defending." Victor Riesel, one of Hoover's favorite Red-hunters in the press, roundly attacked him for these comments.

Robert Sherwood displayed courage all his life. He enlisted in the Canadian Expeditionary Force in 1917 before America entered the First World War to fight for his beliefs; served

President Roosevelt during the Second World War; fought extreme antilibertarian views and practices of the cold war; and wrote plays that expressed his deepest concerns about freedom. *Therefore*—in the clouded vision of the FBI—he had to be watched, and be branded an "Internal Security—C" case.

ELMER RICE

Elmer Rice (1892–1967) was a member of the Playwrights' Company, that suspicious group of dramatists. The Dies Committee on Un-American Activities quoted an unnamed individual's testimony on him: "Very prominent in the Playwrights' Company in New York, along with Robert Sherwood, was Elmer Rice, about whose radicalism there can be little question."

The FBI file on Rice included forty-six heavily censored pages; ten CIA pages were denied; two Office of Strategic Services (forerunner of the CIA) pages were received; one OSS document, dated April 17, 1957, was denied in its entirety after my appeal, on grounds of "national defense or foreign policy."

It was enlightening to see how the FBI described Rice for purposes of identification. His "alias" in the file was "Elmer Leopold Reizenstein." In 1944 his file read: "Wears glasses, Jewish appearing features." In 1953, it simply said: "Always wear glasses." Apparently the FBI no longer thought he looked "Jewish"—or someone had removed the stereotyped anti-Semitic description. (Actually, when this writer spent an afternoon with Rice in the 1960s he talked—and even looked—just like a playwright.)

Again and again it is noted in Rice's file that he was active in the Authors League and Dramatists Guild, of which he was president in 1941. The FBI considered the League and its guilds suspect and worthy of an independent investigation.

The playwright began his career in 1914 with *On Trial.* His next success was *The Adding Machine,* in 1923, about the victims of mechanized society. *Street Scene* in 1929 showed a slice of slum life; Kurt Weill and Langston Hughes turned it into a musical in 1947. In 1933 Rice used the stage to protest the Depression in *We, the People,* and, in 1934, he warned against the Nazis in *Judgment Day.* The file includes a Playbill (normally not considered a subversive document or an FBI souvenir) of *We, the People* when it was playing at the Empire Theater on Broadway.

In a report by J. Edgar Hoover in 1942 Rice's file is transmitted to the special agent in charge of the New York Bureau because of a visa and exit-control matter. After his name there appears the now familiar "Internal Security—C" and "Custodial Detention."

Rice's first entry dates from 1925, when the letterhead of New Masses, the leftist political and literary journal that had been suspended by the government the year before, listed him as a contributing editor. In 1932 he was one of the supporters of an injunction to prevent interference with the Hunger March on Washington. In 1936, after serving as regional director of the Federal Theatre Project in New York, he resigned to protest US Government censorship of a proposed play by him with a background depicting Italy's invasion of Ethiopia. He said, "I cannot conscientiously remain the servant of a government which plays the shabby game of partisan politics at the expense of freedom and the principles of democracy."

All of Rice's affiliations that were frowned upon by the FBI were listed in his file: National Council on Freedom from Censorship, National Council Against Censorship of Theatre

Arts of the American Civil Liberties Union, American Federation for Constitutional Liberties, National Committee of the North American Committee to Aid Spanish Democracy, Russian War Relief, Committee to Defend America by Aiding the Allies.

A report by the FBI's New York Bureau in 1944 described Rice in these words: "A trifle to the left, recently a liberal, never orthodox in his radicalism, inclined more toward those who have renounced the revolutionary attitude in favor of one more moderate to our native tradition, a persistent experimentalist, and revolutionist in things pertaining to the arts and theater. He has stated that he is not a Communist and considers them a pretty futile, feeble people. He is, by his own statement, left wing, not a Communist, but a Socialist since he was eighteen. Rice has been openly critical of the Russian-German nonaggression pact and the Soviet mass executions. He is a strong supporter of all things anti-Fascist."

Because of his plays, anonymous letters also found their way into Rice's files. When *Dream Girl* was staged in Pittsburgh in 1947 a letter said that he had a long "Red" record, that he was president of the Authors League and that "the Communists have a powerful voice in the Authors League. Although Reizenstein-Rice violently maintains he isn't a Communist he usually can be found lined up on the Stalinist side on practically every issue."

Rice stuck to his principles during the blacklisting period by the television networks and advertising agencies that moved the merchandise for the broadcasters. He withdrew his plays from a television producing company because the sponsor, Celanese Corporation, and its agency, Ellington Advertising, "cleared" and blacklisted actors for their "political beliefs." Rice's letter cited such blacklisted actors as Frederic March, Florence Eldridge, Jean Muir and Mady Christians. In his eloquent letter he concluded:

"It has been broadly hinted to me that if I took this step and made my reasons public I could expect reprisals: in other words, the banning of my own plays on the airwaves. That is a risk I am prepared to run. I could not live happily with myself if I allowed economic considerations to deter me from exposing an ugly blot upon American life and an ugly threat to American liberty."

The letter, which defied everything Hoover stood for, of course came to the attention of the chief. Hoover obtained a copy of the letter from Rice to Stellar Enterprises, producer of Playwrights' Television Theatre, and asked the FBI's Connecticut office in New Haven (Rice then lived in Stamford) to place it in the playwright's file—and furnish additional information about him.

Into Rice's FBI file also went additional information about the Authors League, Authors Guild and Dramatists Guild. In 1952, "[name and affiliation censored] advised that the Authors League of America is composed of the Authors Guild, Dramatists Guild, Radio Writers Guild and the Television Writers Guild, with national headquarters located in New York City. According to [censored], the Authors League of America is Communist infiltrated, but not Communist dominated."

The falsehood that the league or its guilds had been "infiltrated" was wholly without evidence; the league has taken strong positions on First Amendment freedoms and professional matters, but it has never been subject to political affiliation, infiltration or domination.

The FBI monitored Rice's name in the newspapers, and his file indicates that newspaper morgues—the usually guarded, private staff material—were opened up to FBI agents. Included are citations from both the Hearst-owned New York *Journal American* and the independent New York *Times,* mentioning the morgues of these newspapers as sources of material about Rice.

Thornton Wilder, author of "Our Town," "The Skin of Our Teeth" and other plays, had more than 100 pages in his FBI dossier. Because he was active in writers' organizations and took stands on such issues as aid for the Spanish Loyalists against Franco's Fascists, his file continued to grow. During World War II (he is shown in a captain's uniform here), he was promoted to lieutenant-colonel and served in Air Force intelligence in the Mediterranean Theatre.

Elmer Rice, author of "Street Scene" and other plays, had a heavily censored file of more than fifty pages, kept by both the FBI and CIA. All of his federal theatrical affiliations were frowned on; all of his civil liberties activities were duly noted, especially his attacks against censorship. The FBI also included the fact that he had been a president of the Dramatists Guild—which had its own dossier.

Jane Bown/Camera Press

Tennessee Williams, author of "A Streetcar Named Desire" and other major American plays, had a small but revealing FBI file. (The FBI mistakenly called "Streetcar" a book, not a play.) Both the State Department and Office of Naval Intelligence also made note of the fact that "Thomas Lanier Williams has the reputation of being a homosexual"—and therefore was a "security" risk in their files.

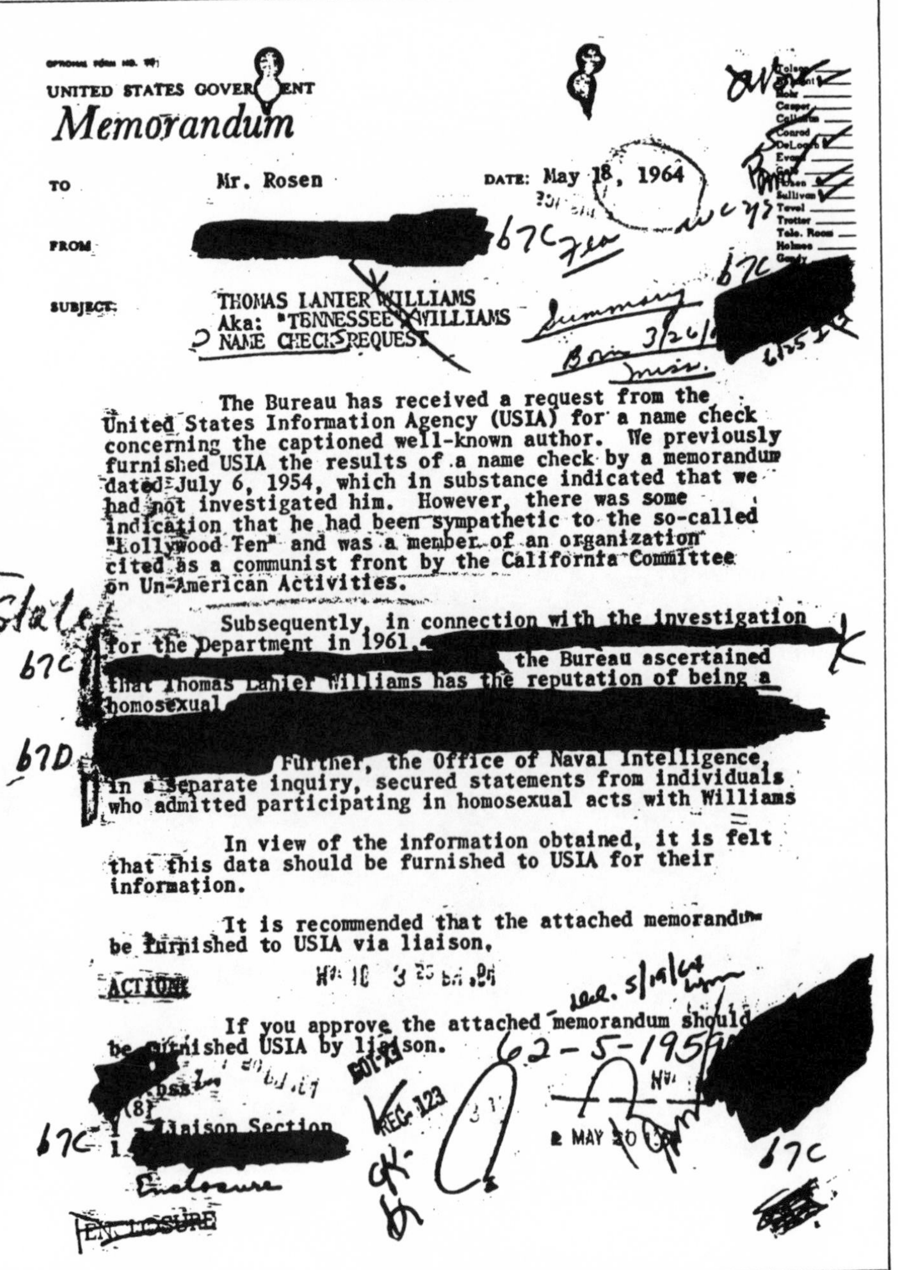
OPTIONAL FORM NO. 10

UNITED STATES GOVERNMENT

Memorandum

TO: Mr. Rosen

DATE: May 18, 1964

FROM: [redacted] b7C

SUBJECT: THOMAS LANIER WILLIAMS
Aka: "TENNESSEE" WILLIAMS
NAME CHECK REQUEST

The Bureau has received a request from the United States Information Agency (USIA) for a name check concerning the captioned well-known author. We previously furnished USIA the results of a name check by a memorandum dated July 6, 1954, which in substance indicated that we had not investigated him. However, there was some indication that he had been sympathetic to the so-called "Hollywood Ten" and was a member of an organization cited as a communist front by the California Committee on Un-American Activities.

Subsequently, in connection with the investigation for the Department in 1961, [redacted] the Bureau ascertained that Thomas Lanier Williams has the reputation of being a homosexual [redacted] Further, the Office of Naval Intelligence, in a separate inquiry, secured statements from individuals who admitted participating in homosexual acts with Williams

In view of the information obtained, it is felt that this data should be furnished to USIA for their information.

It is recommended that the attached memorandum be furnished to USIA via liaison.

ACTION

If you approve the attached memorandum should be furnished USIA by liaison.

Enclosure

(8)

1 - Liaison Section

1 - [redacted]

ENCLOSURE

62-5-1959

REC-123

2 MAY 20 1964

Tennessee Williams was mentioned in three separate files—FBI, State Department and Office of Naval Intelligence. On this FBI page, it is noted that individuals were interrogated who had engaged in homosexual acts with Williams. The reason for the blacked out lines, according to the FBI, was to conceal the identities of confidential sources used for "law enforcement purposes."

According to Rice's file there were two "Security-type investigations" conducted by the FBI—in 1944 and in 1952–53. This investment by the FBI of its resources in wartime and again during the McCarthy era produced nothing to incriminate the playwright—or to silence him.

MAXWELL ANDERSON

Another member of the Playwrights' Company, Maxwell Anderson (1888–1959), had twenty pages in his dossier. As if unwholesome or illegal, the FBI labeled his political thinking in these words: "A person interested in social legislation."

Anderson's verse plays—*Elizabeth the Queen, Winterset, Mary of Scotland, High Tor*—earned him a secure place in American theatrical history. But not in the files of the FBI, whose keepers were moved to protect the Republic from a person "interested in social legislation." An internal memorandum in 1941 noted that he was "one of a group of American writers and playwrights who have formed The Free Company to prepare dramatic broadcasts as a counterattack against foreign propaganda in the United States, the purpose being to restate in 'moving terms' our own beliefs rather than attack foreign propaganda directly. It is noted that under date of April 12, 1941, an article appeared in the San Francisco *Examiner* setting forth a 'resolution of protest' adopted by the American Legion protesting the radio plays given by The Free Company as being 'red' plays designed to encourage radicalism in the United States."

During the Spanish Civil War Anderson was marked in 1938 as a member of the Committee to Save Spain and China, an organization "reported to be under the direction of the Communist party of America." An internal memorandum reported that seventy-eight of America's leading writers, including Ernest Hemingway, Pearl Buck and Maxwell Anderson, had appealed for money to buy arms to defend the Spanish Republic.

"The above résumé of the activities and associations of Maxwell Anderson," the FBI memorandum concluded, "is by no means a complete picture; however, it is believed that sufficient information is set forth to present a clear picture as to his activities in the past." His "past" also included branding him as one of a number (other names censored) of "left-wing individuals."

The FBI special agent in charge of the New York office received a communication in October 1942 from J. Edgar Hoover labeled *"Maxwell Anderson—Internal Security—C."* The message from on high said: "The New York field division is requested to conduct an appropriate investigation to develop background and activities of subject Anderson with reference to his possible Custodial Detention. A summary report should then be submitted in accordance with prior bureau instructions summarizing all pertinent information concerning this individual contained in the files of the New York office and including the information incorporated in this letter."

A month later, the Anderson case was placed in a "deferred status" and, in August 1943, in a "closed status" pending "additional information." (The FBI lived in hopes—we'll get you . . . if not today than maybe tomorrow.) So the bureau continued to track Anderson after the war. His file states that in 1947 the Authors League of America issued a statement criticizing the House Committee on Un-American Activities for its investigation of communism in the motion-picture industry. It is noted that "one of the proponents of this statement was Maxwell Anderson." In 1948 Anderson was listed as one of the writers who would do the narration for a Hollywood Bowl memorial program by the Hollywood Writers

Mobilization, an organization designated as a Communist front by the attorney general. The next year Anderson was listed as one of the signers against the activities of the House Committee on Un-American Activities, which committee, headed by Representative J. Parnell Thomas, had denounced the National Institute of Arts and Letters as "a Communist front for writers, artists and musicians." Anderson was a member of this most distinguished American honor society.

In 1956 a *confidential* document reprised all previous information in the Anderson record of associations and statements, but not one of the documents mentions that the playright had ever written a play. The FBI file, in behalf of the nation's security, disassociated the man from the fruits of his creativity.

WILLIAM SAROYAN

Although forty-five pages in the file of William Saroyan (1908–1981) were reviewed, only thirteen pages, heavily censored, were released to me. His file included documents from the FBI, CIA and State Department. After I appealed the CIA excisions still remained on grounds that they were "secret in the interest of national defense or foreign policy." That phrase might well have delighted the freewheeling California author of *The Daring Young Man on the Flying Trapeze* and *The Human Comedy,* and such plays as *My Heart's in the Highlands, The Time of Your Life* and *The Beautiful People.*

In 1965, at the request of an aide to President Johnson, the FBI provided a name-check to the White House. Much of it is blacked out, except for noting that Saroyan was born on August 31, 1908, in Fresno, California. Although the FBI summary said that no investigation had been made of Saroyan, nevertheless the Bureau had maintained a file on him that included statements that tarred him with the same brush as was applied to several other contemporaries in the theater:

In 1940, it was reported (name censored) that Saroyan spoke at a "Committee of Publishers Pan-American Dinner for Writers in Exile" at the Hotel Commodore in New York. The unnamed informant advised that the dinner was "an extremely left-wing affair" and some literary figures (unnamed) refused to participate when they learned it was a "Communist-sponsored affair." All the speakers were called "front people" for the Communist party.

In 1941 it was reported that a group of American writers and playwrights had formed The Free Company to prepare broadcasts against foreign propaganda in the United States. Saroyan was listed among them. The American Legion protested the radio plays, calling them "Red" and "designed to encourage radicalism in the United States."

In 1948 Saroyan joined a list of signers in the National Institute of Arts and Letters that denounced the House Un-American Activities Committee, and the FBI reported that the California Committee on Un-American Activities had cited the National Institute of Arts and Letters as a "Communist front."

One of the FBI's favorite columnists, George E. Sokolsky of Kings Features, the Hearst syndicate, attacked Saroyan in 1959. The column "revealed" that Saroyan had visited Russian cities, had been interviewed, and had been favorably impressed. "He witnessed an utterly brainwashed society," the omniscient Sokolsky wrote. After seeing this column J. Edgar Hoover asked for a check on Saroyan, and a handwritten note, possibly by Hoover, added to Saroyan's summary: "This pretty well pegs Saroyan."

The following year, during a trip to Moscow, Saroyan was monitored by the State Department. He registered at the American Embassy in Moscow and traveled to Soviet Armenia before continuing on to India. Interviews with him in the Soviet Literary Gazette and Moscow *News* were enclosed. Saroyan had said he was pleased that 150,000 copies of his *The Human Comedy* had been printed in the Soviet Union.

A heavily censored page stamped *Secret* included data on Saroyan from the 1966–67 edition of *Who's Who in America.* (This "secret" source book can be found in most libraries.) The entry notes that Saroyan is "a noted author and playwright residing at 74 Rue Tait-bout, Paris."

A blank sheet, dated February 28, 1977, reveals nothing more except that the FBI maintained its watch on him at least up to that year. Nothing in the FBI records indicates, for example, that Saroyan served honorably in the European Theatre of Operations in wartime. Nor does anything show any awareness of what Saroyan wrote or what was written about his work. In this respect, the FBI, CIA and State Department policed a phantom.

LILLIAN HELLMAN

The plays and memoirs of Lillian Hellman (1905–1984) may well outlast the continuing criticism of her by old and new-right professional Red-baiters. They have judged her, above all else, by her strong liberal views and not by her writings. In this writer's opinion, some of her critics envied her long romantic association with Dashiell Hammett, the idealized author of *The Maltese Falcon* and other pioneering works in the field of detective fiction. Hellman-haters fell in step behind J. Edgar Hoover and witch-hunting congressional committees who despised what she had to say, the organizations she belonged to, her admittedly abrasive style and her financial rewards from writing.

Miss Hellman's FBI file contained 307 censored pages; 37 of these pages were denied to me altogether. In addition, there were several army, State Department and CIA documents. In an effort to obtain more information I wrote to Louis J. Dube, the CIA appeal officer:

"While a play has been put on at the Kennedy Center in Washington about Lillian Hellman, called *Lillian,* the CIA is saying that a document about her is not allowed to be read after her death. During her lifetime she was never put on trial and no violation of the law was ever noted, not even a misdemeanor. How can you withhold a document about her on grounds that it is in 'the interest of national defense or foreign policy'—your official printed reason? Miss Hellman never threatened her country; she merely irritated officials in Washington who did not like her politics or her plays. To withhold a document now is a mockery of the Freedom of Information Act, not some high-level intelligence matter. I notice in the newspapers that the CIA had moles working within your organization, passing information on to other countries. Did Lillian Hellman?"

My appeal was accepted by the CIA, but I did not expect anything to result from it. Nothing did. After a year of waiting there was only a negative response. William F. Donnelly, chairman of the CIA's Information Review Committee, cited Exemption (b) (1) of the Freedom of Information Act for denying the document "in the interest of national defense or foreign policy." Generally, I found, the CIA has stonewalled requests while—comparatively—the FBI has been more forthcoming. However, in the final years of the Reagan administration all the federal surveillance agencies set up bureaucratic roadblocks to information under the Freedom of Information Act.

The FBI files reveal that surveillance of Miss Hellman began by [unnamed] informants before World War II—independently and also because of her relationship with Dashiell Hammett. Surveillance was maintained by FBI informants and also by a mail-watch of her correspondents and what she read.

In 1938 she was one of the speakers at a rally to support the Abraham Lincoln Brigade volunteers with the Loyalists during the Spanish Civil War. The same year she joined thirty-six other authors in a petition to President Roosevelt to bar German-made goods from entering the United States. Her file also noted that she was a sponsor of a suspect (in the clouded vision of the FBI) group: the League of Women Shoppers! In 1941 she attended a testimonial dinner for Theodore Dreiser. The FBI was there. A phrase appears in her file: "extremely close to the Communist party in recent years." In addition to Miss Hellman, the "close" list includes Dashiell Hammett, Marc Blitzstein, Clifford Odets and Richard Wright.

On a wartime plane flight to see Hammett, then serving as editor of an army newspaper in the Aleutians, her baggage was searched. An agent dutifully reported that she carried such books as *The Little Oxford Dictionary* and H. W. Fowler's *The King's English.*

Miss Hellman's plays—including *The Little Foxes* (1939), *Watch on the Rhine* (1941), *The Searching Wind* (1944)—also came under official scrutiny. Later her memoirs—*An Unfinished Woman* (1969), *Pentimento* (1973) and *Scoundrel Time* (1976), the latter an account of her experiences and those of her friends during the McCarthy era—infuriated the neoconservatives and small-bore literary warriors.

An unnamed FBI theatrical "critic" noted that her play, *Watch on the Rhine,* appeared to have "great social significance." (Everyone understood what *that* meant.) Also, that it had received an "extremely favorable" review in the *Daily Worker,* the Communist party newspaper.

The documents reveal, surprisingly, that the FBI somehow had access to the presumably exclusive New York *Times* morgue. Commenting on *Watch on the Rhine,* Hellman's dossier reads: "The morgue files of the New York *Times* reflected that *Watch on the Rhine* was awarded the New York Drama Critics award in 1941." Again, a reference appears to an "undated article in the morgue files of the New York *Times*" listing her as a sponsor of a theater group in Greenwich Village that had turned the stage into "a social weapon."

In 1940 a "reliable source" informed the FBI that Hellman had been assigned by the Communist party to "smearing the FBI in connection with her work on the newspaper *PM.*" No documentation supports this wild claim. In 1941 an FBI agent reported that he had not yet checked the bank accounts of Hellman and (name censored) but would do so.

J. Edgar Hoover himself took a personal interest in Miss Hellman's activities. In a letter written to the FBI special agent in New York in 1943—in the middle of World War II, when Nazi agents and the German-American Bund were operating in the United States—Hoover called for a comprehensive report on her. In a surprisingly uncensored letter in her file, dated October 20, 1943, Hoover wrote: "You are reminded that this subject has a national reputation through her writings in which she has opposed nazism and fascism. Under no circumstances should it be known that this bureau is conducting an investigation of her. It should be handled in a most discreet manner and under no circumstances should it be assigned to the local police or some other agency."

Thereafter, she was branded a "key figure" in the FBI's New York Field Division. Her writings were interpreted in a "confidential" biography. For example, she was identified as the author of the wartime screenplay, "North Star." The FBI summarized the film in these words: "A movie which depicts the outrage committed upon the peaceful people of Russia by the invading armies of Nazi Germany and those who have sacrificed their homes and themselves in resisting the Fascist hordes." Inclusion suggests an Alice-in-Wonderland set of values—Hellman a suspect because the Russians are victims and the Germans bad guys.

Under the heading "Communist Activities" she was condemned in her "confidential" biography for participating in the film, "The Spanish Earth," that helped to raise money for the Loyalists during the Spanish Civil War. Condemned with her for the same cause were Archibald MacLeish (spelled "Mac Leach" by the FBI), John Dos Passos and Ernest Hemingway.

In 1941, she participated in the Fourth Writers Congress, branded "definitely a Communist gathering" by (censored) informant "whose name is known to the bureau." It was also noted that she, as author of *Watch on the Rhine,* the composer Marc Blitzein, and Richard Wright, author of *Native Son,* all received prizes for their work.

During the war, in 1944, the FBI sought two pictures of her from the New York Field Division and also "if possible to do so in a discreet manner, attempt to obtain handwriting specimens of the subject." The effort to get a handwriting sample failed and continued for at least another year—until someone woke up and realized that her passport application included her signature.

The FBI also found it a matter of suspicion—and watched her—when she supported President Roosevelt for a fourth term: Her file includes an "Open Letter from Lillian Hellman to the Voters of Westchester County" that appeared in the New York *Times* on October 2, 1944. The advertisement called upon her Westchester neighbors to support the President: "I agreed to serve on the Roosevelt Committee of Westchester. I want to urge you to do the same. This election is the most crucial of our lifetime. Let us not return to the days of closed banks, business failures, home foreclosures and mass unemployment."

After the war, when her file grew thicker, she continued to be tracked whenever she moved. In 1948 Headquarters Second Army, Security Group, in the Northeast, kept a file on her, according to a document in her dossier. The military document labeled her as a "Communist adherent." In 1949 Hoover told his New York office that a new report was needed on her because of "the tense international situation." A watch was then maintained on her at 63 East 82nd Street, her Manhattan home, and also at her country place in Pleasantville north of Manhattan.

Her FBI file was embellished in 1950 when all the previous material was repeated. This time, what was "alleged" or simply reported by an unnamed "informant" became accepted as fact without qualification. The mere existence of such raw data in the file gave the material acceptability.

During the Eisenhower era, Miss Hellman was called before the House Un-American Activities. Availing herself of her rights under the Fifth Amendment, she declined to say if she had been a member of the Communist party and denied that she had been a Communist in 1952 or the previous two years.

By 1955 the FBI's New York office recommended that Miss Hellman's name be removed from the Security Index—a high priority in the bureau's records. No evidence of any Communist affiliation or disloyalty were uncovered, disproving the accusations against her in the file. The New York office reported: "She is not known to belong to a basic revolutionary organization or to have been engaged in a leadership capacity in front groups during the past three years." The response by Washington to this recommendation is blacked out or omitted for several pages. Apparently Hoover would not let her case drop. When she went abroad in 1963, she was still being tracked by the State Department, which kept the FBI informed of her whereabouts. Again, in 1966, State sent copies to London and Paris as part of a confidential report on her stamped *Subversive Control.* When she spent her summers on Martha's Vineyard the FBI enlisted the help of her local post office to see what she read and to whom she wrote that could be determined by watching the mails. Postmaster Walter Stone, Vineyard Haven, advised the FBI of her forwarding address when she moved back to New York.

When the Committee for Public Justice was formed in New York in 1970 a *secret* FBI memorandum said that Lillian Hellman was the main organizer of the organization and that she supported New Left and anti-Vietnam war groups. The FBI then listed the names of other distinguished members of the Committee for Public Justice, which was designed to provide legal assistance to those accused of political protest and other activities that displeased the government. All appeared, with derogatory biographical information, in the Hellman file.

Among them was Burke Marshall, a former assistant attorney general of the Department of Justice Civil Rights Division in the Johnson administration. He was judged by this peculiar standard: "We had frequent contact with him and he was not considered a friend of the FBI." Telford Taylor, former chief prosecutor at the Nuremberg trials and a professor of law at Columbia University, was also condemned: "Member of National Lawyers Guild . . . member of Carnegie Endowment for International Peace which cooperated with the Soviet government . . . has represented many Communist party members in court and before congressional committees." Dr. Jerome B. Wiesner, special assistant to

President Kennedy on science and technology and former president of Massachusetts Institute of Technology, was accused in these words: "He admitted past membership in the American Association of Scientific Workers, a Communist-front organization and allegedly indicated sympathy for Communists in the 1940s . . . several of his associates at MIT were publicly identified as having been affiliated with the CP . . . attended the Second Pugwash Conference in Quebec, Canada, in 1968, sponsored by Cyrus Eaton, and more recently has been outspoken in opposition to an antiballistic missile system for the US." The list also included Robert B. Silvers, formerly with Harper's magazine, later coeditor of the New York Review of Books, who was described in this fashion: "In 1964 [the New York Review of Books] reportedly used individuals with 'leftist tendencies' to review books dealing with security matters and the US Government. . . . Allegations that this publication was directed or controlled by the CP were not substantiated. . . . Silvers, who visited Cuba in late 1968, was one of the board of directors of 'Center for Cuban Studies,' New York City, the subject of a current Registration Act–Cuba investigation."

Beyond any professional or political associations, being considered "a friend of the FBI" was regarded as a significant measure of devotion to God, country—and J. Edgar Hoover. In this respect, Miss Hellman was "disloyal"; she was clearly no friend of the FBI or the congressional investigating committees. She had her literary and political enemies and was engaged in all the public wars—some very small, indeed, and, in retrospect, unimportant outside the family of intellectuals. But she was consistent in her boldness, speaking up and dramatizing her beliefs in the theater and in print. She would not, in her memorable phrase to the House Committee on Un-American Activities in 1952, "cut my conscience to fit this year's fashions."

TENNESSEE WILLIAMS

The FBI file on Tennessee Williams (1914–83) includes only seven pages, but they are telling. My appeal to the Department of Justice to obtain additional information was denied on several grounds: some of the information consisted of "investigatory records compiled for law-enforcement purposes," I was told, or would involve disclosing "the identities of confidential sources and confidential information." During the McCarthy era, when Williams' plays were being staged all over the country, the FBI maintained a file on him stamped *Security Information—Confidential.*

Apparently what made Williams a danger to the security of the United States, in the view of the FBI, was that his name had turned up several times in the *Daily Worker.* The bureau noted that *A Streetcar Named Desire,* which first appeared on Broadway in 1947, was praised in the Communist party newspaper. (The FBI mistakenly called it a book, not a play.) A year later, his FBI file notes, Williams sent greetings to the Moscow Art Theatre at a time when an effort was being made to exchange plays between the two countries; the Moscow troupe came to New York in 1965. Again in 1950 the *Daily Worker* mentioned Williams, pointing out that he was among a group of " 'top show business cultural names' . . . who had been assembled to speak on a radio show condemning the jailing of the 'Hollywood Ten,' " and adding, "This radio show was refused by the major networks." The FBI memorandum that reports this also reports that in 1951 a catalogue of the Dramatic Workshop and Technical Institute showed Williams to be a member of the institute's board of trustees. The memorandum adds that the workshop was cited as a Communist front by the California Committee on Un-American Activities.

A 1964 memorandum in his file says that, in connection

with an investigation made for the State Department, "the bureau ascertained that Thomas Lanier Williams has the reputation of being a homosexual." Some of what follows has been censored, and then the file continues, "Further, the Office of Naval Intelligence, in a separate inquiry, secured statements from individuals who admitted participating in homosexual acts with Williams."

The file fails to reveal why the FBI thought that a playright's sexual proclivities might make him a threat to America's security.

VII.

POETS AND ESSAYISTS

Major American poets, essayists and critics have not been immune from the reach of the Federal Bureau of Investigation and other police arms of the government. In most of the nontotalitarian nations of the world, creators of artistic material are honored; in the totalitarian states, their writings are sometimes imprisoned, yet even when their work is feared it may be recognized as having national merit. In the United States many distinguished authors have been catalogued and, at times, considered so politically suspect that they have required secret government dossiers—of which they were unaware.

In front of me are thousands of pages of official records that I obtained on authors—after an increasingly long wait during the second term of the Reagan administration, following several years of trying and appealing for denied material under the Freedom of Information Act. Nearly all the documents are censored; the reasons for the blacked-out material range from protecting the names of FBI informers inside suspect organizations to accusations of subversion and endangering the national security.

This point must be underscored: not one of the accused authors, dramatists and artists upon whom so much policing manpower and funds were expended—sometimes they were watched for half their lives and records were maintained even after their deaths—were ever tried and jailed for the crimes they were suspected of in these files.

The field of writing mattered little to the FBI. I also obtained dossiers on such poets as Archibald MacLeish, Robert Lowell, Robert Frost and W.H. Auden, and such essayists as H. L. Mencken and Edmund Wilson. All were considered suspicious or potentially dangerous persons on the watch-lists of the federal government.

ARICHIBALD MACLEISH

Archibald MacLeish (1892–1982) is of particular interest because he held the highest government posts of any American author during the Roosevelt administration. He was librarian of Congress (1939–1944), director of the wartime Office of Facts and Figures, assistant director of the Office of War Information, assistant secretary of state (1944–45). MacLeish, a friend of the president, contributed to his speeches, as he later would for the 1952 and 1956 presidential campaigns of his friend Governor Adlai E. Stevenson.

MacLeish won the Pulitzer Prize three times for his poetry and verse plays, including *Conquistador* in 1932, *Collected Poems* in 1952, and in 1958 *J.B.,* which treated Job's trials in a modern context. He was a kind of American poet laureate of New Deal social reform, democracy and anti-Fascist activism against dictatorships, from Franco's Spain to Hitler's Germany. His file shows that this did not endear him to congressional investigative committees, who saw only Red and suspected authors like MacLeish who supported the Loyalists in Spain and were (in the tortured phrase) "prematurely anti-Fascist."

The MacLeish file contains over six hundred pages. In the documents I found a remarkable exchange of letters and memorandums—stamped *Secret*—between MacLeish and J. Edgar Hoover that served to expose the differences in thinking between the two directors on the subject of liberalism and witchhunting. MacLeish, as head of the Office of Facts and Figures, could speak as a Washington equal; Hoover, knowing he was dealing with a friend of the president (and that he had an ace in the hole—an existing file on MacLeish and his associations with writers and anti-Fascist organizations in the 1930s), was cordially evasive. The exchange reveals a great deal about Hoover's political maneuverability and the FBI's attitude toward all authors who were under surveillance for their beliefs and writings.

The *secret* exchange began a few weeks after Pearl Harbor, in January 1942. The FBI put a summary headline over MacLeish's letter to Hoover: "MacLeish's Criticism of the Bureau and its Investigative Policies."

The polite MacLeish letter to Hoover, in part, reads:

"As reports on employees in the Office of Facts and Figures come to me through the Division of Investigation at OEM [Office for Emergency Management], I notice the recurrence of the phrase that the applicant is said to be 'associated with various liberal and Communistic groups.' This suggests that investigators have been told to consider liberalism as suspicious. Knowing your feeling on this matter, I am sure that no such instructions ever came from you.

"For the sake of our reputation in the history books, don't

you think it would be a good thing if all investigators could be made to understand that liberalism is not only not a crime but actually the attitude of the president of the United States and the greater part of his administration.

"In the same way, I note the frequent recurrence of references to membership in organizations set up to aid the Spanish Republic in its fight against the Fascist Revolution of 1936. The implication is that people who were against the Nazis and Fascists in '36 were suspect. Here again, and for the sake of the reputations of all of us in the history books, wouldn't it be possible to instruct all investigators that the people we are at war with now are the same people who supported Franco in the Spanish Civil War."

Hoover responded cautiously a week later in a *secret* letter:

"As you know, the FBI is a fact-finding organization. The special agents who conduct and report on these and all other investigations are trained and instructed to do so with absolute integrity. These investigations are conducted primarily for the purpose of determining the patriotism, loyalty and character of the individuals concerned.

"In the event an opinion is expressed by the person interviewed, the special agents attempt to obtain the basis for the opinion. It is true that in some cases biased or prejudicial statements may be made by some persons interviewed and comments by others may be objectionable or conceivably false. However, in the interest of obtaining available data for submission to the employing agency, all information, regardless of its nature, is fully and accurately reported as received and in no way do the individual comments reflect any opinions or the policy of the FBI."

MacLeish sent a *confidential* letter, in March 1942, directly to Hoover's superior, Francis Biddle, the attorney general, who forwarded it on to Hoover. To Biddle, with whom he was on a first-name basis, MacLeish could speak more openly:

"You have a lot to worry about these days and I hope I am the last man to add to your worries, but the whole business of the investigation of citizens offering their services to the government has at last gotten me down. Particularly in the case of writers and scholars and above all in the case of liberal writers and scholars the investigations have reached a level of humiliating absurdity which would be laughable if it were not often sinister.

"Malcolm Cowley has been driven to resign from the Office of Facts and Figures by an attack carried on through Westbrook Pegler by, presumably, members of the Dies Committee or of the Dies Committee staff. Pegler very obviously had access to information in the possession only of the Dies Committee or the FBI, and I am certain the FBI is not engaged in the business of trying its cases in the newspapers.

[MacLeish, who was a lawyer himself, probably knew that his letter would be transmitted to Hoover by Biddle, nominally Hoover's boss; he surely must have known that Hoover had certain favored journalists, including Pegler, who sang his praises in exchange for leaked information.]

"Now on top of the Cowley case come investigations of [name censored] and of [censored] which take the entire cake—frosting, candles, and all. I enclose [censored] letter, in which you may wish to read the two underlined sentences. I enclose also the interim report on [censored] in which you may wish to glance at the long list of items which are stated to reflect unfavorably upon [censored] character, reputation and loyalty.

"I ask you—can you beat it?

"[Name censored] statement that FBI investigators are 'out of touch with intellectual currents' is a princely understatement. They seem not only to be out of touch with intellectual currents, they seem to be in other currents of a most suspicious nature—and I don't think I am seeing things. For example, report after report coming to me links the words 'liberal' and 'Communist' as though in the opinion of FBI investigators they were the same thing. In report after report, support of the Spanish Loyalists against Hitler and Mussolini is put down as one of the worst of the black marks, and any association with Loyalist Spain is given as a basis of suspicion of loyalty to the United States.

"I have already written Hoover about this general matter and have had a very pleasant but not precisely responsive answer from him. My suggestion to him was that FBI agents ought to be given a course of instruction in recent history, American and other, to inform them of a few basic facts, such as the fact that this country is now at war with the men who attacked Spain in '36 and '37—such as the fact that President Roosevelt is a liberal—such as the fact that the founders of this country believed in and practiced democracy—and a few other simple items.

"I agree with you that the present attack upon liberals in the government is dangerous. I think, too, that one of the most dangerous aspects of that attack is to be found in such documents as the enclosed 'investigation' of [name deleted]. That investigators of [censored] should go to a notorious America first leader to inquire about [censored]'s loyalty and that investigators of [censored] should turn to [censored] for evidence leaves me absolutely breathless and flabbergasted.

"Forgive this long rant. I know the whole thing makes you just as sick as it makes me. But can't we do something about it?"

Attorney General Biddle innocently passed along MacLeish's letter to Hoover, trying to educate Hoover's men about liberalism. Hoover, a far more experienced bureaucratic in-fighter, wrote a *secret* memorandum to Biddle stating that the FBI was a fact-finding agency whose agents had an obligation to develop "a full and complete picture" of an individual's background without "coloring" its reports. Hoover denied that his bureau was judgmental and added, "To use Mr. MacLeish's phraseology, I am left 'breathless and flabbergasted' by Mr. MacLeish's disregard of the facts."

MacLeish wrote to Biddle: "What is really involved is the education and experience of the investigators themselves." In the exchange with Hoover, both Biddle and MacLeish retreated cordially. So ended the futile attempt to change Hoover's methods and long-held convictions—going back to the early twenties—equating liberalism with radicalism.

Of course, Hoover knew something that MacLeish did not know: the FBI had been keeping a file on him.

One of the first entries in MacLeish's file, dated September 1941, noted that as Librarian of Congress he was on the mailing list of the National Federation for Constitutional Liberties and the Washington Spanish Refugee Relief Committee. Hoover asked for more. The Washington field division responded that it had derogatory information on him and his writings: The FBI records showed that in 1936 MacLeish contributed to Common Sense magazine; was a sponsor of American Friends of Spanish Democracy; in 1937, he was on the board of trustees of the New School for Social Research (which gave teaching jobs to a number of refugees from Hitlerism); was on a citizens committee for the American Civil Liberties Union; was a sponsor of Friends of the Abraham Lincoln Brigade; in 1939 was a sponsor of the International League Defense Milk Fund; a sponsor of Spanish Refugee Relief; in 1940 was on the board of sponsors of the American Guild for German Cultural Freedom, an anti-Nazi group; a former chairman of the Second American Writers Congress; a member of the Committee to Defend America by Aiding the Allies. Furthermore, the MacLeish records included a statement by one of the FBI's allies, J. Parnell Thomas, chairman of the House Committee on Un-American Activities, that MacLeish was a "fellow traveler," aiding the Communists, "but for some reason does not want to become a member of the Communist party."

After the war, whenever MacLeish's name came up for public service, including an appointment as deputy chairman of the American delegation to the United Nations Educational, Scientific and Cultural Organization (UNESCO) in 1946, the FBI repeated all his associations and added more information, indicating that the bureau was keeping its nose on his trail. For example, he was listed as a sponsor for a dinner of the National Council of American-Soviet Friendship and the National Federation for Constitutional Liberties. The FBI records also included quotations from such rabid columnists as John O'Donnell of the Washington *Times Herald:* "The slippery fashion by which fellow travelers and the Roosevelt pinks have wormed their way into high positions . . . Poet Archibald MacLeish's Office of Facts and Figures—fuss and feathers it was merrily called before suspicion grew of its sinister link with Moscow internationalists and native pinkos."

In 1962 MacLeish was being considered for a minor post as an adviser on the arts by the Kennedy administration. This resulted in an alert by Hoover to FBI offices all over the United States to dig up any useful information on him: "Determine from persons interviewed their opinion concerning appointee's loyalty from his written works," Hoover advised. (Here was a case where the FBI specifically sought to determine an author's loyalty by examining his writings even though then, and later, bureau officials have said that they do not interfere with freedom of expression.) MacLeish was highly recommended by many people interviewed around the country and was expected to be named to the unpaid post, but President Kennedy's death ended the Advisory Committee on the Arts. After listing all his affiliations, the FBI noted that he was a "liberal of the New Deal type." (*Q.E.D.*)

In the bureau's effort to discredit MacLeish, involving scores of interviews and a rehash of old accusations about his liberalism, the most damning information the FBI could come up with was that in 1928 MacLeish had been arrested for "illegal fishing on private property" in Massachusetts. He was fined $10, the fine was suspended, and he paid court costs of $4.35. So ended the FBI's exposure of the wayward poet.

ROBERT LOWELL

In his thirty-two page, heavily censored dossier, Robert Lowell (1917–1977) is described in an FBI memorandum: "The subject is a Pulitzer Prize–winning poet who is very prominent in the literary field. During 1965 he refused an invitation to the White House because he did not agree with the president's foreign policy." This referred to Lowell, along with a number of other writers, declining to participate in President Johnson's first (and, as it turned out, last) White House Festival of the Arts during the Vietnam War. Those who protested to the president by telegram then had a second name-check ordered from the FBI by the White House.

The New England poet bearing the famous Lowell name achieved an international reputation with *Lord Weary's Castle* (1946), *For the Union Dead* (1964), three one-act plays, *The Old Glory* (1965), and for his translations of the classics.

In 1942, Lowell tried to enlist in both the army and the navy but was turned down because of poor eyesight. The next year he decided to become a conscientious objector and did not report for induction, explaining, without explaining, that he no longer felt the war was justified. In 1943 he was sentenced to a year and a day in the federal prison in Danbury, Connecticut.

In 1965 Lowell was one of the signers of the "Writers and Artists Protest" document against the continuation of the American war in Vietnam. The FBI then checked his fingerprint files in its Identification division to see if he had an arrest record other than his wartime prison sentence as a conscientious objector. He again came to the FBI's attention as one of the anti-Vietnam war leaders—together with Norman Mailer, Dr. Benjamin Spock and others in the arts and sciences—of the peace march on the Pentagon in 1967. At that time, a *secret* memorandum in his file noted that there were "numerous references to a Robert Lowell."

The file contained a summary of a 1967 article in the New York *Times* saying that Andrei Voznesensky, the Soviet poet, had dedicated a poem to Lowell. Lowell had described him as one of the great poets in any language and was to read a translation of his work during a recital at Philharmonic Hall in Lincoln Center. The translation of a renowned Soviet poet was sufficient to be included in Lowell's suspect file. No mention was made of the fact that Voznesensky had written poems against anti-Semitism and was an outspoken advocate of greater freedom for publication of literature in his own country. Half of the page is blacked out and marked *Secret.*

Whenever Lowell applied for a renewal of his passport the FBI kept track of his travel plans and whereabouts. How closely he was followed abroad cannot be determined from his blacked-out file, but passport photographs that he had supplied were duplicated in his FBI file. Several pages in the Lowell file were withheld—that wonderful catch-all again—"in the interest of national defense or foreign policy."

ROBERT FROST

The FBI file on Robert Frost (1874–1963)—by contrast with the extensive file on Carl Sandburg, the poet, historian and journalist with whom he was frequently paired—is slight. That he was invited to read a poem at President Kennedy's inaugural goes unmentioned.

Although according to the FBI no central record existed on Frost, his file did show a translation of an article from *Narodna Volya (People's Will),* a foreign-language newspaper that had been forwarded from Detroit to FBI headquarters in Washington:

"This article reflects that the American poet, Robert Frost, returned to the United States on Sept. 9, 1962, from a visit to the Soviet Union, where he met with Nikita Khrushchev. The article states that Frost advised he is not a Communist or a Socialist but he believes that socialism is the only system that can deal with the economic problems of the millions of people in the world."

Missing in the Frost file is any awareness of his near-exalted ranking in American letters.

W.H. AUDEN

W.H. Auden (1907–1973), one of the greatest poets of the twentieth century, became a naturalized American citizen in 1946. His work included *Spain, The Age of Anxiety* and collections of his essays. The British-born poet was part of the brilliant group of authors that included his friends Christopher Isherwood, Stephen Spender and C. Day Lewis. Auden was affected by the Depression, Marxist theory, and the anti-Fascist struggle during the Spanish Civil War. He later would call their interest in Marxism "more psychological than political."

Inevitably Auden became a subject of attention by the FBI. His file included twenty-eight pages. Of these, eighteen pages were released initially, I obtained two more after an appeal, and eight were withheld from me. In addition to the FBI, his file included documents from the State Department, Central Intelligence Agency and the Justice Department's Immigration and Naturalization Service. The two pages obtained after an appeal were from the CIA; however, they were so blacked out as to be almost useless as a source of information. Had he seen his file, Auden might well have been inspired to write an ode to the censorial mind.

In 1945, as World War II was winding down, the FBI told the State Department's Visa Division that one of the contributors to an issue of New Masses in 1939 was Wystan Hugh Auden of 16 Oberlin Avenue, Swarthmore, Pennsylvania; at the time he was lecturing at Swarthmore. This began his file and an investigative report.

In a *confidential* memorandum the FBI wrote a so-called biographical account of his schooling and friends and politics that included literary views in which it was said that he belonged to a "group of young poets who were all strongly oriented to the Left, some of them being orthodox Communists." An unnamed (censored by the FBI) person has said that "Auden was never in complete agreement with the Communist doctrine" but was "simply in rebellion" against the opinions of "the upper bourgeoise into which he was born." In 1937 he was described as an ambulance driver for the Loyalists during the Spanish Revolution. "He is married to Erika Mann, daughter of Thomas Mann," the report continues, "and in 1939 he came to the United States as a permanent resident."

The file also includes that he attended school with the missing British diplomats, Donald MacLean and Guy Burgess. Apparently he attended school with MacLean and knew Burgess at Cambridge. A British article is quoted as saying that Stephen Spender, "another prominent ex-Communist," had had a telephone conversation with Burgess before the two men disappeared. Going a step further, the file says that Auden was "believed" to be a Communist party member in the early thirties and a "contact" for the defecting British diplomats. (None of this was claimed by British Intelligence; Auden was not linked to MacLean or Burgess or anyone else politically.)

What appears to be intercepted mail in 1959 includes a birthday greeting to Auden "from a secret admirer" and a letter by an unknown correspondent. Did Auden surmise that his mail was being watched by the FBI? A puzzling page in the file includes a line: "A happy Independence Day to you, G-man." It is not clear who wrote it. What is known is that Auden had written to a group of young poets in New York, proving himself to be prescient: "Try to think of each poem as a letter written to an intimate friend, not always the same friend. But the letter is going to be opened by the postal authorities, and if they do not understand anything, or find it difficult to wade through, then the poem fails."

In 1965 Jack Valenti, one of President Johnson's assistants and political operatives, requested a name-check on Auden from the FBI when he was being considered as a possible candidate to receive the Presidential Medal of Freedom. The response is omitted from the Auden file. Auden never was given the award.

Major essayists and critics who helped to mold the American language and set literary standards for generations of authors and journalists were also found to have dossiers. In all cases the bureaucratic summaries of their careers were plodding and wholly unenlightened about their true importance.

Influential writers whose works were studied in schools all over the country, they were nonetheless viewed as potential menaces to the United States.

H.L. MENCKEN

H.L. Mencken (1880–1956) had fifty-five pages in the file provided to me; two more pages were added after I appealed. Parts of his dossier were censored in the "interest of national defense or foreign policy." Because of his German background he came under suspicion during both world wars. His writings clearly show that he was an Anglophobe, and often wildly off the mark in his political prognostications. However, his acerbic style and posturing in print were not sensibly to be confused with acts of disloyalty.

Mencken was well-known as editor and columnist for the Baltimore *Sun;* founder and coeditor with George Jean Nathan of the American Mercury; author of *The American Language* and *A Mencken Crestomathy.* He did much to alert American readers to the works of Theodore Dreiser, Sinclair Lewis and Sherwood Anderson.

His first entry appears in 1922—from the Secret Service Division of the Treasury Department to the Bureau of Investigation (then the FBI's name) in the Justice Department. It includes a clipping from the Baltimore *Sun* about Mencken's "alleged interview" with former German Crown Prince Friedrich Wilhelm. (The name of the woman who sent the clipping to the Secret Service is censored; her letter fears that Germany is planning to regain its pre-1914 power "with sinister motives regarding America.") The interview was not "alleged." It ran as a lead article in the paper from North Holland.

CENTRAL INTELLIGENCE AGENCY
WASHINGTON 25, D. C.

TO: Director
Federal Bureau of Investigation
Attention: Mr. C. D. DeLoach

FROM: Robert A. Schow
Assistant Director

SUBJECT:

1. Reference is made to your memoranda dated 2 December 1949, 14 June 1950, and 17 October 1950,

4.

a. Wyston Hugh AUDEN, American citizen, born at York, England, on 21 February 1907, a writer. He is bearer of a United States passport number 156327 issued at Washington on 17 February 1948.

He is reportedly in contact with

RECORDED - 20 FEB 5 1951

INDEXED - 20

REVIEWED FOR RELEASE
Date 10 SEP 84

Approved for Release
Date 28 JAN 1985

The Central Intelligence Agency and the FBI shared information about W. H. Auden, who had become an American citizen. The State Department also maintained a file on the poet. Among other reasons, the CIA blacked out his file "in the interest of the national defense or foreign policy."

Houghton Mifflin

Archibald MacLeish held key posts in the Roosevelt Administration during World War II: Librarian of Congress; assistant director of the Office of War Information; assistant Secretary of State. But the FBI branded him a "liberal of the New Deal type" and he clashed with J. Edgar Hoover, whose agents tried to prevent the hiring of "liberals" in MacLeish's departments. The FBI accumulated more than 600 pages in the MacLeish dossier, watching his every move long after he had left government service.

H.L. Mencken, editor and columnist for the Baltimore Sun and founder with George Jean Nathan of the American Mercury, was author of "The American Language." He had fifty-seven pages in his file, sections of which were heavily censored. This photograph was taken by Alfred A. Knopf, his friend and publisher, who had a file of his own.

Alfred A. Knopf

The interview does reveal antagonism to the Versailles treaty. Nevertheless, why an open interview in the press caused Mencken's name to be placed in the Secret Service and FBI files is puzzling—except that this was the Harding era of Attorney General A. Mitchell Palmer's raids against aliens and alleged radicals. Indeed, J. Edgar Hoover first made a name for himself by providing Palmer with information and direction for the antiradical roundups.

Hoover became acting director of the FBI in 1924 and almost immediately revealed a talent for ingratiating himself politically and with the press. The Mencken file shows that in 1934 FBI Director Hoover told one of his assistants that Mencken should receive press releases about the bureau. Hoover had admired a Mencken article in Liberty magazine entitled "What to Do with Criminals" that used FBI statistics. Hoover invited Mencken to visit the bureau. In 1935 Mencken thanked Hoover for sending him material on "civil identification."

Hearts and flowers between the Director and the German sympathizer.

On the eve of the Second World War another entry in Mencken's file appeared—a letter from (name censored) to Stephen Early, President Roosevelt's White House aide, calling Mencken a "fifth columnist" and a German and asking the Department of Justice to "do something" about his writings. Mencken was indeed an isolationist and a Roosevelt-hater. The letter enclosed a column from the Baltimore *Sun* that opposed a third term for Roosevelt. It included such outrageous lines as these: "The United States has broken just as many treaties as Hitler, and got just as much territory by the arts of the burgler." Mencken often let his phrases sabotage his mind. "If it is on the books that the werewolf Hitler shall wreck England," he wrote, "that wrecking will be duly achieved, Roosevelt or no Roosevelt."

In a censored letter stamped *Secret* and signed by Hoover in November 1941, the FBI director wrote: "During the last war there was no indication according to the records of this bureau that Mencken was involved in espionage activities." He also noted that Mencken was a director of both the Baltimore *Sun* and of his book publisher, Alfred A. Knopf.

The FBI included in the Mencken file an interview with the Associated Press in 1956, the year he died. In the article, which appeared in the Washington *Star,* Mencken made his usual acerbic remarks about how a forthcoming book of his, *Minority Report,* would be denounced in the press. The interview included this quotation from the book: "The fact that I have no remedy for all the sorrows of the world is no reason for my accepting yours. It simply supports the strong probability that yours is a fake."

In general the Mencken file contains little worth recording. There is a big blank: what he was saying and writing during World War II when he had been proved so wrong in his anti-Roosevelt, anti-British comments. The file ends abruptly and so lacks a rounded picture of Mencken: what was at the core of his Anglophobia, were his writings incendiary, was he (rather than his words) dangerous to the Republic and, fundamentally, was an FBI dossier on him really warranted?

EDMUND WILSON

From the FBI file of Edmund Wilson (1895–1972) fifteen heavily censored pages were released. The excisions originally omitted Central Intelligence Agency documents; after an appeal I received one CIA document stamped *Secret,* for reasons best known to the agency since its information (not quite accurate about his political views) had frequently appeared in his own writings and in press interviews.

The CIA document, dated November 7, 1957, was labeled "Document No. 2," but "Document No. 1" was not released to me. In a memorandum to J. Edgar Hoover, the CIA director of security (name blacked out) wrote:

"Edmund Wilson was born in Red Bank, New Jersey, in 1895. He is a former editor of the New Republic and was connected with the New Yorker from 1944 to 1948. He has written several books, including *To the Finland Station.* He currently resides in Wellfleet, Massachusetts. This office has recently received information that Wilson was a Trotskyite during earlier years and is now actively anti-Communist."

The FBI had a second, smaller file on Wilson that it refused to release at all because of an exemption under Executive Order 12356—"in the interest of the national defense or foreign policy, for example, information involving intelligence sources or methods." Buried in his researches, books, diaries and writings, Wilson seemed to me one of the least likely authors to have a file and, having one, for it be be censored or denied to a request under the Freedom of Information Act.

Wilson, the most respected literary historian and critic during his lifetime, first served as managing editor of Vanity Fair, then as associate editor of the New Republic, finally as book critic and essayist for the New Yorker. Might any of his scholarly works have threatened the United States? They included *The Dead Sea Scrolls* (for which he learned to read Hebrew); *Apologies to the Iroquois* (on the status of the Indian Confederacy); *To the Finland Station* (European revolutionary traditions, with Lenin and Trotsky); *The American Earthquake* (social reporting on Russia and the United States); *Memoirs of Hecate County* (stories about suburbanites that encountered censorship because of alleged obscenity); *The Cold War and Income Tax* (his objections to federal taxation); *A Window on Russia* (essays on Russian literature). Clearly, Wilson wrote on themes that included controversial ideas and personalities.

But did the government filekeepers actually read his essays, reviews and books?

The partial FBI file that was released to me indicates no familiarity with Wilson's writings. It begins in 1951 as a "Security Matter—C" (Communist). It is not known when the concealed file on Wilson began. A report to J. Edgar Hoover from the special agent in charge of the Boston FBI office reported that Wilson was interviewed "in connection with an Applicant investigation." Wilson had said that he had visited Russia in 1935 and was interested in the future of the Soviet Union. In the FBI interview Wilson said he realized that "the Soviet Union under Stalin could never improve the plight of the masses and that the Russian Revolution had failed." Wilson acknowledged that he had long been a student of Marxism and said, "I have a certain amount of Marxist writing equipment," this by way of explaining his scholarly background. The FBI reported that Wilson "described himself as a Socialist who voted for Norman Thomas in the last presidential election" (the 1948 election of Harry S. Truman).

His file shows that in 1953 and 1957 requests were made to the FBI by the State Department and the CIA for information on Wilson. In reply, Hoover repeated the data in the FBI files based on the 1951 interview. In 1963 the United States Information Agency was furnished more information about Wilson, the FBI adding that a confidential informant in 1956 supplied a letterhead that listed Wilson as a member of a civil rights committee to defend James Kutcher. The matter concerned a book, *The Case of the Legless Veteran,* published in 1953 by James Kutcher, who had been dismissed from his job with the Veterans Administration because of his membership in the Socialist Workers party.

Wilson's attitude about the relationship of the artist and the government was expressed in a letter he wrote to William Faulkner in 1956, a letter that does not appear in either writer's dossier but is most revealing. Faulkner had asked Wilson to participate in a People-to-People program on behalf of the Eisenhower administration (Faulkner himself walked out on the program in less than six months, perhaps enlightened by letters such as Wilson's). From his home in Wellfleet on Cape Cod, Wilson, in part, replied: "I don't believe in these national propaganda schemes and have always refused to take part in them. I was surprised to hear that you were involved in this. I have just come back from Europe and found your books being sold in London, Paris and Munich. How can you, or any other writer, make any better propaganda than by books that get themselves translated because they have something to say to people in other countries? There is a lot of anti-American feeling in Germany, England and France, and propaganda can do nothing to improve relations. In fact, my impression is that our own—which is often puerile—has, if anything, contributed to making them worse. The American ideology is not to have any ideology, and the Soviets and the States, for good or ill, have all along had a good deal in common, more perhaps than either now has with Europe, and have in various ways been imitating one another. The Russians have been learning, and will learn, from us, not what we want to tell them, but what they find is valuable to them."

Wilson's name appeared in a New York *Times* advertisement on May 10, 1961, signed by seventy individuals, that took the form of an open letter to President Kennedy urging the United States to give no further support to exile groups for an invasion of Cuba. The FBI file also noted that Wilson was among fifty signers of an affidavit in 1961 to reduce the sentence of one Junius Irving Scales, who had been convicted under the 1940 Smith Act that prohibited "certain subversive activities."

In 1965, during the Vietnam War, Wilson signed a letter,

called "Writers and Artists Protest," that was strongly opposed to American policy and military engagement in Vietnam. A final note in Wilson's file said that, in connection with a name-check request by the White House in 1966, "the fingerprint files of the Identification Division of the FBI contain no arrest data identifiable with captioned individual."

A familiar refrain: in all these entries there is no mention of the contents of any book or book review written by Edmund Wilson as a possible guide to his thinking or activities. It also is worth noting that nothing appears in Wilson's own diaries to indicate that he had any awareness that the FBI and CIA were keeping watch on him, a fact that might well have led him to produce a New Yorker piece on freedom of expression vs. the policing state.

VIII.

FOREIGN AUTHORS

Kobo Abe, Japanese novelist. Dennis Brutus, South African poet. Julio Cartazar, Argentinian novelist. Carlos Fuentes, Mexican novelist. Graham Greene, British novelist. Primo Levi, Italian novelist and essayist. Gabriel García Márquez, Colombian novelist and Nobel laureate. Csezlaw Milosz, Polish-American poet and Nobel Laureate. Alberto Moravia, Italian novelist. Farley Mowat, Canadian wildlife writer. Jan Myrdal, Swedish essayist. Ignazio Silone, Italian novelist. Stephen Spender, British poet.

What all these authors have in common is that, at one time or another, they have been denied visas or experienced visa difficulties under the "ideological exclusion" section of the McCarran-Walter Act, one of the greatest blots on the traditional American ideal of freedom of expression.

Ever since the onset of the cold war renowned foreign authors have encountered difficulties entering and remaining in the United States. Even when allowed to come here some have lived under a cloud, their words and persons watched, according to experts familiar with FBI and intelligence agency practices. Such treatment applies not only to writers from the Soviet Union and the Eastern bloc; in recent years most of the authors who have been barred or watched have come from Western Europe and Latin America. It has mattered little to the FBI and other agencies that their writings were completely out in the open: published, read, often imitated and regularly taught in this country. Because of sections of the immigration law that are a vestige of the early years of McCarthyism, an unknown number of reputable authors and journalists continue to be at risk and harassed when they are invited to speak or write or teach in the United States. For these writers, as well as for artists and performers, the golden door has sometimes been slammed shut at America's borders.

Before Congress overrode President Truman's veto and approved the McCarran-Walter Act in 1952, Truman said that the bill would perpetuate injustices of long standing against many other nations of the world, hamper the efforts to rally people in the East and West to the cause of freedom, and intensify the repressive and inhumane aspects of immigration procedures. He found the onerous provisions too high a price to pay for other concessions that abolished racial and natural barriers to naturalization:

"I do not approve of substituting totalitarian vengeance for democratic justice," President Truman said. "To punish undefined 'activities' departs from traditional American insistence on established standards of guilt. To punish an undefined 'purpose' is thought control. These provisions are worse than the infamous Alien Act of 1798, passed in a time of national fear and distrust of foreigners, which gave the president power to deport any alien deemed 'dangerous to the peace and safety of the United States.' Alien residents were thoroughly frightened and citizens much disturbed by that threat to liberty. Such powers are inconsistent with our democratic ideals. Conferring powers like that upon the attorney general is unfair. Once fully informed of such vast discretionary powers vested in the attorney general, Americans now would and should be just as alarmed as Americans were in 1798 over less drastic powers vested in the president."

Nevertheless, the bill sponsored by two congressional cold warriors was enacted and remains on the books. It affects not only authors but people in other endeavors—including those who hold political beliefs that are contrary to those of a president or attorney general in office—who may be of importance to the well-being and progress of a nation. Consular officials and border inspectors should not be pressed into service as thought police. That is contrary to the Helsinki Accords, which were designed to encourage free travel and the free exchange of ideas.

The roll call of foreign authors whose names repose in government files and records and/or have run afoul of Messrs. McCarran and Walters comprises a pantheon of creative artists.

STEPHEN SPENDER

Sir Stephen Spender (b. 1909) is the last of the galaxy of British poets and novelists, including W. H. Auden, Christopher Isherwood, Day Lewis and Louis MacNeice, who especially inspired generations of writers and readers, beginning in the 1930s and continuing up to the present.

At his home near St. John's Wood in Northwest London not long ago, Spender told me of a few peculiar experiences that had happened to him after deplaning at Kennedy International Airport in New York. During the course of several meetings with him in New York and London we had discussed the limitations on freedom of travel and especially freedom of expression that existed on both sides of the Iron Curtain. Much of Spender's time—between writing his memoirs and lecturing at American universities—is devoted to raising funds for Index on Censorship, the publication he helped to establish that reports abuses around the world. Spender attributed his experiences to early left-wing affiliations and his Loyalist sympathies during the Spanish Civil War. These incidents at the borders took place despite the fact that, although a British subject, he had once served as poetry consultant to the Library of Congress, the highest honor that can be attained by any poet in the United States.

The first incident occurred when he came to teach at Sarah Lawrence College in Bronxville, N.Y., some years ago. After being questioned closely about his passport by an immigration officer, he suddenly noticed a surprising change in the official's tone. His name sounded familiar . . . ? The immigration officer asked, "Are you Stephen Spender, the poet?" Spender, surprised, admitted that he was. The immigration officer expressed his pleasure at meeting the famous author and passed him through without further questioning. Nevertheless, Spender remained puzzled about why he had been singled out.

The reason why became clear a few years later in 1983. He was carrying an old passport. Again a friendly immigration officer recognized his name. This time the immigration officer told him that there was something peculiar with the passport, something arcane from the distant past. "There are two 'i's with special dots on them, meaning Socialist or Communist or some shit like that, but they don't use that now," Spender was told. Then the immigration officer asked him, "Do you know W.H. Auden?" Spender said that of course he knew him (he had privately printed Auden's first book of poetry). Again, Spender recalled, "I was admitted without further questioning by another intelligent and welcoming man."

Spender then called his old friend, Christopher Isherwood (1904–1986), author of the Berlin sketches that were dramatized in *I Am a Camera* and the musical and film "Cabaret," to tell him what the immigration officer had said about their mutual friend, W.H. Auden, who had died in 1973. Auden and Isherwood had emigrated to the United States and were naturalized American citizens; Spender had remained in England. Isherwood said that he too was impressed by the official's recognition of Auden's work, but he was not too surprised that Spender had been subjected to questioning about his *political* past.

Since Auden did have a dossier (he is included in this study among the poets), after his death I inquired to see if Isherwood had similarly been honored by the FBI bureau in Los Angeles. FBI headquarters at first said no, then raised the possibility that he too had a file. Washington responded: "Documents have been located which may pertain to Christopher Isherwood." However, under the slowdown of Freedom of Information requests during the second term of the Reagan administration, they have not been forwarded to me. Meanwhile, Spender has not encountered new border problems; in 1987 he taught at the University of Connecticut without having his passport examined for any hidden radical symbols.

GRAHAM GREENE

Graham Greene (b. 1904), perhaps the best-known living British novelist in the United States, discovered that he had an FBI dossier by applying through an American lawyer under the Freedom of Information Act. "In about forty-five pages of material which were sent me," he noted in The Spectator in 1984, "nearly sixteen pages were blacked out in heavy ink. So much for 'freedom of information.'" In a cordial response to me from his home in Antibes two years later, Greene said that the material from his FBI file had been sold at Sotheby's for "a fair sum and I don't know who the purchaser was."

The novelist said that he found some amusement but very little instruction in his FBI file. Many of the legible entries confused him with his cousin, Felix Greene, whom he described as a well-known friend of China. "Guilt by relationship?" he commented.

His file included a gossip column by the late Walter Winchell—as mentioned, one of J. Edgar Hoover's favorite leaking journalists—complaining that Audie Murphy, the highly decorated American soldier-turned-actor, would play the lead role in Greene's *The Quiet American.* Winchell reported that the film libeled Americans in Vietnam and that "the author of the book admits being an ex-Commy." Greene added sardonically that he was equally unhappy because he would have preferred a better actor.

Greene said that he was glad to find an account of his being "placed under guard" in Puerto Rico and his deportation from there by Delta Airlines to Haiti. That incident he later described in his 1980 autobiography, *Ways of Escape.* Under the McCarran Act he had become a prohibited immigrant to the United States because, at the age of nineteen, he had joined the Communist party in Oxford as a probationary member and remained in it for four weeks. The FBI account in his file was not fully accurate—they missed the fact that he refused to leave the plane when it reached Haiti and instead flew free of charge to Havana.

Nor was the file, which depended so heavily on his brief affiliation with the Communist party, accurate in other respects. "The authorities seem to have missed my attempt to organize a mass resignation of the foreign members of the

American Academy of Arts and Letters as a protest against the Vietnam War, an attempt which failed," he noted. His only supporters were Herbert Read and Bertrand Russell.

In general, he said that the "press-cuttings" section of the FBI had produced a large number of insignificant pages. Greene's dossier listed his weight correctly at about 180 pounds (that pleased him) but it had the wrong date of his birth (making him older, which displeased him).

HANNAH ARENDT

Hannah Arendt (1906–1975), the distinguished German-born philosopher, author and professor at the New School for Social Research in Manhattan, became a naturalized American and wrote her greatest books in the United States but had her roots in Europe. Her FBI file had nine pages under the classification "Internal Security—R" (Russian). An additional six pages, in a State Department file, were withheld; my appeal failed to produce them. Among the reasons given for the censored material in her FBI file were "in the interest of the national defense or foreign policy."

Miss Arendt wrote and reported on controversial as well as scholarly matters. She was author of *The Origins of Totalitarianism, The Human Condition, On Revolution* and *Eichmann in Jerusalem.* The last first appeared as trial coverage in the New Yorker and included her brilliant phrase about the essence of the Nazi war criminal: "the banality of evil."

Her file includes a "supplementary biographical statement," undated but probably written for her naturalization papers soon after the end of World War II. Her remarkable intellectual background and experience are set forth: graduate studies at the Universities of Marburg, Freiburg and Heidelberg with a major in philosophy and minors in Greek and theology. She received her doctorate in philosophy from Heidelberg with a thesis on St. Augustine. The personal statement, which helps to define her major writings, continues in these words:

"The rapid growth of the anti-Semitic movement in Germany caused me already to start some of my later research on modern Jewish history and the rise of anti-Semitism in Western and Central Europe. A few months after the establishment of the Nazi regime, I left Germany for France, where I lived until 1940. There, in Paris, I decided to leave the field of scientific research to become acquainted with the real life and, above all, to try to help as best as I could in the catastrophe of the Jewish people. From then on with few interruptions I worked as a social worker in connection with different relief and rehabilitation organizations. Together with my husband and my mother (the latter has lived with me since the pogroms of 1938 in Germany), I came to this country in 1941. I have lived here as a free-lance writer trying as best as I could to put down the lessons present and past history has taught us about the causes and consequences of anti-Semitism."

It is not clear from her blacked-out file why Miss Arendt should be considered an Internal Security case. What may well have brought her to the FBI's attention was an article that appears in her file that ran in the Washington *Post* on May 3, 1953. It is an abridgment of a longer article that was first published in Commonweal, the liberal Catholic magazine. The article—illustrated with a photograph of Whittaker Chambers, the ex-Communist who testified against Alger Hiss—carries this headline: " 'Ex-Communists' Remain Totalitarian at Heart."

In the article Miss Arendt wrote that she chose as her model Mr. Chambers because of his articulateness and gifts as a writer and because he has been accepted as the spokesman for all ex-Communists:

> The ex-Communists are not former Communists, they are Communists turned upside down; without their former communism, they insist, nobody can understand what they are doing now. . . . Ultimately, others don't count; we are only bystanders in the great battle of history. . . . Informing, which plays such a great role in Chambers' book [*Witness*], is a duty in a police state where people have been organized and split into two ever-changing categories: those who have the privilege to be the informers and those who are dominated by the fear of being informed upon. . . .
>
> If you try to "make America more American" or a model of democracy according to any preconceived idea, you can only destroy it. Your methods, finally, are the justified methods of the police, and only of the police. . . . As long as you insist on your role as former Communists, we must warn against you. In this role, you can only strengthen those dangerous elements which are present in all free societies today and which we do not want to crystallize into a totalitarian movement or a totalitarian form of domination, no matter what its cause and ideological content.

Miss Arendt's article—singling out Chambers as the government's prize witness, attacking ex-Communists who think they are the only ones capable of directing American thought against totalitarianism, questioning the role of police informers in general—could hardly have been appreciated by Messrs. McCarthy and Hoover.

In 1956 two mostly blacked-out pages from the special agent in charge of the FBI office in Los Angeles to J. Edgar

Hoover simply read: "Information concerning HANNAH ARENDT is being furnished the bureau, San Francisco and New York for information purposes." In a censored response by the FBI New York office to Hoover, the complaint by an apparent informer in Los Angeles about Miss Arendt was said not to warrant an active investigation. It was stamped both *Confidential* and *Subv. Control.*

If anything, Hannah Arendt's "subversiveness" was philosophical and practical: a strong defense of democratic ideals against totalitarianism and police-state methods—whoever espoused them—that could subvert democracy.

ALDOUS HUXLEY

In the Aldous Huxley (1894–1963) file were documents from the FBI, CIA and Army Intelligence and Security Command in Arlington, Virginia. Of the 130 pages, 111 were released to me, many heavily censored. The net of them: he and his daring and original writings were watched.

This British novelist—*Brave New World, Point Counter Point, Crome Yellow, Eyeless in Gaza*—settled in the Los Angeles area in 1938 and became part of the foreign colony there that included his friend, Christopher Isherwood. The Huxley file suggests that his work confused the FBI and other agencies, which did not understand the attitudes of a British writer who believed in pacifism and world peace. No one wearing a holster under his jacket seemed to understand what Huxley was driving at in *Brave New World* with its satirical vision of a future dominated by dehumanizing science.

The FBI began to make enquiries about Huxley almost as soon as he arrived in the United States in 1938. The bureau became interested because of a book he edited, *An Ency-*

Herbert Mitgang

Sir Stephen Spender, poet, essayist and critic, is one of the foreign authors who occasionally has had difficulty entering the United States because he was on a "watch list." Spender was informed by a friendly Customs agent that his passport had secret markings that indicated an unfavorable political past. The "ideological" section of the McCarran Act has delayed or barred a number of distinguished artists, writers and performers. This photograph was taken at Spender's home in London before one of his periodic visits to teach at American universities.

Samuel Beckett, Nobel Prize-winning playwright, shown here near his home in Paris, was one of many European and American authors who supported the Loyalists during the Spanish Civil War and contributed to "Authors Take Sides on the Spanish War" in 1937. That book and those who supported the Loyalists and the Abraham Lincoln Brigade were noted in the FBI files. The anti-Fascist position was one of the benchmarks of "radicalism" for the FBI recordkeepers.

Herbert Mitgang

Simon & Schuster

Graham Greene was one of the British novelists who obtained his FBI dossier and discovered it was filled with errors and opinions. Sixteen of the dossier's forty-five pages were heavily censored. He was amused by the fact that, while the FBI had his weight right, it had the wrong date of his birth. Mostly, he told the author of this book, the file was filled with trivia from newspaper clippings about him. He is shown here with General Omar Torrijos, the subject of Greene's book *Getting to Know the General.*

Hannah Arendt, the German-born philosopher who became a naturalized American and covered the Eichmann trial for The New Yorker, was the subject of an FBI file. The Bureau watched what she said and wrote, including her attack against ex-Communists who thought that, as informers, they were the only ones capable of directing American political thought. Miss Arendt is shown here during an address before the Bar Association in New York while she was a member of the faculty of the New School for Social Research.

New School for Social Research

Herbert Mitgang

The FBI and other government agencies kept files on foreign artists and authors. Among them was Ignazio Silone, the novelist and essayist, shown here on the balcony of his apartment in Rome. Silone, author of *Fontamara* and *Bread and Wine*, was listed in the FBI file as a matter of "Internal Security—Italy." Nine of the twelve pages in his FBI dossier were released to the author in heavily censored form.

clopaedia of Pacifism, printed in 1937 by Harper & Row. The book was bought by special agent (name censored) at the Rand School bookstore and was found to be distributed by the War Resisters League in New York.

Huxley became the subject of an "Internal Security–Alien Enemy Control" file in 1943 because of *Brave New World* and the fact that it was published as an "Albatross Book." The book was even subjected to "cryptographic examination," but nothing subversive was discovered.

An unnamed FBI informant, so far as one could make out from a heavily blacked-out document, kept track of stories that appeared in magazines and books in the 1940s, the list including several by Huxley and two by J. D. Salinger ("Sergeant Sousa's Arm," "Last Day of the Last Furlough"). *Why* the FBI should maintain such a reading list cannot be determined from the censored pages. One explanation for the security dossiers kept on those who scribbled for a living—especially if they were "foreigners"—is that they tried to inject "anti-Americanism" into their writings.

Counterattack, Facts to Combat Communism, a private blacklisting newsletter feared and heeded by the three commercial networks and used as a pressure and, to put it bluntly, shakedown sheet, included Huxley's name in a 1952 issue, naming him as one of the leading authors who still believed in peaceful coexistence with Russia. Huxley's esoteric lectures for Pacifica Radio, considered leftist or worse by the FBI, also made him suspect, and his and other broadcasts were monitored for subversive ideas.

A publication of the House Committee on Un-American Activities in 1951, entitled "Communist Infiltration of Hollywood Motion-Picture Industry," had Huxley's name indexed. Nevertheless, a blacked-out page in Huxley's file includes the statement that in 1953 he was far removed from pro-Russian or Communist party sympathies.

The name of another British author, Sir Charles P. Snow,

was in the Huxley file because of a speech he made in 1960 at the University of California at Los Angeles on human values and science. Sir Charles said that his book, *The Two Cultures,* had been acclaimed all over the world, "including in the Communist countries." Huxley, on the same panel, spoke of totalitarianism and the need to persuade people to vote for rational policies. The transcript of this university panel was obtained and summarized by the FBI and is in Huxley's file.

The Fund for the Republic, a liberal think tank and study center headed by Robert M. Hutchins, former president of the University of Chicago, also was mentioned in the Huxley file. Huxley was among a number of authors and editors and scientists—including Jerome Weisner, Barry Bingham, Andrew Heiskell, Max Lerner, Lillian Smith and Dory Schary—who had checks next to their names as sponsors of the foundation. The Fund for the Republic often came under attack because of its outspoken pamphlets in defense of civil and constitutional liberties.

Undoubtedly the most detested document in the Huxley file was a 1963 publication called "U. S. A," which said that one of the aims of the Fund for the Republic was "Abolition of the FBI's counterintelligence activities and removal of J. Edgar Hoover from office as director of the FBI."

IGNAZIO SILONE

Ignazio Silone (1900–1978) puzzled the FBI. Could he have been both anti-Fascist and anti-Communist, and where in the world did he stand on the cold war? Was he on Our Side? In the black-or-white world of those who policed authors—especially suspicious foreign authors—there were no nuances. (Nobody among the investigative authorities that I encountered while examining government documents from several agencies seemed to have read any cited passages from an author's novels or even essays as clues to where he or she stood artistically and, therefore, politically.)

I decided to take a shot in the dark and see if the government had a dossier on this Italian novelist—one of the first to alert American and British readers before World War II to the barbarities of Mussolini's Fascism—because I had spent some time with him in Rome when he was adjusting to postwar society after his escape and long exile in Switzerland.

Once, in the mid-sixties, while Romans still rubbed sleep from afternoon eyes, I entered his terraced apartment house on the Via di Villa Ricotta in the comfortable middle-class Piazza Bologna section. I pushed out the toy flaps of the open-ceilinged elevator on a high floor and immediately saw the neatly printed name in the slot above the doorbell. It came as something of a shock; there seemed to be a missing element, perhaps an honorary title from the Italian Republic or, at least, a crest, emblazoned: "Silone of Fontamara." In title-conscious Italy, Silone had no title, but he had something all his own—an international reputation greater abroad than at home, a moral position respected by the neoright *and* neoleft.

Silone emerged from shadows into his shuttered drawing room, a figure of crisis in a country that for the first time in decades was without any. He seemed assured, with neither inner torment nor enthusiasm for lost causes. His penetrating black eyes were at once quizzical and melancholy; from time to time, as we talked, the corners of his mouth lifted into a sweet smile. He appeared more dignified and less embittered than I had expected—as if he, too, had undergone revisions in his character as well as in his fiction. He had rewritten *Bread and Wine,* his best-known work, published in 1937—the first Italian novel to become a Book-of-the-Month Club selection. It had followed his small gem of a novel, *Fontamara,* which also described the resistance of peasants to the inroads of the Fascist regime.

After Silone returned to Italy he became one of the voices disillusioned with Stalinism, and his reasons appeared in the collection, *The God That Failed.* But he continued to write about politics and literature. "Society itself remains the same in any land," he said. "Morality remains the same. What interests me is man: his same faults, his difficulties, his greatness. In the end, men are given over to themselves, left to themselves, faced with a failure of hope and moral crises—that is my story." Silone compared himself to Malraux in his preoccupation with the human condition. "The novelist's function is to place the individual within the state," he told me, "and to expose the state when it encroaches upon the individual's freedom."

This was not a man who was a danger to the United States or any other country. Above all, he was a man of letters. He told me that he desired to come to America because he had been sustained, while in exile, by his publishers in New York and London. He asked me many questions about the wonders of New York, about Italian-Americans, about the many religions and immigrants who had made their homes in Manhattan and Brooklyn and the Bronx. He wanted to see all these places. But he never would.

Silone, it turned out, had twelve pages in his FBI dossier. Nine were released to me, heavily censored. Two more were sent to me, after I filed an appeal, by the Department of Justice's Immigration and Naturalization Service. The fact that he should have had a record in Washington at all had faint echoes of the black-shirted bureaucracy that had once driven him out of his own country.

An entry in his file noted that, in 1951, Silone was one of 150 persons planning to attend a three-day "anti-Cominform peace conference" (which should have earned him high marks) in Zagreb, Yugoslavia. This information was forwarded from Italy to Washington, possibly through an FBI liaison official stationed in the embassy. Significantly, if Silone's activities were reported it indicated that other Italian writers were also being watched.

The Immigration and Naturalization Service, according to his blacked-out file, first sent an urgent request in 1954 for information about Silone. The file on him noted—information that could only have come from Italian sources—that Silone's real name was Secondo Tranquilli. The next year he was listed as a matter of "Internal Security—Italy," and the State Department and Immigration and Naturalization Service passed information to each other about Silone on a document stamped *Secret* and labeled "Espionage."

On one censored page the FBI noted in 1955: "This bureau's files reflect that the subject is a prominent Italian author and politician who, in 1921 reportedly participated in the foundation of the Italian Communist party. According to his own writings and other public sources, he left the Italian Communist party in 1930 and since then has been prominently associated with various Italian Socialist factions."

Finally, after an appeal and a wait of nearly two years, in the Spring of 1987 I received one uncensored document from the Department of Justice's Immigration and Naturalization Service. This 1963 document read:

"IGNAZIO SILONE aka Secondo Tranquilli.

"The applicant, a native and citizen of Italy, born at Pescina, L'Aquila, Italy, on May 1, 1900, has been found by the Consular Officer at Rome to be ineligible to receive a visa because of past membership in the Communist party.

"Mr. Silone is the author of numerous anti-Communist and anti-Socialist novels and desires to visit the United States. Mr. Silone's (true name Tranquilli) admission was previously authorized on December 21, 1954, and amended on July 30, 1956. The waivers were not utilized as he was unable to enter the United States at that time. The responsible consular officer reports there is no information available that was not known at the time of the previous order and recommends that the admission of Mr. Silone be authorized in view of his anti-Communist activities and the interest of the Embassy in having him visit the United States. He is the recipient of a Leader grant.

"It is ordered that the admission of Mr. Silone be authorized, valid for one entry within six months of the date of this order and subject to revocation at any time."

The document, dated April 5, 1963, was signed, "Claude B. Kidder, acting officer in charge."

There were several inaccuracies in this half-hearted permission that could be revoked "at any time." While Silone continued to write novels after returning to Italy, they were rather unimpressive compared to his fiery anti-Fascist work while in exile. His postwar novels were not "anti-Communist and anti-Socialist." These interpretations were obviously included by Embassy officials to make his application more attractive to the Justice Department. In his conversations with me, Silone said he did hope to visit the United States. . . . "But not as a political instrument of any party, Italian or American," he said. "I am an independent—and a writer." Unfortunately, Silone could never bring himself to come to the States; he was too deeply aware that he might be used as a political rather than literary symbol.

Thereafter, the Silone documents fade away into silence and secrecy. But nothing in his file suggests that he, even by the wildest distortion of his record, could have been guilty of espionage against the United States. He had been sustained by royalties from this country while living in Switzerland. *Bread and Wine* was first published in London and New

York; it was not printed in Italy until Fascism was defeated by Anglo-American arms and he had returned to his country. This was a man who repeatedly expressed his affection for the United States and Great Britain in his postwar writings.

There was no reason why J. Edgar's men should have been interested in Silone, who was even something of an enigma to his own countrymen. A number of other Italian novelists were partisans (and Communists and Socialists) who had served in the Resistance during the German Occupation. It is not unlikely that they too were subject to surveillance by Washington's sleuths.

IX.

ALFRED A. KNOPF, PUBLISHER

The government maintained two dossiers on Alfred A. Knopf (1892–1984), one of the most esteemed publishers of the twentieth century and who introduced many of the greatest treasures of American and world literature to readers in the United States. Both dossiers raised questions about his own loyalty and devotion to the United States. Both included material that went to the heart of privacy in his role as a publisher: the subject matter of some of the books that he chose to publish and suspicion about the Communist proclivities of some of the distinguished authors on his list.

One of the most revealing comments in his FBI dossier, written on February 9, 1965, some ten years after the lower depths of McCarthyism, reads: "The files of the FBI reflect that Alfred A. Knopf, Inc., has published numerous books written by persons concerning whom allegations have been made which were of such a nature as would raise questions as to their loyalty."

Alfred A. Knopf, of course, was not the only American book publisher of interest to government investigative and intelligence agencies. For example, editors and publishers (not to mention authors and other professionals in the arts and sciences) who took open stands against the Vietnam War through petitions, speeches, donations and demonstrations often acquired records of their own. So some discovered, they told me, after applying for their files under the Freedom of Information law.

There were twenty pages in the dossier on Knopf maintained by the Office of Personnel Management, Office of Federal Investigations, in the Federal Investigations Processing Center in Boyers, Pennsylvania. Some of these pages were censored because they either were said to constitute an invasion of another person's privacy (usually that of an informant) or revealed the name of a confidential source. In the FBI's file on Knopf in Washington, I was allowed to see 102 pages; an additional 51 pages were withheld in their entirety. Several reasons were given for the censorship, including the possibility of disclosing "the identity of a confidential source" and also because of an Executive Order that allowed documents "to be kept secret in the interest of national defense or foreign policy."

Knopf's publishing company carried his own name plus the imprint, Borzoi Books. These books symbolized quality for more than half a century, and his name and the imprint still continue within the Random House fold. He founded his own firm in 1915 and remained an independent publisher for most of his life. His list of authors included more Nobel laureates in literature than any other American house; it included scores of illustrious authors in every field of fiction and nonfiction. The works of Knopf authors bridged the history of modern literature. They ranged from Thomas Mann's *Death in Venice* to Willa Cather's *Death Comes for the Archbishop,* from John Hersey's *Hiroshima* to John Updike's *The Centaur*, from Sigrid Undset's *Kristin Lavransdatter* to Albert Camus' *The Stranger*. Among the Knopf authors (some published by other houses as well) who won the Nobel Prize were T.S. Eliot, Ivan Bunin, Yasunari Kawabata, Ivo Andric and Gabriel García Márquez.

On the House of Knopf's fiftieth anniversary Clifton Fadiman said, "Mr. Knopf has made a profession out of a business and an art out of a profession." Willa Cather wrote, "He has of course published books he thought very second-rate, and he has successfully done business with people who were not congenial to him. But in his own mind, he kept the two sets of values apart, clear and distinct." Noting the books that bore his imprint, Julian P. Boyd, a president of the American Historical Association, told him, "You have done more for the cause of history than any other publisher." Knopf, both a gentleman and a maverick, was described by John Hersey as "the sworn enemy of hogwash, bunk, gas and rubbish, and a scourge of hypocrites and shoddyites." H.L. Mencken called him "the perfect publisher."

In his Office of Personnel Management file, a 1952 United States Civil Service Commission document requested a "personal and confidential" examination of Knopf by the FBI. He had been serving on the Advisory Board of the National Park Service since 1949 and later became chairman of the committee on Historic Sites, Buildings and Monuments. A loyalty-check was requested on Knopf in 1952; the main source of the information on him, according to the document, was the House Committee on Un-American Activities. Knopf's name had turned up in the committee's records because his name appeared on a 1936 letterhead, "Non-Partisan Committee for the Re-Election of Congressman Vito Marcantonio." Marcantonio, the American Labor party candidate, was regarded as a radical in Washington, and his reelection committee was cited as a Communist front. Another document, supplied by the Un-American Activities committee, noted that Knopf was among the sponsors of "The American Pushkin Committee for the Commemoration of the Centenary of the Death of the Great Russian Poet." Alexander Pushkin, who died in 1837, was one of the first modern Russian authors. The Un-American Activities committee described the Pushkin committee of New York City as a Communist front.

The Un-American Activities committee report on Knopf singled out one of his books, *Night Over Europe: The Diplomacy of Nemesis, 1939–1940,* by Frederick L. Schuman, Woodrow Wilson Professor of Government at Williams College, published in 1941. The unnamed agent investigating Knopf relates that he saw Schuman's book among the titles in the outer office of the publisher and then went over to the New York Public Library and studied it. The bureau was interested in the book because Professor Schuman had a file of his own—and here he was, an author being published by Alfred A. Knopf, the subject under investigation for loyalty.

Professor Schuman had called for a break in relations with Franco Spain the year after America entered the Second World War. "We are at war with fascism and Franco Spain is Fascist," he said, on behalf of the Council for Pan American Democracy. Others who spoke up for the same organization included Lewis Mumford, the author, and Deems Taylor, the composer. Nor did he endear himself with the isolationists in Washington in 1942 when he said that if the postwar problems were to be solved and there was to be peace in the future, the answer was to establish a federation of United Nations and a new World Court. On relations with Russia, Professor Schuman wrote in 1950 that "American capitalism and Soviet socialism do not resemble the Fascist economics of yesteryear. Neither one requires war and conquest to avoid collapse. Since Russians and Americans need no war and can win no war, we shall eventually make peace. But we shall not make an early peace because the cold war is much too useful either to be ended or to be spoiled by making it hot."

These were not popular sentiments to hold when Senator McCarthy was riding high. In 1950 Professor Schuman was described by Senator McCarthy, without documentation, as "one of the closest collaborators in and sponsors of Communist-front organizations in America." During the war Professor Schuman had served as a consultant in Washington on Far Eastern affairs, and afterward had become one of McCarthy's targets during his attacks on the State Department. Responding, Professor Schuman was moved to say, "Senator McCarthy is mistaken in supposing that I have ever held any post in the State Department or Foreign Service. He is perhaps confusing this with my lectures at the National War College at the invitation of of Major General L.L. Lemnitzer, Lieutenant General H.R. Bull and Vice Admiral H.W. Hill. I am as opposed to communism as is Senator McCarthy, but I do not believe we shall ever be in agreement as to the definition of Communist-front organizations."

The same agent who had tracked down Professor Schuman's book in the Public Library on 42nd Street and Fifth Avenue also noted other Knopf authors being promoted in the company's outer office at 501 Madison Avenue in Manhattan. His report goes: "Books written by authors such as H.L. Mencken, George Jean Nathan, Carl Van Vechten, Katherine Mansfield, Thomas Mann, Charles A. Beard, John Hersey, Willa Cather and numerous others were prominently displayed on the wall as published by Knopf."

The report prepared by the FBI for the Civil Service Commission continues: "An investigation disclosed another book entitled *Some Random Recollections,* an informal talk at the Grolier Club in 1948 by Alfred A. Knopf. In this book, Alfred A. Knopf reviews his life in the publishing business. There is a sketch, courtesy of the New Yorker magazine, of Alfred A. Knopf, shown smoking a pipe and surrounded by books bearing the names of some of his authors. Still another book where the publishing house is the author is entitled *Quarter Century, Alfred A. Knopf, 1915–1940.* All this heavy intelligence compiled simply for membership on the National Parks Board.

The Knopf file also includes his own "Application for Federal Employ," filled out in 1950, in which he describes his current activities: "General executive work as head of a book publishing business." Answering questions about his loyalty, Knopf checked the appropriate boxes to show that he had never been a member of a Fascist or Communist organization and that he owed allegiance to the United States. At the end of the investigative report in 1951—which also involved his authors and books—Knopf comes out clean: "His reputation in the community for honesty and integrity and general conduct is the highest. He has for over thirty years been the head of his own publishing business and has been a leader in his industry. He has an outstanding reputation both as a person and as a businessman."

Ironically, the Federal Bureau of Investigation file on Knopf begins in 1936 because of a letter he wrote from his then offices at 730 Fifth Avenue to E.P. Coffey, Esq., FBI, Department of Justice, Washington, D.C. Knopf said that he had read an account of a talk that Mr. Coffey had given to a chemistry club about the growing use of science in criminal detection through laboratory analyses. "It seems to me that a very good popular book might be written on this general subject," he wrote, "and if the idea appeals to you at all I should like to discuss it with you."

The answer, on May 12, 1936, came from John Edgar Hoover himself, who immediately saw an opportunity to promote his bureau. After referring to the letter addressed to Mr.

Coffey, the director wrote: "While I would not personally be able to participate in the publication of such a book at this time, I think that there is ample material for such a book and if approval were secured for the writing of such a publication, I would be very glad to make available information in the files of the Federal Bureau of Investigation for such a purpose. Of course, such a plan would have to be passed upon by the publicity officer of the Department of Justice and definite details of the manner in which the book would be prepared would have to be submitted." Hoover added, "You probably know that two books have already been written concerning the work of our bureau, namely, *Ten Thousand Public Enemies,* by Courtney Cooper, and *Farewell, Mr. Gangster!* by Herbert Corey."

A half-year later Knopf reminded Hoover of his continuing interest in the subject of an FBI book on scientific detection methods and again suggested that Mr. Coffey might be its author. The suggestion for such a Borzoi Book on sleuthing was not as surprising as it might appear; Knopf, after all, was the publisher of Raymond Chandler and his Lew Archer and Dashiell Hammett and his Thin Man. Hoover replied, "I am sorry that it will not be possible for any representative of the Federal Bureau of Investigation to participate in the publication of a book, inasmuch as a policy has been established by the attorney general against such participation in a matter of this kind." He then suggested that Knopf find a qualified author and that "it would give me personal pleasure to be able to assist in making available to such an author information from the files of the Federal Bureau of Investigation." Knopf answered routinely that he would keep looking for an appropriate author; but he never found one and that ended his correspondence with the director.

Thereafter, the FBI file picked up its interest in Knopf because of the request in 1952 by James E. Hatcher, chief of the investigations division of the Civil Service Commission, to examine his record as a member of the advisory board of the National Capital Parks and the National Park Service.

As a conservationist and traditionalist, Knopf had a passion to preserve the integrity of the national parks system—a fact that unfortunately does not appear in his dossier and obviously has nothing whatsoever to do with Communist-front organizations. In "The National Park Idea," he wrote, "a National Park or Monument is a scenic or archaeological or in some way unique preserve, and it is also a playground, campground, natural schoolroom, wildlife sanctuary. It is not a resort, though there will always be those who try to make it so. The Parks are set aside for other than dollar uses, to be kept without impairment for the enjoyment of the people. They cannot tolerate exploitation of any resource, for exploitation uses up, makes over, mars, and changes the things that according to wise law must be kept natural. If a tree falls in a Park, unless it blocks a road or endangers a building or human life, it must lie where it has fallen, slowly to return to the earth out of which it grew."

In 1952, his heavily blacked-out FBI file repeats the fact that he had been on a nonpartisan committee to reelect Congressman Vito Marcantonio and that he had also been on the American Pushkin committee. In addition, (censored) an informant related him to membership in the American Russian Institute. Digging deeper into his past, the file says that in August 1931 (whatever he did or belonged to is blacked out), and in December 1937, Knopf was listed on a civil liberties committee to battle Mayor Frank Hague of Jersey City, who had become famous for boasting, "I am the law."

The FBI had to go through the list of the hundreds of authors published by Knopf over the years to single out those with files of their own. Of particular relevance to his role as an independent publisher, the same censored document from 1952 reads: "Bureau files further reflect that the Alfred A. Knopf Publishing Company, New York City, of which the appointee is president, has published numerous books and articles for authors who have been subjects of bureau espionage and security-matter cases. Included among these authors are such prominent persons as Agnes Smedley, Owen Lattimore, and Philip Jacob Jaffe." When Dashiell Hammett appeared before the Senate Permanent Subcommittee on Investigations, what emerged from the record was that Hammett "referred to books published by Alfred Knopf."

The FBI file called attention to a children's book published by Knopf entitled *Yankee Doodle: Stories of the Brave and the Free.* The source of its information was Counterattack, the weekly four-page publication founded in 1947 as Counterattack, the Newsletter of Facts on Communism, published by American Business Consultants in New York. Counterattack also brought out Red Channels, the Report on Communist Influence in Radio and Television, the "bible" that was used by the television networks to blacklist writers, directors and performers. The Counterattack-FBI citation in Knopf's dossier reads: "Howard Fast is one of the authors whose writings appear in the book. Would you want your children . . . or any children . . . to learn about American history from a CP [Communist party] member whose writing is featured in a recent issue of the Moscow-published New Times?"

The Knopf dossier called attention to a 1934 article in Publishers Weekly that mentioned a reception held on the tenth anniversary of the New School for Social Research in New York City. "Among those present in addition to [censored]," the article reported, "was Alfred A. Knopf." The New School had come under suspicion—at least in the eyes of the FBI, which blacked out the names of its informant at the reception—because of the European refugee scholars who had joined the graduate faculty after escaping Hitlerism. Among them was the philosopher-essayist Hannah Arendt (whose file is included in this book).

In the same year Bufiles (Bureau files) included a page from The Arbitrator entitled "Committee Sponsoring Return of Emma Goldman." The name of Alfred A. Knopf appeared on the committee list calling for the return from Europe of the exiled anarchist-feminist-pacifist. What the notation in the file failed to mention was a most relevant fact: Emma Goldman had been published by Alfred A. Knopf.

Some of the items in Knopf's dossier were incomprehensible after being blacked out. A letter from the New York Bureau to Director Hoover in 1948 (censored) included a statement from (censored) boasting that "for years Alfred Knopf had been urging him to write a book disclosing his extensive knowledge of the Russians." This might have included the name of an academic, or a Soviet emigré, or it simply may have been a Red flag at the mention of "Russians." The details are less important than the fact that an informant was involved in passing along the statement and that somehow this cast a shadow of doubt over what a publisher in the United States should publish.

Similarly, the file revealed that a (censored)-born journalist and writer—"believed to be a member of German and Czech Communist party"—(censored) visited the United States in December 1939. "Alfred A. Knopf, publisher, was listed as a friend on application for visa." The very thing that the House of Knopf was noted for—casting a wide net for authors in countries the world over without giving talent a security check—here became a matter of suspicion. However, the special agent in charge of the New York FBI office did note that Knopf "would logically have contacts with numerous persons in various fields and that the contacts of Knopf mentioned were only legitimate business contacts."

In the middle of the 1950s, Knopf was placed in the "Internal Security—R" (Russia) category. He was also upgraded in the stamping on some of the documents in his dossier—from *Confidential* to *Secret.* The apparent reason for this higher security designation was that he had been listed as a "member of the American-Russian Institute as of 1955, which organization is on the attorney general's list [remainder of sentence blacked out]." Furthermore, the FBI appended a note saying: "He and his wife, Blanche W. Knopf, have been associated with various Communist party members and have supported various front organizations." To have made such a broad accusation would have required a certain degree of surveillance upon their personal and business lives. FBI field files list documents pertaining to them from New York, Los Angeles, Baltimore and Washington.

The surveillance extended to Knopf's staff, according to information in the documents. In 1955 an entry in his file read: "The nature of his contact with these persons has never been established. It is also noted that two individuals reliably reported to have been members of the CP were employed by his company in 1941 and 1943; however, there is no indication that Knopf was personally acquainted with these individuals or was made cognizant of their CP activities."

In 1956 Hoover refused to grant authority to interview Knopf, even though he had been a member of the American-Russian Institute and supposedly had been in contact with Communist party members and sympathizers. The reason given: "The bureau advised that the risk in interviewing him appeared to be much greater than possible results would justify." At the end of this caveat, a note was added that kept the possibility alive: "Should information come to your attention in the future which would indicate that an interview with Mr. Knopf is desirable, do not hesitate to request bureau authority."

The FBI had contacts in newspaper and television companies who fed them inside information; furthermore, as indicated elsewhere, some newspaper publishers and television owners allowed agents to use the newspaper's morgue and the station's film files without regard for the fact that they were thereby compromising their independence. Similar cooperation existed in book publishing, judged by this statement in Knopf's dossier: "The New York Division [of the FBI] has no established sources at either Random House or Alfred A. Knopf." In this respect, the Knopf file shows that in 1965 an FBI agent picked up "a current catalogue over the counter at the publisher's office without pretext." The New York bureau special agent in charge reported to Director Hoover in Washington that the Borzoi Books catalogue contained "several thousand titles by about eight hundred authors" and that the Modern Library-Vintage Books catalogue contained "roughly two thousand titles consisting of what could be called old standards, classics, and books in the public domain, including writings of Shakespeare, Tolstoy, Zola, Mark Twain, etc." In the interlocking relationship between Random House and Alfred A. Knopf, a positive note was found—Random was publisher of Don Whitehead's *The FBI Story,* an ideal version from the viewpoint of the FBI.

Unaware of the dossiers mentioning her and her husband, Blanche Knopf sent a cordial but innocent letter to J. Edgar Hoover in 1964, enclosing a copy of Leonardo Sciascia's *Mafia Vendetta.* She described it as a "documentary novel, translated from the Italian, which I believe will be of special interest to you." Mrs. Knopf said that its publication in Italy opened serious speculation in the Italian press about the extent of government involvement with the Mafia. And then she added, seeking what sounded like a request for a promotional plug, "I hope you will let me hear what you think of it."

This was a rather farfetched notion of Mrs. Knopf, assuming as it did that Hoover would comment about the Sicilian Mafia, when he had enough trouble handling, and avoiding, any strong pursuit of the American Mafia. Sciascia's book is, above all, a novelized account of a Mafia execution set in Sicily; Hoover was not known as a reader of fiction other than what he had encouraged to be written about his own G-men. Sciascia, with whom I have held several talks in recent years in Palermo and at his country house in Racalmuto, deep in the Sicilian interior, holds the America Mafia and especially the romance about it in contempt. As an author who has constantly written against the lassitude and corruption of government and police authority, he would have shrugged a Sicilian shrug in amusement if he had been told that one of his novels had been sent to the director of the Federal Bureau of Investigation for approval.

In reply, Hoover's secretary acknowledged receiving the book but said the director was out of town. (This form reply was known as an "in-absence" letter, used to avoid a direct response by the director.) No answer appears from Hoover to Mrs. Knopf in the dossier. However, an internal note at the end of the secretary's correspondence shows that her letter became the occasion for another rehashing of the charges against both Knopfs. "Bufiles indicate that the correspondent is known to have been associated with various Communist party members and has supported various front organizations," goes the note. Also in 1964, Knopf himself sent a copy of a book to Hoover, *The Raymond Chandler Omnibus,* which again resulted in an "in-absence" letter from Hoover's secretary and no comment on the book. A note was also appended to Knopf's correspondence, listing his association with "Communist party members and support of various front organizations."

Under the Freedom of Information Act, in 1975 and 1976 Knopf wrote to the CIA and FBI to see if they had kept a file on him. The CIA responded by telling him that it did have a record on him that had originated with the FBI. According to his present dossier only a few pages were sent to him at that time. These contained a list of exemptions telling him why more material was not sent to him and excised pages that made the file almost useless. There was one reference to Agnes Smedley and another to the Civil Service Commission.

An interesting mistake was made by one of Hoover's top assistants that directly affected the bureau's attitude toward Knopf and helped to explain why the FBI avoided putting the heat on him with a personal interview. On July 1, 1952, Alan Belmont, assistant to the director, appended a handwritten note at the bottom of a memorandum about Knopf: "He has been friendly to the bureau, owns 'This Week' magazine." This comment was thereafter repeated as a fact. Another memorandum went: "Numerous references appear in bureau files on Knopf but do not per se reflect adversely upon his loyalty. He has been friendly to the bureau and owns 'This Week' magazine. Mr. Knopf is listed in Who's Who in American Jewry."

There was only one problem with the reference to the mass-circulation Sunday supplement called This Week—Knopf never owned it. This Week had been affiliated with and distributed by the Crowell-Collier publishing empire. Since the supplement appeared as the magazine for many different Sunday newspapers, it had to be fairly bland in its reporting and opinions. Its power was in its numbers—over twelve million readers in the early 1960s. Mr. Belmont may have confused This Week with The American Mercury, a monthly magazine that Knopf founded in 1924 and on which H. L. Mencken and George Jean Nathan served as coeditors with a one-third interest in the magazine. The iconoclastic American Mercury published major literary figures until it was sold to Lawrence E. Spivak in 1933, when it then became a conservative magazine in its politics and economics—with opinions that were more congenial to those held by Hoover and his FBI.

And so, by a casual error of fact in his dossier, Alfred A. Knopf was inscribed as "friendly" to the FBI. Yet even this did not allow the FBI or CIA to reveal to him the details in his files about what their recordkeeping maintains were this distinguished publisher's questionable authors and his own loyalty.

X.

SEEING RED: REX STOUT

Among professional writers in the United States, the name Rex Stout (1886–1975) calls up memories of his leadership of the Authors League, the Authors League Fund, its charitable foundation, and the Authors Guild. At various times he served as president of all three voluntary national organizations that are devoted to protecting the interests of authors and dramatists in such areas as copyright, contracts, freedom of expression and various professional and personal difficulties.

THE LEAGUE'S STAND

The Authors League traces its origins to the early years of the twentieth century. Through the Depression years, World War II and up until his death, Stout was in the front rank of advocacy for authors' rights and, in some cases, for their very survival in difficult times. He helped them achieve greater professional standing so that authors and dramatists could practice their craft in a cleaner atmosphere of economic and political freedom.

Stout's faithful readers knew him best as the genial author of detective novels featuring Nero Wolfe, gourmet, connoisseur and orchid grower, who, with the help of his assistant, Archie Goodwin, could solve crimes without leaving his Manhattan brownstone.

The Federal Bureau of Investigation files show that J. Edgar Hoover considered Stout anything but genial: as an enemy of the FBI, as a Communist or tool of Communist-dominated groups, someone whose novels and mail had to be watched, and whose involvement with professional writers organizations was not above suspicion. In the vague, bizarre phrase of one of the documents in his dossier, Stout was described as "an alleged radical."

The Authors Guild, Dramatists Guild and Authors League all came under investigation by the FBI because some of their members took strong stands on public issues and because all three organizations defended writers everywhere against blacklisting. (The Authors Guild and Dramatists Guild together form the Authors League of America; membership in either guild automatically includes membership in the league.) By contrast, I was informed by the FBI that their indices produced no file at all on the American Center of PEN.

A dozen years after Rex Stout's death, the FBI did not easily give up his personal file under the Freedom of Information Act. Of 301 pages that were reviewed, only 183 pages were released to me, and these were heavily censored. Among the reasons mentioned for so many denied pages were that they were to be kept secret "in the interest of national defense or foreign policy" and also that they might disclose the identity of "a confidential source"—which indicated that Stout was being watched by informers. This is further evident from his blacked-out file. It is possible that in the many pages denied to me military intelligence agencies also kept track of Stout, a veteran of the United States Navy in his youth, because of his role as chairman of the Writers War Board during the Second World War.

As Rex Todhunter Stout, born in Noblesville, Indiana, he also appeared in the records of the Immigration and Naturalization Service. An excised *confidential* document, dated August 9, 1955, provided by the FBI to the Immigration and Naturalization Service said that he was an author "most noted for his Nero Wolfe mystery stories" and that there are "approximately five hundred references to him in the bureau files." The document called Stout a "joiner," listing his activities as president of the Authors League, chairman of the Writers War Board, and president of the Society for the Prevention of World War III.

Stout's name in the FBI files reached back to his beginnings as an author, but what particularly irked the bureau and possibly other government agencies occurred during the McCarthy era when he served as president of the Authors League. In January 1952, on the eve of President-elect Eisenhower's inauguration, the Authors League Council adopted this resolution—the strongest in its history:

"In the face of today's growing practice of blacklisting writers, particularly those working for radio, television and the screen, the Authors League of America now emphatically reaffirms its position that such 'political screening' constitutes a basic threat to the entire body of free American writing.

"From the earliest days of this nation's life, our tradition has been that writers and writing should be free of political control. Today this tradition is being eroded by fear. Today any

American writer may be subject to dismissal, disgrace and disaster through the organized activities of self-appointed monitors eager to defend the nation on their own terms.

"The Authors League of America, a purely professional organization of writers in all fields, has never had and will never have a political test for its members. The league neither judges nor defends the individual views of its members. But the league, as always, will combat every concerted effort, whether hidden or overt, to determine the employment of any writer or the presentation or publication of his work on any basis other than the merit of his writing.

"This the league can do by campaigning actively against these new political controls. This the league now proposes to do, believing that here, in today's new suppression of writing and writers, lies a 'clear and present danger' to all American freedoms."

The council resolution did not, of course, stop the networks or studios from continuing their blacklisting practices during the hysteria that characterized the times. Stout followed up the resolution with a letter to Wayne Coy, chairman of the Federal Communications Commission, pointing out that radio and television stations were supposed to operate in the public interest. He noted that four issues were involved: A concerted denial by the radio and television industries to writers of employment or presentation of their works; inadequate presentation of the works of writers because of arbitrary blacklisting of actors, directors, scene designers and other personnel; denial to the public of its constitutional right to see and hear the works of established writers of high literary reputation; and the practice by the radio and television industries of organized blacklisting which, if not actually illegal, was wholly at variance with the American traditions of freedom of expression and due process—and wholly against the public interest.

In this respect Stout was pursuing a course that had not endeared the Authors League to Congressional Red-hunters in the past. In 1947 the council had protested against "the radically harmful form of censorship now being exercised on the entire profession of writing by the House Committee on Un-American Activities." The league did not deny the right of Congress to investigate for legislative purposes. But it did continue to oppose the foment of censorship manufactured by publicity-keen politicians and commercial defamers, such as the vicious private publication called Red Channels that was involved in "clearing" names. "The motion-picture industry has cravenly submitted to this censorship by blacklisting from employment a group of writers for their alleged political beliefs," the league stated, adding that the radio and television networks were repeating the pattern of blacklisting developed by the major Hollywood studios.

If anything, network blacklisting affected even more professional writers, actors and directors. Surprisingly, among the worst offenders was the television network with the strongest news tradition—William S. Paley's CBS, which lived off the reputation of Edward R. Murrow and some of his distinguished wartime colleagues, including William L. Shirer, Eric Sevareid, Alexander Kendrick and Charles Collingwood. Yet CBS continued to have a loyalty oath for its news employees long after the demise of McCarthyism, and it continued to maintain a blacklist for certain performers well into the sixties.

(For example, Peter Seeger, the outspoken folk singer, was not permitted to perform on television until, one Sunday morning in 1966, he finally broke through the ban by an appearance on a CBS News religious broadcast. At the time, the author of this book was executive editor of CBS News and, together with a daring and talented executive producer, Pamela Ilott, delightedly helped to break the blacklist against

Seeger. When Miss Ilott came to me and asked for permission to have Seeger "cleared" by the Program Practices Department—the euphemism for the network censor—I told her not to do so and simply to put him on the program without fanfare. We winked, Seeger sang, there was some behind-the-scenes grumbling by the president of CBS News about the use of an anti-Vietnam War folk singer on a religious program, but neither the president nor anyone else at the network chose to protest openly. (It should quickly be added that the Authors League and other organizations told similar tales of resistance by people going on record against blacklisting and loyalty oaths.)

The Authors League appointed a committee of three of its most active and best-known writers—Elmer Rice and Ruth Goetz, playwrights, and Laura Z. Hobson, novelist—after Rice had publicly accused the networks in 1951 of maintaining blacklists. The committee investigated the effects upon authors and dramatists whose names were listed in Red Channels, the private blacklisting publication mentioned earlier that was heeded by the networks, sponsors and advertising agencies. A questionnaire was sent to fifty-one writers listed in Red Channels; thirty-one responded. All said they were aware of blacklisting though not all were as yet affected. At a meeting of the Authors League after the committee reported its findings in 1952, the council decided that it now had positive proof of blacklisting. Most of the writers listed in Red Channels, who said that they knew blacklisting existed, declined to testify before the Federal Communications Commission, admitting that they were afraid of reprisals by the networks.

Such was the frightening mood in the country—exacerbated by the willing cooperation of the commercial networks and Hollywood studios—that affected authors, dramatists, directors and performers. Red-baiting was given the highest priority; but no network, studio, congressional committee or the FBI ever proved that the script of a single program or film followed the so-called "Moscow line"—that is, ever advocated a Soviet system of government or praised collectivism on the farms or in the factories. What puzzled some of the Red-hunters were such films as "Meet John Doe," with a screenplay by Robert Riskin, that was produced and directed by Frank Capra for Warner Brothers in 1941. Like a number of other films growing out of the Depression era, it included talk of the "common man" and the need for people to work and stand together. With clean-cut Gary Cooper playing "John Doe," the tone of the film was mildly populist but hardly revolutionary. (Later, Cooper, together with Ronald Reagan and several other "friendly" witnesses, were praised for their patriotism by J. Parnell Thomas, chairman of the House Un-American Activities Committee investigating communism in Hollywood.)

A heavily blacked-out internal FBI memorandum on Stout, stamped *Confidential,* noted that he was president of the Authors League of America in 1952. The memorandum represented the attitude of the FBI toward authors, including the fact that writers were being watched and files kept on them. Under "Authors League of America," the document flatly declared: "There were numerous Communists in the membership of the Authors League of America. It is pointed out that the Authors League of America in 1941 organized the Writers War Board as a means by which the Authors League of America could aid the war effort."

The claimed linkage between "numerous Communists"—no names or evidence for this wild charge appeared in the Stout file—and the Writers War Board, which included many of the most distinguished writers in the country who had volunteered their skills, was an obvious smear of both the league and the board.

While the war was on, Stout, who had organized the Writers War Board and became its chairman, was placed on something called the "General Watch List." Hoover himself, according to a heavily censored page marked *Confidential,* requested Byron Price, director of Censorship, Federal Trade Commission Building, Washington, to include Rex Stout of Brewster, New York, on "General Watch List No. 49."

The FBI watched what Stout wrote and somehow turned his fiction into suspicious fact. Because, for example, of a story that appeared in the May 1940 issue of American Magazine called "Sisters in Trouble," he was labeled what might be called "prematurely anti-Nazi." A highly imaginative document from Los Angeles (correspondent's name censored) to the FBI's Communications Division in Washington claimed that the story was "either a deliberate attempt to convey a meaning other than the solution of a mystery story—or else the whole thing is full of coincidences. Note the almost exclusive German cast of characters, particularly Fritz Brenner. Could Fritz refer to the German Consul in San Francisco, and could Brenner have any reference to the Brenner Pass? Could 'Nero' refer to Rome by any chance? While for the purposes of the story, April, May and June are the names of three sisters, couldn't it also mean that for three months, or until July, somebody's back was to the door—maybe the door to the Balkans or the Mediterranean?"

When it served its purposes, agents of the FBI could turn into literary critics, finding, however ludicrous, damning symbols in fiction. The same document included the news that a publication entitled "Sequel to the Apocalypse—The Uncensored Story: How Your Dimes and Quarters Helped Pay for Hitler's War," written by John Boylan, carried a foreword by Rex Stout. The FBI report noted that the publication "purports to be a complete history of I.G. Farbenindustrie from its inception in 1920 to the present." Again, Stout was somehow suspect because he was associated with a publication that exposed Hitler's leading arms manufacturer.

Five months before Pearl Harbor and the declaration of war against Japan and Germany, Stout's anti-Nazi views were entered in his file: "On August 1, 1941, Stout made an address over radio station WMCA entitled 'Declare War Now,' in which he advocated an immediate declaration of war by the United States against Germany. This speech was later put out in pamphlet form by the Associated Leagues for a Declared War, of Westport, Connecticut. Stout was listed in this pamphlet as one of the organizers of this group."

An early entry in the Stout file noted that the Western Worker carried an article in 1936 that Rex Stout would be one of the contributors of articles or stories appearing in a special issue of the New Masses, the left-wing magazine that succeeded The Liberator and had undergone various editorial changes, from proletarian to Socialist to Communist oriented. Many prominent writers and artists—including Communists, but some of more literary than political bent, among them Carl Sandburg, Archibald MacLeish and Rex Stout—contributed poems and stories to New Masses at the beginning of their careers.

Stout described himself as a "pro-labor, pro-New Deal, pro-Roosevelt left liberal." Nevertheless he was branded a Communist on an FBI internal memorandum in 1942. At this time he was devoting most of his energies to the War Writers Board. Some of the FBI's favorite writers and conduits, among them columnist Westbrook Pegler and Chesly Manly of the Washington *Times-Herald,* then began to attack him. Manly ridiculed him in these words: "Rex Stout, goat-bearded writer of mystery stories, whose record as a Communist fellow traveler is one of the prize exhibits of the Dies Committee on Un-American Activities, is chairman of the War Writers Board. Stout was interviewed at his country place near Brewster, New York. His long gray chin whiskers bristled against a scarlet shirt, and there was a fanatical gleam in his small brown eyes. He was like a grotesque caricature of a man."

As for the War Writers Board, Stout said it had been created originally in December 1941 as the Writers War Committee to carry out a request by the Treasury Department for assistance in its war-bond drive. Members of the board included many members of the Authors Guild and Dramatists Guild—Pearl S. Buck, Russell Crouse, Elmer Davis, Clifton Fadiman, John P. Marquand, William Shirer and Luise Sillcox (who served as executive secretary of the Authors League). Major writers on the Board's advisory council included Franklin P. Adams, Stephen Vincent Benét, Van Wyck Brooks, Marc Connelly, John Gunther, Langston Hughes, Howard Lindsay, Edna St. Vincent Millay, Clifford Odets, Eugene O'Neill, Elmer Rice, Thornton Wilder—a roll call of some of the most important figures in the book, theater and journalism worlds.

After the war Stout, writing his mystery novels at high speed, continued his voluntary public activities. In addition to the Authors League, his time was devoted to civil liberties and world government organizations. And the FBI kept tailing him, in person and in print, apparently using its network of informers (one reason why so many pages in his file were denied to me, I believe, was to conceal their names). Indeed, the bureau continued to dig into his associations as if he were an arch-criminal.

Stout's dossier also included membership in Americans for Democratic Action (ADA). A 1947 news report in *PM,* the adless New York newspaper that the FBI deplored because of its liberal writers and editorial positions, stated that the

New York chapter of ADA protested "the current probe of alleged communism in Hollywood as generating hysteria and endangering civil liberties." The statement of protest was signed by sixty-five notable figures of the stage, screen and literature. Stout was one of the signers.

In 1948 the New York *Sun* carried a feature story, summarized in Stout's dossier, saying that plans had been completed "in secret" for a campaign to create a new organization designed to attack the House Committee on Un-American Activities and persuade Congress to abolish it. The organization was identified as the "Committee of 1,000," headed by Dr. Harlow Shapley, the Harvard astronomer. The California Committee on Un-American Activities declared that the "Committee of 1,000 was a Communist created and controlled front organization." The Shapley committee issued a statement saying that the Un-American Activities committee resorted to "trial by headlines and encouraged publicity seekers and sympathizers." Stout was one of the signers.

The National Americanism Commission of the American Legion in 1955 attacked the Society for the Prevention of World War III, Inc., and its members. Regarding Rex Stout, identified as the organization's president from 1943–46, the American Legion publication, "Firing Line" (no relation to the television program), said that he had been affiliated with "four subversive organizations."

Again in 1955, while he was serving as president of the Authors League, the FBI assembled a *confidential* twelve-page internal memorandum on Stout that began: "The purpose of this memorandum is to set forth salient information appearing in bureau files concerning Rex Stout, the author, who is most noted for his Nero Wolfe mystery stories. It is pointed out that although the bureau has never conducted an investigation concerning Stout, there are approximately five hundred references to him in bureau files." "Never conducted an investigation"—the by-now familiar self-protective euphemism meaning that the bureau had not conducted a full-scale formal investigation, in case other information should turn up. A totally blacked-out page in this file is labeled "Allegations of Communist Party Membership and Family Affiliations." It is the only reference to Stout's family, but whether his family also came under surveillance cannot be determined from the censored pages, all of which creates an ominous aura.

A partially blacked-out page is labeled "Membership In or Affiliation With Cited Organizations," in which Stout is identified as a member of the League for Mutual Aid, an organization cited for its financial help to "political prisoners, radical agitators and workers temporarily in distress. It operated an employment agency and maintained a bail fund for members of the Communist party, the Young Communist League, (censored). The League for Mutual Aid has been cited by the House Committee on Un-American Activities as a Communist enterprise." And other cited affiliations included this breathy roll call: the Joint Anti-Fascist Refugee Committee, the National Council of American-Soviet Friendship, the National Federation for Constitutional Liberties, the American Committee of Jewish Writers, Artists and Scientists, Emergency Committee to Save the Jewish People of Europe, Friends of the Spanish Republic, American Veterans Committee, Americans United for World Organization, Federation of American Scientists, United World Federalists and the Authors League of America.

Inclusion of the Authors League of America with the other organizations—cited as Communist or subversive by the attorney general, the congressional or California Committee on Un-American Activities—was based on the statement that there were "numerous Communists" in the membership of the Authors League. Not one name, however, was cited as a

Communist, nor was there any documentation about the league, its history, charter and what it had stood for since 1912.

J. Edgar Hoover himself and the FBI's powerful publicity machine came down hard on Stout in 1965 when his novel, *The Doorbell Rang,* was published by the Viking Press. About one hundred pages in Stout's file are devoted to this novel, the FBI's panicky response to it and the attempt to retaliate against the author for writing it. The FBI's internal memorandum for its special agents told them that "the bureau desires to contribute in no manner to the sales of this book by helping to make it the topic of publicity." Orders came from headquarters in Washington that any questions concerning the book should be forwarded to the Crime Records Division, thereby putting book and author in a criminal category.

An internal memorandum by Special Agent M.A. Jones (name suprisingly not censored) summarized the novel and went on to write a critique for the FBI's top command—a rare "literary" honor accorded to few books in its files:

"This vicious book depicts the FBI in the worst possible light. Fred Cook's *The FBI Nobody Knows* [an unflattering portrait of Hoover and the bureau] plays a significant role in the plot. Nero Wolfe, Stout's hero, is contacted in New York City by a wealthy matron, Rachel Bruner, who desires to hire Wolfe to stop FBI harassment of her. Mrs. Bruner claims the harassment began after she purchased ten thousand copies of *The FBI Nobody Knows* and sent them to prominent people. She states the FBI had been tapping her telephones and had placed her under constant surveillance. Wolfe indicates that she could have expected such treatment from the FBI. He accepts the assignment from Bruner and is paid a one-hundred-thousand-dollar retainer fee. In this manner, Rex Stout establishes the FBI as the villain of his book."

Thereafter, Mr. Jones made these observations about the

possible success of *The Doorbell Rang* in the marketplace: "The plot of this book is weak and it will probably have only limited public acceptance despite Stout's use of the FBI in an apparent bid for sensationalism to improve sales. The false and distorted picture of the FBI which Stout sets forth is an obvious reflection of his leftist leanings as indicated in our files."

The FBI book reviewer also said that Rex Stout "has been a member of or affiliated with numerous organizations which have been connected with Communist groups or identified as Communist fronts." As for the novel's publisher, "The Viking Press is a reputable publisher with which we have had little contact." (The phrase, once again, raises the question of what contacts the FBI did maintain with other publishers, especially since FBI files on several authors and journalists make reference to sources within publishing houses and newspaper and magazine offices.)

Following the review came a series of recommendations—first, Stout was designated as a person "not to be contacted" without prior approval by FBI headquarters in Washington; second, that "all SACs" [Special Agents in Charge] of FBI offices around the country be notified about the book and its placement in the Crime Records Division; third, that any inquiries received about the book should be answered with a statement that "the FBI has no comment other than that the book is a fictional work which presents a false and distorted picture of the FBI and that any agents conducting themselves in the manner depicted in this book would be subject to immediate dismissal." Hoover then wrote a memorandum to his top assistants, including the book review and its observations, and saying that Rex Stout should not be interviewed "unless compelling reasons dictate, in which event the matter should be called to my attention."

Several people who read the book and took it seriously as fact wrote to Hoover, deploring the novel's contents and expressing their confidence in the FBI. Hoover replied to these letters personally with words of thanks and praise—especially when writing to sympathetic editors and columnists. What is particularly noteworthy in this exchange of letters is the revelation that the FBI maintained a "Special Correspondents List" that apparently included journalists useful to the FBI as informers or plants. One friendly book reviewer for the Los Angeles *Times* actually sent a copy of her review, attacking Stout and defending the FBI, to Hoover, who wrote her a warm letter. Another letter writer (name blacked-out) said he or she slept better at night "because you and the FBI are on guard."

The controversy surrounding *The Doorbell Rang* led to additional publicity and watchfulness by the FBI. When Stout appeared on NBC's Today Show, Special Agent Jones monitored the program and wrote a report for his superiors in Washington. He noted that Stout was critical of the FBI, and on one occasion referred to Hoover as a "tinhorn autocrat." On the program Stout proved himself to be prescient. According to Jones, Stout commented that the FBI kept dossiers on thousands of individuals and because of the possession of these dossiers the FBI held a threatening weapon against numerous citizens. Stout contended that these dossiers should be destroyed. Jones concluded, "Stout, of course, is known to the bureau. He is nothing more than a bearded beatnik looking for publicity."

The Stout dossier includes numerous reviews and interviews. An amusing combination review-interview by Caskie Stinnett in the New York *Herald Tribune* helped promote *The Doorbell Rang.* In the interview Stout talked about his casual experience with the FBI: "I have never had a personal involvement with the FBI but they had one with me about fifteen years ago. An agent came up here [to his home in Brewster, New York] to ask me some questions about a writer who was a very close friend of mine. His eighth question, if

I remember correctly, was whether or not my friend read The New Republic. After he asked that, I wouldn't talk to him anymore. I will not cooperate with a subversive organization, and to censor or restrict what a man reads is subversion. I got so damned mad, I put him out."

Stout attacked Hoover personally in the *Herald Tribune,* calling him a meglomaniac and on the edge of senility. "I first became suspicious of Hoover years ago when I heard that he had been seen going to horseraces with Senator McCarthy," Stout said. "I couldn't quite see the head of the Federal Bureau of Investigation being pals with a man who at the time was the greatest single threat to American democracy. If he wants to get at me for writing this book, I wish he would try. He can't hurt me at all, so to hell with him."

The *Herald Tribune* review-interview ended by observing that Stout, as president of the Authors League of America, was spending much of his time trying to get the country's archaic copyright law brought up to date—an effort that succeeded in large part because of lobbying by Stout and other members of the Authors League in Washington.

As for the charges made against the Authors Guild and Authors League as being subversive organizations, the FBI eventually had to retreat for lack of evidence. This was finally admitted to me after my inquiry; presumably, special agents are no longer clipping newspapers and magazines and reading the books and filing reports on league and guild elections, as they had done for years. But there is no such admission or formal clearance about the false accusations made against the scores of officers and council members whose names still exist in the government's files. Their dossiers remain, ready to be revived by some important public official who captures the lightning of antilibertarianism at some future time in Washington.

Tom Hollyman

Alfred A. Knopf, the most distinguished American publisher of the twentieth century, had an FBI file of 153 pages, of which fifty-one pages were denied in their entirety to the author of this book. Knopf was considered suspect because of his own views and those of his authors. His dossier notes: "The files of the FBI reflect that Alfred A. Knopf, Inc., has published numerous books written by persons concerning whom allegations have been made which were of such a nature as would raise questions as to their loyalty."

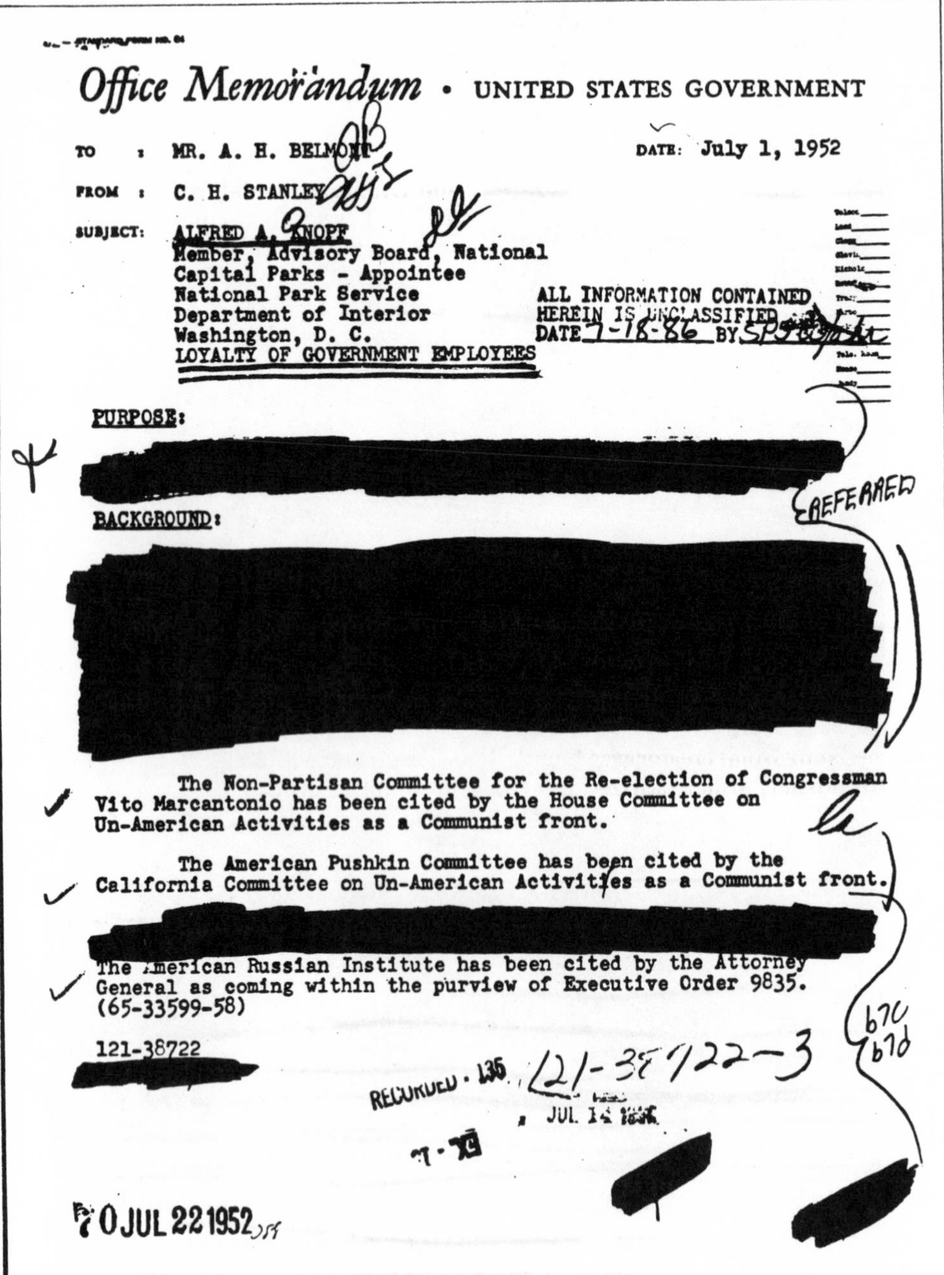

Office Memorandum • UNITED STATES GOVERNMENT

TO : MR. A. H. BELMONT

DATE: July 1, 1952

FROM : C. H. STANLEY

SUBJECT: ALFRED A. KNOPF
Member, Advisory Board, National
Capital Parks - Appointee
National Park Service
Department of Interior
Washington, D. C.
LOYALTY OF GOVERNMENT EMPLOYEES

ALL INFORMATION CONTAINED
HEREIN IS UNCLASSIFIED
DATE 7-18-86 BY SP

PURPOSE:

BACKGROUND:

The Non-Partisan Committee for the Re-election of Congressman Vito Marcantonio has been cited by the House Committee on Un-American Activities as a Communist front.

The American Pushkin Committee has been cited by the California Committee on Un-American Activities as a Communist front.

The American Russian Institute has been cited by the Attorney General as coming within the purview of Executive Order 9835. (65-33599-58)

121-38722

REFERRED

b7C
b7D

RECORDED · 136 121-38722-3

JUL 14 1952

70 JUL 22 1952

A page from the heavily censored dossier on Alfred A. Knopf that raised questions about his "loyalty" to the United States. During the McCarthy era, he underwent a security check because of his membership on the National Parks Advisory Board. Three of the committees that he belonged to, mentioned on this page, were branded Communist fronts.

The Viking Press

The Authors League, which includes the Authors Guild and Dramatists Guild, had an FBI dossier that implicated thousands of its members as coming under "Communist influence." Rex Stout, president of the Authors League, Authors Guild, and Authors League Fund, had a thick file of his own which grew thicker after he ridiculed J. Edgar Hoover and the FBI in one of his Nero Wolfe mystery stories.

Stout presented an award in 1950 from Friends of Democracy to Arthur Miller, playwright, who wrote the narration for the film, "Difficult Years," which dramatized the impact of totalitarianism. The Nero Wolfe creator was branded an "alleged radical" in his FBI dossier; Miller satirized the House Committee on Un-American Activities, assuring him a dossier by the FBI, which cooperated closely with the committee.

FD-72 (1-10-49)

SECU... INFORMATION - CO...IAL

FEDERAL BUREAU OF INVESTIGATION

FORM No. 1
THIS CASE ORIGINATED AT NEW YORK | FILE NO. FC

REPORT MADE AT	DATE WHEN MADE	PERIOD FOR WHICH MADE	REPORT MADE BY
NEW YORK	2/9/53	9/5,9,10,26; 11/18/52;1/5-9,12/53	[redacted] b7C
TITLE			CHARACTER OF CASE
COMMUNIST INFILTRATION OF THE AUTHORS LEAGUE OF AMERICA			INTERNAL SECURITY -C

SYNOPSIS OF FACTS:

The Radio Writers Guild of the Authors League of America considered Communist infiltrated by the Sub-Committee investigating the administration of the Internal Security laws of the Committee of the Judiciary, U. S. Senate. Results of the Radio Writers Guild, Eastern Region, election on 11/6/52 set out. Officers of Authors League of America set out [redacted]

b7C b7D

ALL INFORMATION CONTAINED HEREIN IS UNCLASSIFIED

ALL INFORMATION CONTAINED HEREIN IS UNCLASSIFIED

\# 267,770

APPROVED AND FORWARDED:	SPECIAL AGENT IN CHARGE	DO NOT WRITE IN THESE SPACES	
COPY IN FILE		100-50311-54	RECORDED-36
COPIES OF THIS REPORT		FEB 11 1953	INDEXED-86

COPIES OF THIS REPORT

6-Bureau (100-50311)(REGISTERED)
2-Chicago (info)(REGISTERED)
2-Los Angeles (info)(REGISTERED)
3-New York (100-99705)

PROPERTY OF FBI—This confidential report and its contents are loaned to you by the FBI and are not to be distributed outside of agency to which loaned.

SECURITY INFORMATION - CONFIDENTIAL

The Authors League of America—which included guilds of professional writers for the major publishing houses, the theatre and broadcasting—was penetrated by FBI informers who provided notices of meetings and internal documents. The FBI labeled the character of the case against the Authors League of America a matter of "INTERNAL SECURITY—C" (for Communist). In response to the author of this book, the FBI admitted that it had not produced evidence to document this charge.

XI.

INFILTRATING THE GUILDS

The Authors League of America and its professional guilds were penetrated by the FBI on the eve of the Second World War and continued to be watched all through the war and during the McCarthy era and postwar years of the Eisenhower presidency.

The thick file on the league and its components—the Authors Guild and the Dramatists Guild—adds up to 369 pages. I was allowed to see 295 pages; 74 pages were denied to me entirely because of a revised Executive Order, approved by President Reagan in 1986, that erected a higher fence around access to information under the Freedom of Information Act. The main reason that the FBI gave for the exemption was that the Executive Order allowed the documents to be kept secret "in the interest of national defense or foreign policy." As already indicated, the documents I did receive included many blacked-out pages.

The league and its guilds—voluntary organizations designed to protect the contractual rights and freedoms of creators of books and plays—represent most of the professional writers in the United States as well as a small number of foreign writers whose works are published or staged in this country. As a former president of the Authors Guild for four years, a continuing member of its governing council for twenty-five years, and as current president of the Authors League Fund (a charitable foundation established by the two guilds that helps authors and dramatists in ill-health and economic distress), I was particularly interested in how the federal authorities regarded these author organizations. Over the years I have observed scores of dedicated professional writers willingly devoting private time to the guilds; it is their way of elevating and giving something back to the profession of letters in the United States. The guilds, however, are not political—except insofar as defending the constitutional right to protect their copyrights and enjoy the liberty to write without abridgment have been considered political by federal investigative agencies.

SPYING ON MEETINGS

The first entry in the file was a "personal and confidential" letter, dated October 29, 1941, sent to Director Hoover in Washington from P.E. Foxworth, assistant director, in New York. He enclosed a copy of the actual notice and proxy for the secret ballot of the biennial meeting of the Authors League of America, to be held at the Hotel Lincoln in New York on November 12, 1941, for the purpose of electing officers. The membership document explained the voting methods and listed the names of the officially nominated slate of officers: president, Howard Lindsay; vice-president, Henry

F. Pringle; secretary, Kenneth Webb; treasurer, Arthur Schwartz.

This was followed in the FBI file by a notification to me under the Freedom of Information Act stating that two pages were being withheld in their entirety, under subsection (b)(7)(d) of Section 552 of Title 5 of the United States Code. This exemption—designed to protect informers—reads in part:"Records or information compiled for law-enforcement purposes, but only to the extent that the production of such law-enforcement records or information could reasonably be expected to disclose the identity of a confidential source."

My appeals under the informers' exemption invariably have been denied. The obvious reason is that the FBI does not wish to disclose the names of those members who have spied upon colleagues in their own organizations—as Ronald Reagan did when he was president of the Screen Actors Guild.

The Authors Guild file continued with a clipping from the Chicago *Tribune* Press Service, dated June 3, 1942, written by Chesly Manly, one of the FBI's favored journalists. Among the dozens of authors and dramatists who came under suspicion in the *Chicago Tribune* article because of affiliations with the writers' organizations or because in public meetings they spoke of "winning the war at home" as well as abroad were some of the most respected writers in the nation: Stephen Vincent Benét, Van Wyck Brooks, Pearl S. Buck, Mary Ellen Chase, Russel Crouse, Elmer Davis, Clifton Fadiman, John Gunther, Langston Hughes, John Kieran, Howard Lindsay, John P. Marquand, Edna St. Vincent Millay, Clifford Odets, Eugene O'Neill, Elmer Rice, Mary Roberts Rinehart, William L. Shirer and Thornton Wilder.

An internal FBI memorandum in 1942 from D.M. Ladd, one of Hoover's top aides, addressed to "The Director," summed up the activities of the Authors League, quoting from its bulletin, which supposedly was distributed to members only. The FBI maintained its own file of Authors League Bulletins, going back at least to 1936 when an issue appeared on censorship. It noted that one issue carried a censorship article "which condemns several federal bills pending because of their repressive measures." The Ladd memorandum included interpretative statements about "many prominent writers and authors" who had been connected with "Communist-front organizations."

Another internal memorandum by Ladd in 1944—in the midst of the Second World War—responded to a request by Hoover for more information about the Writers War Board. The memorandum said that while no information was available showing any "Communist influence or control," a number of the writers had been affiliated with Communist groups. Among those so named were Pearl S. Buck, Clifton Fadiman, Dorothy Canfield Fisher, Carl Van Doren and Clifford Odets. "It is also significant to note that the name of Langston Hughes appears with the advisory council," the memorandum went on. "Hughes, you will recall, is the Negro Communist poet famous for the Communistic, atheistic poem, 'Goodbye Christ.' "

The FBI file shows that by 1944 the Writers War Board had grown to include cooperating committees in other fields, among them a high school drama committee of the Council of Democracy, chaired by Barrett Clark and including Ernest Angell, Russell Crouse and Elmer Rice; and a music war committee of the American Theatre Wing, chaired by Oscar Hammerstein II and including his musicals partner, Richard Rodgers, as well as other composers. These writers and musicians cooperated voluntarily with all the branches of the armed forces and government agencies—at the same time that a file was being kept on them.

After the war the Authors League was targeted as an "Internal Security—C" (Communist) matter. On July 31, 1950, the FBI director ordered the special agent in charge of the New York office to investigate "Communist infiltration of Authors League of America." Hoover's order read: "You are instructed to immediately institute a discreet investigation of the Authors League of America to determine whether there is any Communist infiltration, influence or control in the league and the extent thereof." Hoover, always aware of the danger of a public relations boomerang when he undertook investigations of well-known or well-placed authors, added, "In view of the nature of this group, the investigation must be most discreet and at this time should be limited to establishing the history, background, officers and nature of the group and the extent of Communist infiltration, influence or control. A complete review of your field office file should be made and any outside inquiries should be limited to your confidential informants and established and reliable sources of information."

What touched off the investigation was an article in the May 25, 1950, issue of the New York *Compass,* citing an Authors League statement that the refusal of the Supreme Court to review the case of the blacklisted Hollywood Ten writers and directors had perpetuated "a form of censorship dangerous to the rights and economic subsistence of all authors." The strong statement warned that "Hitler lost his leading scientists, writers, artists and teachers because of discrimination against those who were not in step with his totalitarian regime" and that "censorship by defamation, blacklisting, compulsory public disclosure of views and association, is quite as effective as direct prohibition of creative work." The article also noted that in 1947 the league had criticized the House Committee on Un-American Activities—clearly a heresy.

The Hoover memorandum singled out by name Erik Barnouw, Lillian Hellman, John Hersey and Rex Stout. In 1950

Oscar Hammerstein II was president of the league, Hersey was vice-president, Kurt Weill treasurer, and Barnouw secretary; among the prominent authors and dramatists on the league council were Russel Crouse, Ruth Goodman Goetz, Laura Z. Hobson, Howard Lindsay, Richard Rodgers, Lionel Trilling and Ann Petry. It was little wonder that Hoover did not want to take head-on some of the most respected dramatists, novelists and essayists in the United States. However, this did not prevent him from investigating them—to what purpose? as agents of the Kremlin?—surreptitiously, through informers, so they would have no knowledge and no chance to clarify or respond.

An "urgent" communication from Hoover on December 4, 1950, said that it was "absolutely imperative" that the New York office send its report on the Authors League of America. On December 29, 1950, a thirty-five page *confidential* report labeled "Communist Infiltration of the Authors League of America" was sent from New York to Washington. This detailed report, though heavily censored, still clearly showed that it was based on organizational files and documents. It noted that the league was formed in 1913 and was composed of the Dramatists, Authors, Radio Writers and Screen Writers guilds. (The Radio Writers and Screen Writers later established separate organizations because of the specialized nature of their work and left the league amicably.) The report said that the league operated as a labor union, but without the same status as a union, though it sometimes sought relief before the Labor Relations Board. The name of the censored FBI source is described as a person "of known reliability" and (possibly a slip that got by the censor since the informers are normally genderless in the files) is referred to as a "she." Apparently each of the guilds had informers, judging from the blacked-out lines in the report.

The report also includes a copy of the league's constitution and bylaws, normally available to members only. Indeed, league and guild publications were restricted to dues-paying members and not distributed for public relations purposes.

Under the section on the Authors League, this paragraph appears: "Mr. Jay Whittaker Chambers, a self-confessed former Soviet espionage agent and former senior editor of Time magazine, advised in 1949, that John Hersey was chief of the Moscow Bureau of Time magazine in the early 1940s and that the information he supplied to Time was obviously and quite openly quite favorable to the Union of Soviet Socialist Republics." (Hersey's reputation for veracity among his peers and the public, as a war correspondent and contributor to the New Yorker, where his famous report, "Hiroshima," first appeared, could not credibly be tarnished by an admitted liar and Soviet spy. Whittaker Chambers, remembered for hiding State Department microfilms in a pumpkin on his farm, had been the principal witness in the trial of Alger Hiss, the former State Department official accused of espionage and instead convicted of perjury in 1950. The publicly tried case helped to make the reputation of Richard M. Nixon as a Redhunter and directly led to his selection as General Eisenhower's running mate in 1952.)

The report on the league also included a reprint from Hearst's New York *Journal American,* August 3, 1947, that described Lillian Hellman as a playwright "whose affiliations with Red Fascist groups and movements would fill a proscenium arch, according to files of the House Committee on Un-American Activities."

Under a section labeled "Implementation of Communist Party Line," an informant (name blacked out) said that "there has been a leftist or pro-Communist group within the Radio Writers Guild."

An informant (name blacked out) in the report on the league advised the FBI that the organization was "at least

Communist infiltrated." The report finished off by saying that the New York office of the FBI would continue to follow the activities of the League and its various guilds "through confidential informants and official publications."

(The name of one informer, a novelist, became known to the late Peter Heggie, the executive secretary of the Authors Guild, because of the informer's subsequent activities. Mr. Heggie passed along the name orally to one or two people as a caution for the continuity of the guild; the name of the informer, also deceased, cannot be revealed here since there is no written documentation.)

The leadership of the FBI in Washington then recommended that "due to the Communist infiltration"—it had now become a definite fact in the report, without the knowledge of the Authors League officers, council or membership and without an opportunity to confront their accusers—that the thirty-five-page document be disseminated to the army, navy and air force intelligence services. This action undoubtedly resulted in the league's officers and council members having their names placed in the Pentagon's security files.

In 1952 the FBI reported that the Authors League council had issued a public statement defining the organization. The statement said: "The Authors League of America, a purely professional organization of writers in all fields, has never had and never will have a political test for its members. The league neither judges nor defends the individual views of its members. But the league, as always, will combat every concerted effort, whether hidden or overt, to determine the employment of any writer, or the presentation or publication of his work on any basis other than the merit of his writing."

The FBI might have saved a goodly amount of paper, personnel (including informers) time and money if it had accepted the truth of that statement.

THE RADIO WRITERS GUILD

In the same year of 1952 the FBI also reported on the Radio Writers Guild, which had created a fact-finding committee on the blacklist and censorship. That guild issued a statement saying that the committee had been fighting blacklists all along. It noted that "until recently ours was the only labor organization making an active effort to defend its members from this insidious form of discrimination. We are no longer alone in our efforts to get rid of blacklists. Increasing numbers of entertainers are becoming alarmed at the implications of industry blacklists and are joining together to fight."

In a confidential report dated February 9, 1953, the FBI issued a heavily censored fifty-seven-page document—some pages of which were denied to me altogether—headed "Communist Infiltration of the Authors League of America" that covered "subversive infiltration of the radio, television and entertainment industry, the Radio Writers Guild elections, officers of the Authors League of America. . . ."

The report relied on information derived from senators James O. Eastland, Pat McCarran and Arthur V. Watkins, who had held hearings in executive session in New York and Washington. One of the points underscored by the senators was that members of the Radio Writers Guild wrote not only for the national networks but also for the Voice of America and the radio section of the United Nations. To some of the senators on the Judiciary Committee, the U.N. had always been regarded as a suspicious foreign body within the United States.

This influential Senate committee then quoted an unnamed witness who claimed that "the verbiage which flows into almost every American home came from the pens of the pro-Communist faction." The report said that the radio carried "a constant derision of the capitalistic system, and a constant derision of the average citizen, and there is no such thing in their scripts as a decent banker and a decent lawyer." The methods of writing were said to be "subtle," yet filled with "scorn and contempt," so that "simple people" who might otherwise turn off Communist propaganda became "undermined" by listening to the radio programs.

The Radio Writers Guild responded to the public airing of these absurd, undocumented accusations, saying that the organization was dedicated to the constitution of its parent body, the Authors League of America; that its only objective was to promote the professional and economic interests of its twelve hundred members; that it had never aligned itself with any Communist or pro-Communist organization, and that in compliance with the Taft-Hartley Act its officers had signed non-Communist affidavits.

The Eastland-McCarran committee report had charged that "a certain element in the guild followed the Communist line in their script writing." One specific example was cited—a script written for "Cavalcade of America." The committee's informant, Ruth Adams Knight, a leader of the so-called anti-Communist faction in the guild, mentioned "The Swamp Fox," and said that there had been constant identification with the partisans in Yugoslavia to "our early Americans," thus connecting the anti-Nazis who resisted the Germans during the Occupation of their country to "our own revolutionaries." In response, the guild invited its members and the public to examine the script itself. "The script does not deal at all with any Communist situation, in Yugoslavia or anywhere else," the guild council noted. "There is no constant identification of our early Americans with anybody except our present Americans."

In 1953 Hoover stepped up surveillance of the Authors League across the country and in Canada. In a personal memorandum to his "liaison representative in Ottawa," he passed on information about the Radio Writers Guild from three special agents in New York. In addition, he reported to his liaison (usually, his man in an American embassy would be the legal attaché) that he had ordered the Chicago and Los Angeles offices of the FBI to look into the activities of the Radio Writers Guild in their territories. Hoover cautioned that "in view of the nature of these organizations"—meaning the prominence of some members of the Authors League and the Radio Writers Guild and their possible ability to embarrass the bureau—the offices "should be discreet in their investigation" and that contacts should be had only "with established sources." The names of the officers of the Radio Writers Guild, plus all the elected members serving on the councils in New York, Chicago and Los Angeles, were inscribed in the files and exchanged among the three bureau offices as well as with Hoover's liaison in Canada.

At this same time the bureau distributed an article from the August, 1953, issue of the American Mercury magazine by Martin Berkeley, one of its favored journalists, entitled "Reds in Your Living Room." After stating that the Communist party "already had control" of the Radio Writers Guild, the American Mercury pointed to the establishment of another organization, the newly formed Television Writers of America, and said it meant that "the Communist party has set up a potent weapon to assail you right in your living room!" Berkeley and the American Mercury failed to mention which programs had Reds as subliminal heroes, lurking in the soap operas, to overpower the United States and make America unsafe for commercials.

Individually, the members of the Authors League were not monolithic in their political attitudes or about the role that their guilds should play in confronting or cooperating with the federal investigators. For example, while the league's officers and council members approved resolutions against blacklisting and censorship, a minority view was expressed by Maxwell Anderson in a letter to the radio-television editor of the New York *Times* in 1953. Writing from Beverly Hills, Anderson, author of the verse plays *Winterset* and *Elizabeth the Queen*, offered a strong personal view: "The screening of the guilty from the innocent is a very difficult matter. It cannot be done, in the absence of absolute proof, without occasional error, yet it is essential and must be done. It must be done for two reasons—first, because every American Communist is a traitor to his country and to democracy and has forfeited his right to be heard, and, second, because there are many honest and able men named in Red Channels [the frequently mentioned privately owned blacklisting publication that was used by the networks and studios to blacklist writers and performers] whose voices are needed in the worldwide war for freedom and who should not be silenced without a careful consideration of the charges against them. If the Authors League wishes to be of service in this matter, and not merely muddy the waters, it should set up a board to consider the cases of writers accused of communism, a board prepared to condemn those found guilty and to clear the innocent." No such name-clearing and condemnatory board was set up by the Authors League to stand in judgment on its own members—an action that, in any case, would have violated the organization's nonpolitical constitution.

By 1954 the special agent in charge of the FBI's New York office found it necessary to lower the temperature of accusation against the Authors League. He (name blacked out) submitted a thumbnail sketch for the approval of the bureau in Washington: "According to informants of known reliability, the Authors League of America is Communist infiltrated but not Communist dominated."

This slight concession did not, however, change the category for the Authors League in the FBI records. In 1955 the documents continued to identify the organization as a subject of "Internal Security—C." Chicago and Los Angeles reported that "there may be the need in the future for investigative activity," and New York said that it would "continue to follow and report" on the league's activities.

The FBI's New York office noted that, in 1955, the Radio Writers Guild and the Screen Writers Guild had withdrawn from the Authors League of America to form the Writers Guild of America. Furthermore, the Television Writers Guild had become a component of the Screen Writers Guild. Thereafter, the Authors League remained the sole parent body of the Authors Guild and the Dramatists Guild. The unnamed special agent in New York commented to Hoover: "Our sources are of the opinion that the removal of the Radio Writers Guild would tend to make the Authors League of America less subject to being referred to as Communist infiltrated."

Nevertheless, a confidential report to Washington continued to identify the leadership of the writers' organizations—Rex Stout, president of the Authors League of America; Merle Miller, president of the Authors Guild; Moss Hart, president of the Dramatists Guild—and included their affiliations and writings.

Merle Miller, a longtime acquaintance of this author (we had both been wartime army correspondents, he for *Yank*, I for *Stars and Stripes*), was described as an "established author." Someone in the bureau apparently read one of his novels, *The Sure Thing,* and found its theme suspect because "it presented a fictional account of an American faced with a loyalty investigation." Even Miller's writing while a college student was closely examined by the FBI. Its agents had taken the trouble to delve into the files of the *Daily Iowan,* the University of Iowa newspaper, and found that the January 24, 1939, issue contained an article by Miller, "On Being a Subversive Influence," in which Miller had written that he had often been termed a Communist and added that if standing for reform for the underprivileged meant that he was a "Red," then he would plead guilty to the charge. Based on the flimsy evidence of this New Dealish college newspaper writing at the end of the Depression, the FBI with straight face added: "The Communist party, USA, has been designated by the attorney general of the United States pursuant to Executive Order 10450."

Moss Hart, the playwright who received the Pulitzer Prize in 1937 for his drama, *You Can't Take it With You*, and wrote the librettos for Broadway musicals by Irving Berlin, Kurt Weill and Ira Gershwin, was tracked by the FBI because he had been scheduled to attend a luncheon under the auspices of the women's division of the Joint Anti-Fascist Refugee Committee and had also been a sponsor of the American Committee for Spanish Freedom during the Franco dictatorship. In another derogatory listing in his file, Hart was mentioned as a wartime sponsor of the National Council of American-Soviet Friendship—at a time when the United States, Great Britain and the Soviet Union were all fighting on the same side to defeat Hitler's Third Reich. The FBI failed to mention that at this same time Hart's patriotic 1943 play, *Winged Victory*, about the United States Air Force, was being performed by men in uniform all over the United States.

Moss Hart

A WILD-GOOSE CHASE

At the end of 1955 the FBI special agent in New York informed Hoover that "confidential informants" have reported that they had no further knowledge of "current Communist activity to infiltrate" the Authors League of America, and the bureau agreed that the case against the organization of authors and dramatists should be placed in a "closed status."

In a final report filed in 1956, (names censored) New York informants advised that they had "no information concerning Communist activity or infiltration" in the Authors League of America. A "confidential" memorandum followed from William F. Tompkins, assistant attorney general of the Department of Justice's Internal Security Division, to J. Edgar Hoover. Tompkins reviewed the investigative reports on the League and decided that there was "not sufficient evidence to justify filing a petition to the Subversive Activities Control Board" to require that the Authors League register as "a Communist front."

The league file, though, remained alive. In 1957 Sherman Adams, President Eisenhower's principal aide in the White House, requested that a "name-check" be made on the "Authors League of America, Incorporated, 6 East 39th Street, New York, New York." Whereupon a private "personal and confidential" report was delivered to Adams from Hoover. It said that in 1950 the FBI had instituted an investigation of the Authors League "to determine whether or not there was Communist infiltration of this group." Information was developed through "reliable informants," Hoover wrote, "that the Authors League of America was Communist infiltrated but not Communist dominated." Informants stated that the removal of the Radio Writers Guild from the Authors League "tended to make the Authors League less subject to being referred to as Communist infiltrated."

There follow three pages deleted in their entirety. It is not possible to determine why the White House was interested in the Authors League at that time. By 1958 the status of the Authors League had been reduced to a handy abbreviation—*Cominfil* (Communist infiltration). The Authors League was referred to as a "labor union" for the first time; it was not and never had been. As for surveillance, blacked-out lines indicated that there were still informants or special agents involved in "coverage" of the organization.

An article in the Authors League file, clipped from the Boston *Globe* in 1958, reported that Adlai E. Stevenson, the Democratic Presidential candidate who ran against General Eisenhower, had gone to Moscow to represent the Authors League in an effort to obtain royalties for books and plays written by its members and translated in the Soviet Union. Stevenson opened a wedge; the Russians at least admitted that they had a moral obligation to make some payments. In later years a copyright agency was established in the Soviet Union and payments began to flow—slowly and modestly—to foreign authors.

The Authors League, except for its FBI plants, obviously did not know that it was being watched by Hoover's agents. In 1960 Philip Dunning, editor of the Dramatists Guild Bulletin, exchanged warm personal greetings with the director. Hoover had sent him a copy of his latest American Legion address. In return, writing to him on the Dramatists Guild letterhead, Dunning described Hoover's speech as "splendid and timely," enclosed a copy of the bulletin, and added that he was the editor. "I just wanted you to know what I'm doing," Dunning wrote, "in the event I could be of service anytime." An internal FBI note at the end of Hoover's letter of thanks for "your generous offer of assistance" said: "Mr. Dunning is on the Special Correspondents List"—maintained by Hoover for favored journalists and other friends of the FBI who could be trusted to be properly reverential toward the director and the bureau.

Except for what may have appeared subsequently among the seventy-four pages withheld from me in their entirety, the FBI file on the Authors League ends in 1962 with an ironic touch. Mr. Dunning thanks Mr. Hoover for sending him an autographed photograph, adding, "I shall prize it highly." The photograph obtained by the admiring *former* editor does not hang in the offices of the Dramatists Guild today.

XII.

AMONG THOSE PRESENT . . .

The Freedom of Information-Privacy Act enabled Americans for the first time to discover if their government had kept them under suspicion or surveillance by maintaining their names in secret files for alleged violation of laws of the United States. Most authors of my acquaintance resisted the temptation to write away for their files for several reasons. They thought it would be a waste of time because they did not believe that there would be anything there. They could not think of anything that they had done in their personal or professional lives, other than a signature here or a petition there, that would truly warrant the attention of such important branches of government as the Federal Bureau of Investigation and the Central Intelligence Agency. They thought: Didn't the FBI and CIA have enough to do chasing real crooks and spies?

To be sure, there were some authors who were modestly proud of the antiestablishment or antigovernment stuff that they had written in the past. But, truth to tell, they came to realize as the years passed that their words had drifted away on gossamer wings: despite what they believed was their most thundering prose, the corrupt establishments and administrations still stood unshaken, the McCarthys and Nixons turned up in new and even more rueful guise as Meeses and Reagans. And then there were some authors, composers and other artists with long memories, who told me that they preferred not to find out if they did have dossiers. They feared that the mere act of asking might open up old wounds and new files.

After a long article of mine called "Annals of Government: Policing America's Writers," appeared in the New Yorker in the autumn of 1987, friends and acquaintances got in touch with me and said that their curiosity (or that of their grown children) had prevailed and that they, sometimes with the help of lawyers, had obtained their own dossiers. Invariably, they said that what they discovered inside was a little worse than they had expected. Their government had indeed kept an eye on them as if they were potential criminals or political risks to the country. The so-called facts about them were alternately half-truths, undocumented rumor by unnamed informants, full of trivia, and wildly amusing—but only in retrospect. Most surprising of all, they felt, was that the United States Government had bothered to look into their personal lives and writings and careers in the first place.

JOHN KENNETH GALBRAITH

John Kenneth Galbraith—economist, professor, diplomat, author of a score of books, a president of the American Academy and Institute of Arts and Letters—knows, among other things, his numbers. He told me that, counting overhead, the FBI file on him alone must have cost the American taxpayer hundreds of thousands of dollars. "By a wide margin," he said, "it was the most expensively researched enterprise with which I have ever been associated."

Galbraith offered some sound advice for this study. "These people can't stand satire," he said. "Of course, what the FBI did has to be treated as a danger to freedom, but they do deserve a large amount of ridicule." Ridicule is what they got in his memoir, *Annals of an Abiding Liberal,* part of which recounts the FBI's forty-year pursuit of him. They accumulated hundreds of pages about whatever he said or wrote or even thought—right down to their last errors of fact. (One of the documents in Galbraith's file noted that he had a "commanding" appearance because of his height of five-feet-six-inches; he happens to be six-feet-eight-and-a-half-inches tall.) In a separate talk with Professor Arthur M. Schlesinger, Jr., the historian, author, and White House aide to President Kennedy, I was told that these files could be regarded as something of a merit badge and that he believed his own dossier was even thicker than that of his friend Galbraith.

"The file," Galbraith said, "is unparalleled in my experience as a mine of misinformation. It proves conclusively that on the matter of being a security risk—perilous one day, safe the next—the age of miracles is not over. While the impression of other people's paranoia is great, my own was diminished by the fact that while the documents are full of deeply damaging intentions, virtually nothing unpleasant ever happened as a consequence. But one can see how the only slightly more vulnerable must have suffered. The file also proves, and here beyond the most pallid shadow of a doubt, that the government of the United States has, in these matters, a colossal capacity for wasting money."

Among other things, the Galbraith file noted that "the subject leaned as far to the left as President ROOSEVELT." Congressman John Taber, described by Galbraith as "an articulate fossil from upstate New York," deplored Galbraith's postwar work for the State Department directing economic affairs in Germany and Japan. The Congressman fattened out Galbraith's file with this observation: "He is a member of many Communist-front organizations . . . a totalitarian . . . would be a whole lot more effective using a pick and shovel [in the State Department]."

Galbraith said that an unnamed informant—someone he judged to be "an aged Princeton professor of economics"—described him as "doctrinaire" in his views, "in favor of anything Russia was in favor of." The reference to Russia did not survive, but his description of Galbraith as doctrinaire was heard by the investigator as "Doctorware." This was held to imply that Galbraith was a follower of an otherwise unidentified subversive called Doctorware, later promoted, academically, to "Dr. Ware."

"For the next twenty years," Galbraith said, "whenever my file was examined, the superb testimony on my personality, garrulity and loyalty was never reproduced. Only the references to radical theory and to a Dr. Ware." The investigator responsible for the "Dr. Ware" tale turned out to be someone from the Republican National Committee, according to later information. The comedy of pronunciation errors, and other comments about his politics, caused the State Department Security Office to disapprove him in 1946 as a security risk.

In 1950 Galbraith underwent an FFI—a Full Field Investigation—because of his work as a consultant to the Commerce Department. Frightened officials in Commerce and not the FBI were responsible. "It was a very full investigation indeed," Galbraith said, "and it was this that must have run into the real money. Men were deployed, according to a later memorandum, in Washington, New York, Boston, Chicago, Newark, Detroit, Albany and St. Louis. A request went to the State Department for research, via the consular offices, into my Canadian background and my activities while a student thirteen years before in England. No disloyal information was forthcoming."

In addition, Galbraith's book reviews were read by an agent in the New York bureau. The reviews were found not to "reflect any information that may be pertinent to this investigation." There was one exception—a review of Merle Miller's *The Sure Thing,* a novel about the witchhunting practices that were taking place in the early fifties. The same FBI agent in New York gained access to the New York *Times* morgue; the agent called the morgue "The Biographical Morgue file of the New York *Times* newspaper." (Other publications and television stations allowed investigators access to their news resources. The New York *Herald Tribune,* for example, was particularly close to J. Edgar Hoover; the publisher's son, Brownie Reid, served as his catspaw for a continuing series of what might be considered Red-baiting articles and editorial positions.) In any event, no information was found that reflected on Galbraith's loyalty.

FBI plants in the Communist party were interrogated about Galbraith in a half-dozen cities. The reports came through: "Confidential Informants New York City T-2, T-3, T-4, T-5 and T-6, who are reliable and familiar with general Communist activities in New York City area, advised that they are not acquainted with the appointee." And from Harvard: "Boston Confidential Informant T-1, of known reliability, closely associated with activities at the School of Public Administration, Harvard University, advised having been acquainted with Appointee. . . . T-1 expressed the firm belief that GALBRAITH was without question a loyal American citizen."

During his full investigation, informants, known and unknown, branded Galbraith as a "screwball in economics," "a fellow traveler," "a fly-by-night economist determined to inject a Socialist trend in policies and directives of the Office of Price Administration," as someone who sent "chills down the spine of any American with a knowledge of the left-wing conspiracy to take over our Republic."

Galbraith came under attack from J.B. Mathews, research director of the House Committee on Un-American Activities and a notorious Red-hunter, who eventually joined Senator McCarthy and then was fired by him for charging that the Protestant ministry was Communist-infiltrated. Mathews reported in tortured syntax: "J. KENNETH GALBRAITH has had a connection with one of the Communist books, magazines and other literature but it is not indicated as to exactly which Galbraith was affiliated." Galbraith, divining that Mathews meant his former employer, Fortune magazine, described Mathews as "a formidable opponent of communism and good syntax."

In 1960 J. Edgar Hoover called for a full survey of Galbraith's file when he learned that the economist was working for John F. Kennedy's presidential campaign. All the misinformation from the past was repeated, with additions. The Commerce Department was reported as saying that, in his non-employment there, Galbraith had been viewed as one of fifty-one "poor security risks." Galbraith said, "Hoover was also told that, as a Kennedy helper, I was associated with Arthur Schlesinger, Jr. Although there was no mention again of Dr. Ware, it was noted that in 1959, at the suggestion of Adlai Stevenson—with whom, the file read, I was associated during the 1952 and 1956 presidential campaigns—I had 'contacted' the Soviet Embassy. The approach to the Embassy, unless for a visa, was news." Hoover's mixing into politics, despite his oft-repeated remark that his bureau was independent and nonpartisan, led him to report that Galbraith was "left of center" though not "left wing or pink." Surely a featherweight FBI distinction.

Before Galbraith was named the ambassador to India in 1961, a final report was made on him. "The investigation revealed a striking fact about the loyalty of government officials. If you are a member of the administration and about to become an ambassador, things go better. Adverse information disappears or even becomes favorable," Galbraith discovered. "It was noted with emphasis that President Truman had bestowed on me the Medal of Freedom for 'exceptionally meritorious achievement' during the war. There was, of course, the usual misinformation. My birthplace was given as Ottawa or Toronto [he was born in Iona Station, Ontario], and I was described as deeply anti-Communist, which I am not."

The Vietnam War resulted in Galbraith's last important encounter with the FBI. The Johnson White House had asked for a name-check on him because he and several other individuals had helped to raise money for "Dove" United States senators. In 1968 an internal memorandum revealed the FBI once again in the role of literary critic. A review was offered of his novel, *The Triumph:* "The book primarily is a 'spoof' and satire of the State Department, Dean Rusk and American policy to uphold dictators in power for the reason of overthrowing communism. . . . Several miscellaneous references are made to the FBI, but nothing of any pertinence. The references are not derogatory."

Galbraith told me that he was amused by what his friends told him they had said about him when the FBI agents came around to investigate his loyalty and economic views. One said, "Galbraith? He's extremely conservative—really more of a reactionary." Galbraith commented, "Those are the sort of wonderful things your friends did for you. It's impossible not to have fun at the expense of the FBI. But there's also a need to distinguish between the members of the FBI rank and file and the people in the government who so egregiously use them."

WILLIAM H. (BILL) MAULDIN

In front of me is Bill Mauldin's 207-page FBI file. Bill Mauldin, of all people! Two-time winner of the Pulitzer Prize for editorial cartoons. Author of a dozen books, including three that were Book-of-the-Month-Club selections and whose titles—*Up Front, Back Home* and *The Brass Ring*—are a part of our language and modern experience. Wartime rifleman with the 45th Division in Sicily (Purple Heart); editorial cartoonist for *Stars and Stripes* in the Mediterranean Theatre (Legion of Merit); Democratic candidate for congressman from New York; postwar cartoonist for the St. Louis *Post-Dispatch;* and living in his native New Mexico and still producing four editorial cartoons every week for the Chicago *Sun-Times* and North America Syndicate.

Mauldin told me that he was willing to reveal the contents of his file because it exposed the absurdities and falsehoods of dossiers that cast a cold eye on American authors and artists and, at the same time, revealed the leanings of various officials who judged him to be a suspicious character if not a potential danger to the Republic.

Mauldin and I go back a long way together—to a time best described by Ernie Pyle in one of his dispatches from up front in Italy: "Sergeant Bill Mauldin appears to us over here to be the finest cartoonist the war has produced. And that's not merely because his cartoons are funny, but because they are also terribly grim and real. Mauldin's cartoons aren't about training-camp life, which you at home are best acquainted with. They are about the men in the line—the tiny percentage of our vast army who are actually up there in that other world doing the dying. His cartoons are about the war. . . . After the war he wants to settle down in the Southwest, which he and I love. He wants to go on doing cartoons of these same guys who are now fighting in the Italian hills, except that by then they'll be in civilian clothes and living as they should be."

The Mauldin file is chock-full of ironies. A report discloses that while Mauldin was a guest of the army at Fort Bliss, invited to speak to troops in training at the invitation of the commanding officer, he was also kept under surveillance. "I was the army's fair-haired boy and there they were investigating my ass!" he told me. One letter in it, addressed to J. Edgar Hoover, recommends that he use Bill Mauldin's drawings to help him carry on his work at the FBI. Not in the file is a visit made to him about a year ago by an FBI agent to check on a neighbor of his, a retired three-star general who was going to do some work for a defense contractor. Mauldin was amused at the fact that he, a onetime sergeant, was called upon to vouch for the character of a former general. "The agent asked me all kinds of things, like does the general snort dope," Mauldin said. "I was appalled at the nature of the questions."

Appropriately, the file begins with a "Willie and Joe" cartoon that ran in the Washington *Daily News* in January 1946; the FBI saw fit to clip and save it. (Willie and Joe were the names of his two army infantry characters, now back home adjusting to civilian life.) The cartoon was a crack at the House Committee on Un-American Activities, which appeared on the door of a congressman's office as "Un-American Committee for Investigating Activities (Free Speech Division)." Later that year, the FBI included a clipping from the Communist *Daily Worker* that slapped Mauldin because, in

John Kenneth Galbraith, writer, economist and professor, described his dossier as "unparalleled in my experience as a mine of misinformation" and that it proves that "the Government of the United States has, in these matters, a colossal capacity for wasting money." In a conversation with the author, Professor Galbraith said that his FBI file alone cost the American taxpayer hundreds of thousands of dollars.

University of Guelph, Canada

Christine Lund Mauldin

Bill Mauldin (adorned with beard, like his famous wartime riflemen, Willie and Joe, the characters in "Up Front") is shown here with Herbert Mitgang in front of Mauldin's home in Santa Fe, New Mexico. Mauldin and Mitgang served together on the Mediterranean edition of Stars and Stripes, the Army newspaper. The cartoonist, who has a 207-page FBI dossier, continues to comment on the state of the nation and the world as a syndicated editorial cartoonist.

"*Investigate* them? *Heck, that's mah posse.*"

Bill Mauldin

Several of Bill Mauldin's postwar editorial drawings showed up in his FBI dossier because they attacked the methods of the House Committee on Un-American Activities. This cartoon appears in "Back Home," one of his three books that were chosen by the Book-of-the-Month Club.

Word Processor

Bill Mauldin told Herbert Mitgang that Mitgang's article in The New Yorker on FBI dossiers resulted in this drawing.

a radio address, he had urged the Russians to allow reciprocal freedom of travel for American journalists in the Soviet Union. In 1947 another Mauldin cartoon from the Chicago *Sun,* in a lighthearted fashion illustrated a "loyalty check." A handwritten note over the cartoon ordered it to be placed in the "Mauldin File." In the eyes of the FBI, the days of wine and roses were over for Willie and Joe's creator after the war.

Mauldin did his usual number on the "brass" in 1948 when he was invited to speak at the Naval Academy. The headline in the Washington *Evening Star* read: "Mauldin Cheered by 2,000 Middies in Annapolis Talk." But, in addition to calling for enlisted men to be able to bring their grievances to chiefs of staff without going through channels, Mauldin said that the most important goal for today's world was to implement a world federalist movement through "a United Nations with teeth in it." To the FBI, it was a dangerous statement to be clipped and placed in his file.

By 1949, Mauldin had become a "Security Matter—C." (Mauldin was a bit surprised to hear, when we recently talked about it, that in FBI shorthand the "C" stood for "COMMUNIST.") An urgent teletype was sent from the FBI office in El Paso to the FBI Director in Washington. It read: "WILLIAM MAULDIN, AKA BILL MAULDIN, SECURITY MATTER—C. SUBJECT WELL-KNOWN CARTOONIST IS VISITING FT. BLISS, TEXAS, AS GUEST OF US ARMY AND IS BEING KEPT UNDER CONSTANT SURVEILLANCE BY CIC [Counterintelligence Corps] REPRESENTATIVES HERE ON INSTRUCTIONS OF DEPARTMENT OF ARMY, WASHINGTON, D.C., WHO HAVE MERELY INSTRUCTED LOCAL CIC TO SURVEIL HIM. TELETYPE SUMMARY ANY SUBVERSIVE BACKGROUND KNOWN TO BUREAU AND WHETHER ANY ACTION DESIRED BY THIS OFFICE." It was signed "BROWN." (The Mauldin file had been obtained by him through his attorney under the

Freedom of Information Act in the mid-seventies so Special Agent D.K. Brown's name was included; by the nineteen-eighties the names of FBI bureau agents were usually blacked out.)

Now J. Edgar Hoover himself got into the Mauldin case, establishing his own territorial rights independent of the army. His "Urgent" message to the special agent in charge of the FBI bureau in El Paso read:

"WILLIAM MAULDIN SM DASH C [Security Matter—C]. BUREAU FILES REVEALED THAT THE SUBJECT HAS ACTIVELY PARTICIPATED IN VARIOUS AFFAIRS SPONSORED BY THE AYD (American Youth for Democracy], PARTICULARLY THE "WELCOME HOME JOE" DINNERS SPONSORED BY THAT ORGANIZATION. IN ADDITION, HE WAS A MEMBER OF THE BOARD OF DIRECTORS OF THE INDEPENDENT CITIZENS COMMITTEE OF THE ARTS, SCIENCES AND PROFESSIONS IN FEBRUARY, FORTY-SIX. FURTHER, HIS SERVICES HAVE BEEN SOUGHT IN VARIOUS COMMUNIST-FRONT ORGANIZATIONS INCLUDING THE JAFRC [Joint Anti-Fascist Refugee Committee]. BUREAU'S FILES CONTAIN NO INFORMATION INDICATING THAT MAULDIN IS A MEMBER OF THE COMMUNIST PARTY. HOWEVER, IT HAS BEEN ALLEGED THAT HE IS SUCH WITHOUT PROOF. BUREAU DESIRES THAT YOU CONDUCT NO INVESTIGATIONS IN THIS MATTER, HOWEVER, IMMEDIATELY UPON SUBJECT'S DEPARTURE FROM EL PASO, YOU SHOULD FORWARD TO THE BUREAU ALL THE INFORMATION YOU HAVE CONCERNING THIS MATTER TOGETHER WITH THE INFORMATION YOU RECEIVE CONCERNING HIS ACTIVITIES WHILE THERE. NO CONTACT SHOULD BE MADE DIRECTLY WITH THE ARMY, HOWEVER, FOR THIS PURPOSE. HOOVER."

Apparently both the army and the FBI hit a dry hole trying to unearth anything subversive on Mauldin at Fort Bliss. An FBI memorandum sought to know from Army Intelligence the purpose of "this surveillance of a civilian." No army response appears in the file. The El Paso bureau of the FBI reported that the CIC found "nothing of significance" and discontinued tailing Mauldin. Special Agent Brown then told Hoover that in the absence of further instructions, "this case is being considered closed."

At a time of ferment on behalf of minorities for civil rights, education and housing, Mauldin, like other liberal-minded Americans, stood for equality of opportunity. His drawings and activities found their way into his FBI file under: Internal Security—Communist; Racial Matters; Housing.

Mauldin did not endear himself with the FBI as early as 1946, when one of his cartoons appearing in the Washington *Daily News* took a direct swipe at the bureau and insured that they would consider him suspect for at least the next quarter of a century. The drawing showed two commuters reading a newspaper whose headline read: STILL NO CLUES ON LYNCHERS OF 4 IN GEORGIA. In the caption one commuter turns to the other and comments: "I see the FBI cleared up another big postage stamp robbery." The drawing, of course, was placed in his file, and surely stuck in Hoover's craw.

Except if they were black, many veterans moved into the fine new Peter Cooper Village–Stuyvesant Town apartments, erected after World War II with tax-exempt concessions to the Metropolitan Life Insurance Company, that bordered on the East River in Manhattan. Mauldin and this writer were neighbors, and continued our friendship, there. What none of us who signed petitions against discrimination in the housing project in 1949 knew was that Big Brother in Washington was watching. The only rumor at the time was that Metropolitan Life would look with disfavor at lease-renewal time upon those who signed petitions, a rumor that proved groundless. But Big Brother did not relent. A clipping in Mauldin's FBI file reported that a conference by the Town and Village Committee to End Discrimination would be held at the Henry Hudson Hotel. Among the sponsors were people with check marks next to their names, indicating that the FBI had files on them. They included several religious figures, among them Dr. Algernon Black and Congressman Adam Clayton Powell, and writers, among them Langston Hughes and Bill Mauldin. As with many similar documents in such raw FBI files, there was no explanation and no follow-up. The petitioners, some three thousand strong, eventually did cause Metropolitan Life and the City of New York to break down the racial barriers in the housing project.

From January to April, 1952, Bill Mauldin took Willie and Joe to the Korean War. But—another case where a man's professional career was placed in jeopardy because of a dossier—the decorated army combat veteran correspondent-cartoonist learned that he almost never made it there because an FBI file hung over his head. When he applied for a visa in 1951 to go to cover the war it did not come through. He then got his friend W.L. White, a roving editor for the Reader's Digest, to write a letter on his behalf to Hoover. White, who knew Hoover and knew that Hoover knew the power of the Reader's Digest, wrote that his good friend, Bill Mauldin, had an unexplained visa delay and added: "Now it so happens that a few years ago Bill was mixed up in some left-of-center journalism for which he has no reason to apologize, and it has occurred to me that some subordinate in your department may be wavering for this reason on the subject of granting him a visa and clearance. Having known Bill for years (and having often disagreed with him), I can give you my solemn word that he is not, never has been, nor never could be a 'microfilm liberal,' and actually is as good a security risk as I am, if not better." Hoover responded by referring him to the State Department and Defense Department and nothing that his comments on Mauldin would be "filed for future reference."

Mauldin also checked with another friend, Chet Hansen, a lieutenant colonel who had served as General Omar N. Bradley's aide during the Second World War and was now working at the CIA. Hansen told Mauldin to call him back in a half-hour. When he did Hansen informed Mauldin that they had an FBI record on him, and that he would try to straighten things out. He did, Mauldin at last got his visa, and went off to cover what he later described as "a slow, grinding, lonely, bitched-up war."

When Mauldin ran for Congress in 1956 from his then home in Rockland County, New York, his Republican opponent, a radical conservative from Tuxedo Park, apparently obtained the raw FBI files on him. "I could tell," he recently said, "because her campaign ads used some of the same language as the stuff in the file. They accused me of being a Communist party-liner. I sued to stop them from telling a pack of lies about me in their ads, but I later dropped the suit when the campaign was over. Anyway, I got more votes in that district than any Democratic candidate received in the past."

Nonetheless, Mauldin did indeed have a dossier that kept building up. An FBI memorandum the same year he ran for Congress provided a summary of his activities. "Bufiles reflect Mauldin had numerous contacts shortly after World War II with Communist-front and other type organizations," his file reads. "Cartoon by Mauldin in October 1946 by inference critical of FBI in lynching investigation. Mauldin critical in 1947 of Congressional committees in Gerhart Eisler Case; claimed subject of this type was up to FBI; added he had no warmth for native Communists and realized their aims full well. 'Reader's Digest' sought accreditation as war correspondent for Korea, 1951; army conducted investigation at that time."

The report on Mauldin accreted in greater detail about his participation in the American Veterans Committee: "It was proposed that the Communists would try to organize a Veterans Action Committee in connection with other veterans organizations which should be composed of such men as Bill Mauldin, a member of the AVC." A pamphlet included a quotation signed by him that said that the American Veterans Committee should be "liberal without being revolutionary, progressive without being radical; which advocates individual freedom without subscribing to the idea that a rich, powerful man has the right to be a tyrant; which is patriotic without believing that ours is a master race or that we have the right to put our national interests ahead of the interests of humanity as a whole." This admittedly high-flown language, prevalent at the time when World War II veterans were trying to raise the level of discourse and idealism in the country, countered the veteran's first, conservative stand of the American Legion with its own slogan of "Citizens first, Veterans second."

The file further says that "a self-admitted former Communist party member" advised that "Bill Mauldin was installed in a high position" in an American Legion post in New York "with the purpose of assisting in a Communist domination of the post." Mauldin's language in the AVC pamphlet indicates the falsity of this statement. The actual story was better than the incomplete and inaccurate one provided by the ex-Communist informer. A number of former *Stars and Stripes* and Yank magazine staff members had formed the Duncan-Paris Post, named after Gregor Duncan and Pete Paris, two of their colleagues who had been killed in action during the war. Their aim was to liberalize, not communize, the legion from within. It was an abortive effort that provoked the Legion to take away their charter.

Mauldin was not intimidated by knowledge that the FBI kept watch on him and his work. One of his 1972 cartoons—dutifully placed in his file—foretold the mood of sting operations and Watergate. It showed an FBI man collaring one of his plants in front of a judge's bench. The caption reads: "He's guilty. We planned the job, conned him into it, equipped him for it, and caught him at it."

Commenting on the cartoon, Clyde A. Tolson, Acting Director of the FBI, said: "Mauldin has always resorted to muckraking in portraying the FBI." It was one of the rare accurate remarks in Mauldin's dossier, and in retrospect a sign of his courage.

NORMAN MAILER

Norman Mailer—novelist, chronicler of American life, former president of American PEN, member of the American Academy and Institute of Arts and Letters—once said: "J. Edgar Hoover has paralyzed the imagination of this country in a way Joseph Stalin never could." That statement, guaranteed to arouse the FBI, was made in early 1960 on At Random, Irv Kupcinet's popular syndicated television show out of Chicago. Eighteen years later, when he obtained his FBI file under the Freedom of Information Act, Mailer said that thirty out of the three hundred pages in his heavily censored record were devoted to his appearance on "Kup's" show. In his *Pieces and Pontifications,* Mailer included a section from his own dossier as it was reported by the special agent in charge in Chicago to Director Hoover in Washington. Without a political category but simply for information, part of what the FBI said about him reads:

"NORMAN MAILER is an admitted 'leftist.' He is also an author, his most popular novel being *The Naked and the Dead.* His remarks clearly reflect his animosity toward the bureau. The enclosed text clearly reflects that other noted panelists on the program definitely and specifically disagreed with and refuted his observations. [Mailer pointed out that among the other panelists were the former president of B'nai B'rith, the Lord Mayor of Dublin, a national police chief from the Sudan—and, he said, "all were in a hurry to swear their allegiance to Hoover."]

"A number of persons in Chicago have personally commented to me that MAILER made an ass of himself on the program, and all such comments received have been definitely pro bureau and anti MAILER. MAILER went on to say: 'I said the other day in an interview that we have a very subtle totalitarianism here, a pleasant totalitarianism, in that we don't have concentration camps. We don't have a secret police everywhere. We do have an FBI which is one of the two religions left in America. There's the FBI and medical science. This country was softened up but not by the Communists. It was softened up by the FBI, by Joe McCARTHY, by the House Unk-American Affairs [sic] Committee, by the peculiar, subtle psychological reign of terror that went on in this country five years ago.' "

As the ideal television guest for keeping a moderator, panelists and the audience awake, Mailer continued to speak about the FBI without pulling his punches—as inscribed in his dossier:

"The man in the street does not have a specific knowledge of the right things and the wrong things that the FBI does. He has a general knowledge of them and a general fear of them and a general respect for them which, I say, is too great. Because what I am getting at is this. There has been so much damn fear in this country for the last five or ten years that people in this country are being worn down and they are being softened. There's very little passion left in American life, and this was about the most passionate country in the history of the earth at one time, and the most adventurous and the bravest and the boldest, and it has become a cowardly, sleek, soft, fat country. What I am saying is that this is exactly the climate which the Russians adore, and if they ever come over here, the first thing they would do is that they would have their secret police chief get together with the FBI, and you would be amazed at how little time it would take."

In another part of his FBI file, Mailer found a 1960 letter from the special agent in charge, New York, to Director Hoover: "Information has been received that Mailer, in an appearance on the Chicago television program, At Random, advocated the abolition of the FBI. He said the FBI was too efficient against communism and was connected with McCarthyism and the House Committee on Un-American Activities. He also said that the FBI efficiency 'created a psychological atmosphere on the part of the public and that the public is being protected from communism' and that the public, and not the FBI, should be allowed to decide for itself what is good for it. You are requested to bring the investigation of Mailer up to date."

Afterward, Mailer commented that he thought that the FBI had bit on his words and he had "pricked their blood." If so, not sufficiently to divert them from carrying on their activities—just as Mailer persevered in carrying on his.

ALLEN GINSBERG

Allen Ginsberg, poet, social activist and member of the American Academy and Institute of Arts and Letters, also engaged the attention of the FBI recordkeepers. "I have a stack of documents three-feet high," the Pulitzer Prize–winning poet said, and showed me a sampling of them. He has devoted much of his time to challenging the government on issues of privacy and personal freedom—including sexual preference—and arousing his fellow writers to campaign for freedom of expression.

Ginsberg recently told me that Pacifica Radio, the group of radio stations that airs public events, contemporary verse, drama and other literature, may no longer broadcast much of his poetry, including the well-known *Howl* and *Kaddish*. Under the Reagan administration's policy of destroying the power to regulate of the regulatory agencies, the weakened Federal Communications Commission has carried out Attorney General Meese's diktat against "obscenity" and "indecency." The final report of the Meese Commission on Pornography is a legacy for book-censors and book-burners that could affect authors, editors and elements of the publishing community for a long time to come.

Ginsberg said that some of the papers in his file come from related customs and Treasury Department investigative bureaus. His file crisscrosses those of other writers. "They include Leroi Jones, who was the victim of much more attack than people understand and, in that context, his anger is understandable," Ginsberg said. "Most people don't realize what he and other black literati have been through, assuming that all past injustices have been redressed or somehow disappeared out of mind. The waste remains, the waste remains and kills. The section on Tom Hayden in Newark intersects with Jones, since Jones was influenced by an FBI misinformation campaign to denounce Hayden as an [FBI] agent and drive him out of Newark. The section on Black United Front and Ann Arbor intersects with John Sinclair, poet director of Detroit Artists Workshop, a multiracial press that is one of my publishers."

Commenting on the FBI's activities in the literary-political arena, Ginsberg said, "Why did the FBI lay off the Mafia and instead bust the alternative media, scapegoating Leroi Jones, ganging up on Jane Fonda, Tom Hayden, Martin Luther King, Jr., antiwar hero David Dellinger, even putting me on a 'Dangerous Subversive' Internal Security list in 1965—the same year I was kicked out of Havana and Prague for talking and chanting back to the Communist police? 'The fox condemns the trap, not himself,' as Blake wrote in *Proverbs in Hell.*"

In a memorandum from Hoover to the Secret Service in 1965, Ginsberg was cited as an "Internal Security—Cuba" case, and a potential threat to the president of the United States. On the document, stamped *Secret,* Ginsberg was listed as "potentially dangerous" and a "subversive," with "evidence of emotional instability (including unstable residence and employment record) or irrational or suicidal behavior," as having made "expressions of strong or violent anti-U.S. sentiment," and as having "a propensity for violence and antipathy toward good order and government." All such items were checked on a form in his file.

A photograph of Ginsberg was placed in the Federal Narcotics files in 1967 as if it were a dangerous explosive, and a copy of the photograph was sent to the FBI. Ginsberg had openly campaigned against what he regarded as harsh antimarijuana laws that were used to arrest anti-Vietnam War and other protesters. "He is pictured in an indecent pose," the report said. "For possible future use, the photograph has been placed in a locked sealed envelope marked 'Photograph of Allen Ginsberg—Gen. File: ALLEN GINSBERG. The locked sealed envelope has been placed in the vault of this office for safekeeping."

The nature of his case was described as "antirioting laws" in 1968 by the Chicago office of the FBI. "[Name blacked out] advised he observed GINSBERG at Grant Park in front of the Conrad Hilton Hotel in conversation with associates," his report read. "GINSBERG chanted unintelligible poems in Grant Park on August 28, 1968." Ginsberg explained that the "unintelligible poems" were William Blake's "The Grey Monk."

Ginsberg was tracked in this country and abroad. When he returned from a trip to Montreal in 1969, his valise was opened, bonded and held for customs inspectors at Kennedy Airport. It contained his manuscripts, poems, what were described by authorities as obscene photographs, a position paper on narcotics that he had prepared for Senator Edward Kennedy, and newspapers. The Ginsberg file reveals that when he gave a poetry reading in 1970 at Quincy College in Illinois the FBI bureau in Springfield was alerted to be on the lookout for him because he was an "IS" (Internal Security) case. It was duly and soberly noted that he was billed as the "Hippie Poet."

During the first term of the Reagan administration, a list of eighty-four people deemed "unsuitable" as government-paid speakers abroad was prepared by the United States Information Agency. Among the names were Ralph Nader, the consumer advocate; Coretta Scott King, the black leader; Betty Friedan, the feminist; John Kenneth Galbraith, Paul Samuelson and Lester Thurow, economists; and Allen Ginsberg, poet. It was, most felt, the equivalent of the Nixon administration's "enemies list"—and an honor to be included, a disappointment to be left off.

* * *

As he demonstrated in one of his recent poems, "Industrial Waves," Ginsberg is unstoppable when it comes to defying the authorities with verse that outrages: "Free computerized National Police!/Everybody got identity cards? At ease!/ Freedom for Big Business to eat up the sea/Freedom for Exxon to examine your pee!"

He remains at the cutting-edge of controversy. His only weapons are chants and poetry that may be depended on to arouse Washington officialdom and delight his admiring peers and readers. He continues to campaign openly for causes he believes in. Ginsberg's plots thicken, and so undoubtedly does his FBI file.

XIII.

WATCHING ARTISTS

It seemed inevitable that artists as well as authors would come under the scrutiny of investigative and law-enforcement agencies in Washington. They did, and usually for the same reasons: the government did not like what they signed, or with whom they associated, or their political opinions. So Pablo Picasso, perhaps the century's most celebrated artist, appeared on a document in the file of Dorothy Parker, the America writer, because he had served as honorary chairman and she the chairman of the Joint Anti-Fascist Refugee Committee to aid the victims of Franco Spain. Of course, Picasso deserved the honor of being inscribed in the FBI's records. He called himself a Marxist (albeit one who belonged to its unofficial capitalist subdivision); had received the Lenin Peace Prize even though few of his paintings were displayed in Moscow or Leningrad because they did not uphold the official style of Socialist Realism; and his painting of a peaceful dove had been adopted as a Communist symbol.

The FBI seldom could point to writings they found offensive when dealing with artists, American or foreign. Nevertheless, where artists committed their ideas to print, federal lawmen made note of their words for the files. Obviously it would have been more difficult, though probably irrelevant, to study their paintings and sculptures and drawings for hidden messages and subversive squiggles.

I decided to look into the records of several distinguished artists—Alexander Calder, the painter and sculptor who invented the mobile and stabile; Ben Shahn, painter, graphic artist and photographer; Georgia O'Keeffe, painter of desert scenes and symbolic abstracts; Henry Moore, the great British sculptor whose bronze reclining figures can be seen from Washington to Jerusalem, from Toronto to Hong Kong. I had never met Miss O'Keeffe but, independently, I had talked with Calder and Shahn on several occasions—including their opinions of the cold war and of the B-52 bombings of jungle villages during the Vietnam War. I frankly admired them for their individuality when they took public stands in demonstrations against that war. And while writing a documentary film about the creation and development of his two-piece reclining figure that was placed in the reflecting pool at Lincoln Center in New York, I visited with Moore at his homes and studios in England and Italy, and met his two closest friends and philosophical influences, Herbert Read and Kenneth Clark. His ideas about the human family became transformed into statements in sculpture.

All four of these artists had dossiers maintained on them by the FBI or other government agencies.

ALEXANDER CALDER

The sculpture of Alexander Calder (1898–1976) is probably more visible in museums and in public places than that of any artist in the United States. He is widely considered to be America's most inventive sculptor; his gouaches and sculpture can be seen in many countries in the world. Calder's creations are sophisticated works of engineering and artistry that, at first glance, seem playful and innocent and then, on second thought, celebrations of freedom.

Calder's file contained thirty-one pages; twenty-four were released to me. The pages were heavily censored or denied "in the interest of national defense or foreign policy" and for various unspecified "investigatory" reasons. And what transgressions had Calder committed to be inscribed in the government's records? The "subject" and "character" of the investigation by the United States Air Force was labeled: "PEACE MOVEMENT—Mouvement de la Paix. Participation in Peace in Vietnam. Demonstrations in the United States. Planned by American Resident of France.

Some of the Calder documents that were denied came from the department of the air force's Office of Special Investigations at Bolling Air Force Base in Washington, D.C. In my letter of appeal I took a shot in the bureaucratic dark and mentioned that I had once been in Air corps Counterintelligence in wartime North Africa, thinking it might help; it didn't. The response came back: "The Office of the Secretary of the Air Force has considered your appeal and . . . determined it should be denied." One of the reasons given was that "this material must remain privileged to prevent circumvention of the agency's law-enforcement purpose."

And so, in addition to its assigned role of protecting the western world from the perils of war by surprise or accident, the United States Air Force in Europe was watching Alexander Calder. A 1966 air force document sent from France (where Calder kept a home and studio) alerted Washington that the sculptor was headed for the States:

"[Informer's name censored] advised that ALEXANDER CALDER, an American sculptor resident in Sache (Indre et Loire), France, was scheduled to depart for the United States within eight days for a stay of approximately a month. The purpose of CALDER's visit was purportedly to engaged in demonstration for Peace in Vietnam. Bureau did not know CALDER's destination in the US or the exact nature of the activity in which he is participating. [Name censored] advised that CALDER resides in France at a place called The Green Mill, Sache. Source continued that CALDER, an American citizen, is an artist and creator of mobiles. Source could furnish no further identifying information concerning CALDER."

By 1966 Calder was well-known in France as well as the United States but, apparently, the air force sleuths could not identify him. However, its informer noted that he would be alert to Calder's departure from Orly Field; later he advised that he could not say for certain that Calder had left for the United States. Indeed, Calder did go to Washington for the large peace demonstration against the Vietnam War on May 15, 1966, in front of the Washington Monument. He was accompanied by his wife, Louisa, and other artists and writers from their home area in Roxbury, Connecticut.

Calder's name first appeared in the FBI files in a 1954 document marked *Confidential,* initiated as a name-check and furnished to the United States Information Agency. The FBI report indicated that it had been aware of his whereabouts and activities since 1941: "It was reliably reported in late 1941 that Alexander Calder, 244 East 86th Street, New York City, was a member of the American Artist Congress.

The American Artist Congress is cited by the California Committee on Un-American activities as 'typical of Communist created and controlled organizations.' "

Similarly the FBI reported that a folder had been issued in 1944 by the American-Russian Institute listing Calder's name as one of the many sponsors who endorsed the campaign of the American-Russian Institute for funds to permit the expansion of its facilities and services to the American public. This was followed by the familiar statement that the American-Russian Institute was on the United States Attorney General's list as a Communist or Communist-dominated organization.

When in 1957 Calder's name surfaced again in a State Department request to the FBI for a check on him, the FBI repeated the (by its canons) derogatory information about the American Artist Congress and the American-Russian Institute from its file on Calder.

Responding to a White House request about the facts on Calder in 1964, the FBI once again repeated his endorsement of the American Artist Congress and the American-Russian Institute. It added that an announcement in the National Guardian on April 17, 1961, indicated that a rally was going to be held in New York City on April 21, the purpose of which was to abolish the House Un-American Activities Committee. "The name of Alexander Calder, artist, appeared among others as one of the sponsors who would sponsor this rally. . . ."

For reasons unclear because of censored material, Calder's name also appeared in the files of the Bureau of Personnel Investigations, United States Civil Service Commission. One can speculate that some agencies looked into his background before acquiring a Calder mobile or stabile for their public buildings. The public must be protected, presumably, from the sympathies of its artistic creators.

Before Calder made his trip back to the States from France in 1966 for the anti-Vietnam War rally, the American Embassy in Paris forwarded certain material (censored) about Calder for the information of FBI field offices in New York, New Haven (the bureau office closest to Calder's Roxbury home) and Washington. And a *Confidential* memorandum in 1967 from the American Embassy in Paris to the FBI director in Washington noted that Alexander Calder and seven other individuals (their names and those of informers censored) were part of the Paris American Committee to Stop the War in Vietnam. Calder was not hiding his feelings against that war at home or abroad.

The Calder folder continued to fatten. A confidential informant in 1968 furnished the FBI with a "throwaway" entitled "Resist," 763 Massachusetts Avenue, Cambridge, Massachusetts. It stated that over twenty-six hundred concerned citizens pledged to "raise funds to organize draft resistance unions, to supply legal defense and bail, to support families and otherwise aid resistance to the war in whatever way seems appropriate." Among the active participants, the file notes, was "artist Alexander Calder."

In 1970 leaflets were handed out under the heading, "Committee to Defend the Conspiracy," at a public gathering at the University of New Mexico. The leaflets asked for contributions to help the so-called Chicago Eight—including the then notorious Bobby Seale—who were to go on trial in the federal court in Chicago in September of that year. The Chicago Eight, which later became the Chicago Seven, was a group of antiwar activists convicted for violation of federal antiriot statutes during the 1968 Democratic National Convention in Chicago. "Listed at the bottom of the page were about sixty names," the file reads. "Among them was Alexander Calder."

A final entry in 1974 (in the material I was permitted to see; it is not known if any withheld and censored pages followed) included "Mr. and Mrs. Alexander Calder." A staff assistant involved in security at the White House had requested a name-check on the artist and his wife. The FBI then provided a summary of all the material it had previously supplied two years earlier. The summary included every statement Calder had ever endorsed on national affairs and in opposition to the Vietnam War.

Two years later Alexander Calder died; but he did live to see the war that he had openly denounced and publicly marched against end—and his art placed all over Washington.

BEN SHAHN

The FBI considered Ben Shahn (1898–1969) an outright "Red." In Shahn's case, J. Edgar Hoover and his agents looked beyond the artist's associations and causes to what he actually put on canvas and walls as signs of suspicion and possible subversion. In his file he was branded a "left-wing artist." I was denied 7 pages from his 146-page file on various grounds, including the monotonously familiar overkill: "in the interest of national defense or foreign policy." Two of his passport pages on trips to Europe were provided by the State Department, indicating that he was observed whenever he traveled abroad.

In response to my appeal for access to denied and censored material, the equally familiar and predictable Richard L. Huff, the codirector of the Office of Information and Privacy, Department of Justice, said: "After careful consideration of your appeal, I have decided to affirm the initial action in this case. Ben Shahn is the subject of one bureau main file—Security Matter—Communist, and is alluded to briefly in seven files, the subjects of which are other individuals or organizations."

Shahn used his art for ideas and causes that interested him. Picasso painted a dove of peace; Shahn painted "The Passion of Sacco and Vanzetti." That 1932 painting, in the Whitney Museum of Art in New York, shows the two executed anarchists in coffins, attended by top-hatted Massachusetts dignitaries. Shahn, an immigrant from Lithuania, came to this country as a child, studied at City College and New York University, and became a painter of social protest during the Depression. But his murals and graphic work went well beyond realism. His handwritten and illustrated biblical work, *Ecclesiastes,* showed him to be a master calligrapher.

Shahn was being watched as early as 1940, acording to a heavily blacked-out page in his FBI file. A memorandum written for J. Edgar Hoover noted that, in 1935, the Farm Security Administration employed "a man named Ben Shahn" as a photographer. At the same time the Rural Electrification Administration had an employee named (censored), also a photographer. The memorandum says: "[Censored] recalls that Shahn and [censored] used to argue furiously at times about Communism and each characterized the other as being a soapbox Communist. This took place at the Farm Security Administration laboratory."

Another memorandum, in 1943, mentioned his name during hearings of the House Appropriations Committee, when questions were asked about the background of employees of the Office of War Information. Among the dozens of names listed (blacked out) was this description of Shahn at the time: "Bureau of Graphics and Printing, New York—speaks and reads French—entered on duty August 15, 1942, mural painter in Washington, October 1940 to June 1942—Social Security Building."

After the war a Republican Congressman from Michigan, George A. Dondero, charged that "left-wing" art was being exhibited under government auspices. He said that "radical" paintings had been exhibited in Veterans Administration hospitals and that the State Department should not allow the works of such artists to be toured abroad. After congressional criticism, Secretary of State George C. Marshall halted the art tour. Representative Dondero said that among the artists with left-wing affiliations and who contributed to left-wing publications or who have been favorably reviewed in left-wing publications were Reginald Marsh, Jack Levine, Max Weber, Rufine Tamayo, Yasuo Kuniyoshi and Ben Shahn.

A report marked *Confidential* on a page labeled "Security Matter—Communist," quoted an unnamed informant in 1951 as saying that "Shahn denied being a Communist; however, according to informant, Shahn has definitely been identified with pro-Communist activities." The FBI memorandum said that his early work was making posters "for various trade unions in New York City, and he has been very successful in the modern art field." (Unions and modern art—the stuff of security files.) The unknown FBI "art critic" continued: "Ben Shahn's work in the modernistic art field has shown a tendency to play up the lower class and he has had occasion to do work which in former years appeared in the *Daily Worker.*" (The lower classes—obviously a suspect theme.)

Shahn, who lived in Roosevelt, New Jersey, was also the subject of surveillance by the FBI's Newark office. Keeping track of his getaway car as well as his palette, the FBI found it necessary to report: "Owner of 1948 blue Chrysler convertible, bearing 1952 N.J. plates LO 84 U." (There is something so portentous about plate numbers—"calling all cars,"as in all good Los Angeles Freeway chase shows.) The FBI also noted that in 1952 appeared a biography, *Portrait of the Artist as an American,* by Seldon Rodman, published by Harper & Row. The FBI files even included a review of the book by

James Thomas Flexner in The New York *Times Book Review,* that said: "His pictures—as is to be expected of an artist—have been much profounder than his politics."

Together with others in the arts and sciences and professions, Shahn put his signature on an open letter to the motion-picture industry in 1947. It went: "The decision of the Motion Picture Association of America to purge and blacklist those writers, directors and producers who deny the Un-American [Activities] Committee's right to inquire into the political opinions of private citizens is a submission to government censorship and dictation."

In 1952 the FBI advocated that the Shahn file be activated as a possible deportation matter. An FBI memorandum noted that the Immigration and Naturalization Service had no record of his applying for American citizenship. That year, this "negative" statement turned up in his file: "Ben Shahn had painted peace Christmas cards which are being sold by the New Jersey Committee for Peaceful Alternatives." To the FBI, even the sacred wasn't sacred.

The following year the special agent in charge of the Newark FBI office received permission from FBI Director Hoover to interview Ben and Bernarda Shahn as a "Security Matter—Communist," and to attempt to extract information from them on Communist activities in New Jersey. Two unnamed FBI special agents conducted the interview and reported:

"Mr. Shahn stated that he had never been a member of the CP but felt that he may belong to seven or eight organizations that might have been cited by the Attorney General of the United States as subversive. Mr. Shahn said that he was interested in peace and would offer his assistance to any group that he thought was working for a good cause.

"Mr. and Mrs. Shahn refused to name anyone that they considered to be Communists.

"This case will remain in a pending status in the Newark

Office in order to verify subject's naturalization and foreign travel."

When the Shahns moved to Cambridge, Massachusetts, in 1956, where the artist held the chair of Charles Eliot Norton Professor at Harvard, the Newark FBI notified the Boston FBI of his whereabouts.

The FBI summarized a 1962 article in *The Worker,* the Communist Party daily, that linked Ben Shahn with Alexander Calder in a common protest. According to the article, the painter and sculptor were co-chairmen of the "Artists Committee to Free Sequeiros." Two hundred artists and art students had picketed the United Nations demanding release of David Alfaro Sequeiros, the Mexican muralist, who had been sentenced to eight years by a Mexican court for "intellectual authorship of demonstrations by teachers and other unionists."

In 1963 Shahn joined other artists in an exhibit to help the Abraham Lincoln Brigade's campaign to aid imprisoned opponents of Franco Spain. In that same year the Newark FBI office requested permission from Washington to interview him again and then to take his name off the Security Index. Hoover denied the interview request this time, saying that "little information" could be gained; furthermore, "subject is employed as an artist-writer by profession and might possibly exploit an attempted interview in an effort to embarrass the bureau." As usual, Hoover's top priority was his personal image.

The next year the White House asked for a name-check from the FBI on Shahn (page blacked out; reason unknown). In 1966, when Shahn traveled to Europe, the FBI alerted legations in Paris, Rome and London to be on the lookout for him.

From his beginnings as a government muralist and photographer during the Depression to his final years as an acclaimed international artist, Ben Shahn never stopped being his own man—or subject to surveillance by Hoover's men.

GEORGIA O'KEEFFE

There were 117 pages in the file on Georgia O'Keeffe (1887–1986); of these, 28 pages were withheld. The released pages that I received were heavily blacked out. They were censored on various grounds; the main reason given was that disclosure would reveal the names of those who acted as informers about her life for the Albuquerque, New Mexico, field office of the FBI. In addition to her New Mexico file, another file was maintained by the New York field office that dealt with forgery of her artworks.

When Miss O'Keeffe died in Santa Fe at the age of ninety-eight, the works in her estate were reported to have a market value of sixty-five million dollars. Eight major museums were named as beneficiaries of her paintings. In the last half of her life Miss O'Keeffe was recognized as an artist in her own right. She no longer lived in the shadow of her husband, Alfred Stieglitz (1864–1846), the photographer, photography magazine publisher and pioneering art exhibitor who introduced the works of Cezanne, Picasso and other modern French masters to the American public.

Miss O'Keeffe's file was first opened during the reign of Senator McCarthy. An entry in 1953 characterizes her case as a "Security Matter—Communist." She was living and working at her home in Abiquiu, New Mexico, when an informer (name blacked out) reported:

"Subject was the only person in Abiquiu who was pro-Wallace in the 1948 election [when former Vice-President Henry A. Wallace ran independently on the Progressive

Party ticket for president]. Also that the subject had made remarks which were not with his [the informer's] line of thinking and remarks that would not be made by a loyal American. The informant stated [blacked out] the subject, who is an artist and spends much of her time in New York and has a house at Ghost Ranch and also in Abiquiu, regarding Henry Wallace whom the informant called a bolschevick [sic] and the subject replied that she believed in Wallace's theory that we should have closer relations with Russia." (One wonders what language was native to this informer. Certainly not English.)

This semi-illiterate complaint was followed by a recommendation from the FBI special agent that a "case" should be opened on Georgia O'Keeffe for this strange reason—"due to the closeness of Abiquiu to Los Alamos." By this topsy-turvy reasoning, the fact that she had voted for Henry Wallace apparently made her a potential espionage agent at—or some variety of security threat to—the atomic testing facility.

Thereafter, Miss O'Keeffe and her friends and business associates were tracked by the FBI. A "confidential informant of known reliability"—a familiar phrase in FBI documents—reported the news that guests stayed at her house in Abiquiu while she remained at her ranch. One of these guests "appeared to be either Chinese or Filipino and did not speak any English"—also familiar, an FBI whiff of implied racism. Later the informer noted that Miss O'Keeffe had gone to New York City and could be found in room 1608 at 509 Madison Avenue. Copies of this report were sent to Washington, to Albuquerque and to New York.

The whereabouts of the artist were well-covered by these FBI's field offices. The special agent in charge of the Albuquerque field office, for example, sent a memorandum directly to J. Edgar Hoover about Miss O'Keeffe. The unnamed agent described her house in Abiquiu as "a pretentious re-

Alexander Calder, the pioneering American sculptor who devised the mobile and stabile and whose work is exhibited all over the world, had an FBI dossier of thirty-one pages, but only twenty-four were released to the author. Calder was an outspoken critic of the Vietnam War and participated in the peace movement in France and the United States. He is shown here at one of his exhibitions in New York, with a mask sculpture he created in the background.

Alexander Calder was tracked in the United States and in France, where he maintained a home and studio. Both the FBI and the Air Force Office of Special Investigations kept files on him. This FBI document notes several of his positions as artist and private citizen.

Herbert Mitgang

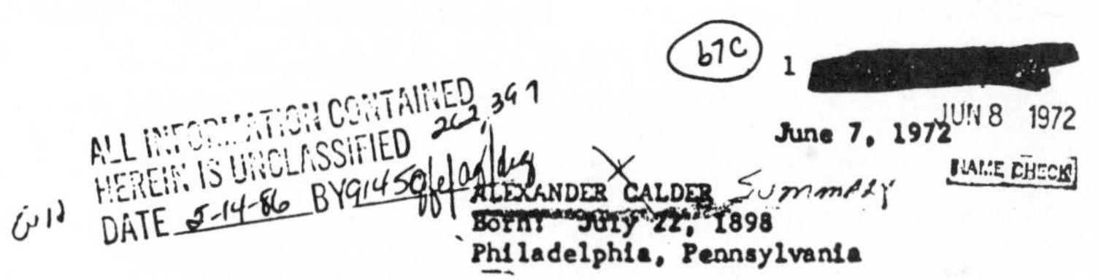

(b7C) 1

ALL INFORMATION CONTAINED HEREIN IS UNCLASSIFIED DATE 5-14-86 BY 9145

June 7, 1972 JUN 8 1972

NAME CHECK

ALEXANDER CALDER Summary
Born: July 22, 1898
Philadelphia, Pennsylvania

No investigation pertinent to your inquiry has been conducted by the FBI concerning the captioned individual. However, the files of this Bureau reveal the following information which may relate to the subject of your name check request.

A confidential source, who has furnished reliable information in the past, reported in late 1941 that Alexander Calder, 244 East 86th Street, New York City, was a member of the American Artist Congress.

The American Artist Congress has been cited by the California Committee on Un-American Activities as "typical of communist created and controlled organizations."

In November, 1944, the American-Russian Institute, New York City, issued a folder captioned "American Information Center on the U.S.S.R." This folder listed the name of Alexander Calder as one of the many sponsors who endorsed the campaign of the American-Russian Institute for funds to permit the expansion of its facilities and services to the American public.

EX-116 REC-2005-153076-4

An announcement in the "National Guardian" of April 17, 1961, indicated that a rally was going to be held in New York City on April 21, purpose of which rally was to abolish the House Un-American Activities Committee. The name of Alexander Calder, artist, appeared among others as one of the sponsors who would sponsor this rally.

Original and 1 - NASA JUN 8 1972
Request received - 5-24-72

This document contains neither recommendations nor conclusions of the FBI. It is the property of the FBI, and is loaned to your agency; it and its contents are not to be distributed outside your agency. This reply is result of check of FBI investigative files. To check arrest records, request must be submitted to FBI Identification Division. Fingerprints are necessary for positive check.

Felt, Mohr, Rosen, Bates, Bishop, Callahan, Campbell, Casper, Cleveland, Conrad, Dalbey, Miller, E.S., Ponder, Soyars, Walkart, Walters, Tele. Room, Mr. Kinley, Mr. Armstrong, Ms. Herwig, Mrs. Neenan

NOTE: This documentation of Chicago Seven per

55 JUN 15 1972

MAIL ROOM ☐ TELETYPE UNIT ☐

Ben Shahn was branded a "left wing artist" in his FBI file, which contained over 150 pages. The FBI took note of the fact that Shahn's themes on canvas included "The Passion of Sacco and Vanzetti" and that he had done "radical paintings" that were exhibited in Veterans Administration hospitals. He was labeled a "Security Matter—Communist" in his file.

Delacorte Press

Whitney Museum

Two great American artists with something in common: FBI files. Alexander Calder, sculptor, and Georgia O'Keeffe, painter, were watched by Federal sleuths because some of their views and associations were considered suspect. Miss O'Keeffe came from her home in New Mexico to honor Calder during an exhibition of his work at the Whitney Museum of American Art in New York in 1976. Behind them is a Calder stabile.

Bill McClure, CBS News

Henry Moore, the greatest British sculptor of the twentieth century—his work can be seen all over the world, including in front of the East Wing of the National Gallery in Washington and in the reflecting pool at Lincoln Center in New York—was not unknown to the FBI. Because he joined other artists and writers in condemning the use of the atom bomb in some future war, his name was placed in a file. Moore is shown here in one of his studios at home in Perry Green, England, with Herbert Mitgang, who wrote the CBS News and BBC-TV documentary film, "Henry Moore: Man of Form."

Henry Steele Commager, Professor Emeritus of History at Amherst College and author of major works of American history, served as a member of the War Department Committee on the History of the War during World War II. The United States Information Agency did not allow his book *Freedom and Order* on its bookshelves overseas because, said the USIA, "The value of the rest of the book does not begin to overcome the liability of the thirty-plus pages condemning American policies in Vietnam." Professor Commager is shown here on the Amherst campus.

Herbert Mitgang

Inspired by Herbert Mitgang's article in The New Yorker on the dossiers kept on authors, M.G. Lord, the political cartoonist for Newsday, drew this comment for her newspaper.

treat." (Leave it to the FBI to spot tastelessness in the home of an artist.) He said that she "frequently entertains guests of foreign extraction," that she is "ultra-liberal" and that his informant reported that "her political philosophy doesn't sound entirely American."

A mail-watch was placed on her correspondence, including individuals—names, addresses and telephone numbers are blacked out in the released documents—who lived in Arizona, New York and France. Apparently her bookshelves were also scrutinized by "an anonymous source of known reliability," who advised that *The Tiger in the House,* by Carl Van Vechten, was in her possession. Why the informer found this noteworthy is anyone's guess: the book is about cats.

Despite the surveillance an FBI special agent (name and place blacked out) recommended to the Albuquerque office that both the Washington and New York files failed to reflect any new information of a derogatory nature about her, and in 1954 a recommendation was made that the file be closed "at the present time."

It was not reopened until 1981 when a grandnephew, James E. Stieglitz, was accused of forgery and attempting to sell her paintings as signed lithographs. The FBI records state that he pleaded guilty and that the counterfeit lithographs were withdrawn from the market. The FBI still maintains a five-volume main file in its New York field office about the case.

However, what *is* significant is that nothing further exists in the record to remove the false accusation attached to Miss O'Keeffe's name: that the FBI once considered her a possible Communist "Security Matter" because of whom she voted for and where she made her home and even its architecture. Had Miss O'Keeffe not been a well-known artist, and therefore almost automatically in a suspect category, it is highly unlikely that the FBI would have pursued her all across the country.

HENRY MOORE

When Stephen Spender delivered a memorial address for Henry Moore (1898–1986) at Westminster Abbey, he recalled that Kenneth Clark had once remarked to him that if the inhabitants of earth found themselves having to send an ambassador to represent the human race to the inhabitants of another planet, they could not choose better than to send Henry Moore.

Moore did not like to explain either his work or his politics, preferring his sculpture and his activities to speak for themselves. According to his friends, he remained a moderate Socialist all of his life. He came out of a coal-mining family in Yorkshire, which he celebrated in sketches as a war artist, together with his more famous shelter drawings of sleeping Londoners in the Underground during the Blitz by the German Luftwaffe. He had served in the frontline trenches in France and suffered from mustard-gas poisoning during the First World War. One of his most moving sculptures depicted a fallen warrior, with shield, who symbolized the timelessness of war's finality on the battlefield. He opposed military solutions to mankind's problems.

Like most of the major artists and writers in Great Britain during the Spanish Civil War, Moore sided with the Loyalists against Franco's Fascist columns. In the early thirties he supported the Marxist-oriented Artists International Association; but he was not a Communist. "To be a member of the Communist party was an active role which I didn't want to have," he said. In 1938 he was invited by the Republicans to go to Spain with a British delegation, but the Foreign Office declined to issue him a permit to travel there. He also served as a member of the Artists Refugee Committee, helping to settle German artists escaping nazism on the eve of the Second World War.

In the postwar years he continued his involvement on humanitarian issues, lending his name in opposition to the Russian tanks' invasion of Hungary and the Soviet Gulags, the imprisonment of Mexican as well as Polish intellectuals, and against the bias in the Commonwealth Immigrants Bill. He signed letters to *The Times* of London against apartheid in South Africa, and supported the Campaign for Nuclear Disarmament but declined to become a founding member because he opposed civil disobedience. Yet, he said, it was necessary for protests to be made even when wrongheaded so that people would be allowed to express their feelings.

But what had any of these opinions and positions—spoken or signed in his own country by a British subject—to do with United States laws and, in particular, the business of the Federal Bureau of Investigation? Might not someone in authority, in some future era of darkness, question the fact that one of Moore's finest works stood at the entrance to the East Wing of the National Gallery in Washington?

The FBI does not respond to such questions; that would require a policy opinion about internal methods or, worse, a possible admission of wrongdoing. Instead, the FBI diligently replied that, after a search of "the index to our central records system at FBI headquarters," that two pages of materials had been located in its files concerning Moore.

The first, in October 1944—while Britain remained a target for the Luftwaffe and buzz bombs and the war against Germany still raged on the Continent—cited a dispatch by the Overseas News Agency from London that reported that an International Arts Guild had been created "to strengthen the spiritual and artistic intercourse of artists of all nations." Three sections of the guild had been established—a literary section under Stephen Spender, a music section under Benjamin Britten, and a sculpture, painting and architecture section under Henry Moore. There would also be a publicity department, a translation department, mobile exhibitions and "exchange visits of thinkers and artists between various countries." It was an idealistic statement of unity that existed at the time among the Allied nations that, a few years later, found a similar effort in UNESCO when it had such distinguished delegates as Julian Huxley and Archibald MacLeish.

An FBI comment at the end of the dispatch noted: "In utilizing the above material in any communication going outside the bureau, its source should be specifically identified as the Overseas News Agency. For bureau purposes evaluation of it should be with the realization that the news of this agency is received principally through leftist emigre channels, official and unofficial, and that its correspondents regularly take a slant consistent with such channels in reporting." This gratuitous reflection on the Overseas New Agency reporters did not coincide with the experience of other correspondents who had served alongside the ONA's feature writers. It was inaccurate to say that their main sources came from "leftist emigre channels." The ONA, like the other wire services, newspaper and magazine correspondents, included a mixture of ordinary and outstanding talents, of all political stripes.

The second document on Moore, a clipping from a January 1951 issue of the *Daily Worker,* listed the names of sixteen men and women in London who had issued a statement condemning the use of the atom bomb. Without any changes, the statement repeated a letter to the editor of *The Times* of London:

"We who have signed this letter are not actively concerned in politics, and probably differ widely among ourselves in such political opinions as we hold. We are all profoundly convinced that in no circumstances should our country associate itself with the use of atomic weapons against people who have not used them against us. Without sacrifice of our honor or security, our government should take the lead in a new and realistic endeavor to resolve by mutual agreement the international conflicts which now imperil the peace of the world and human civilization itself."

The signers included notables in all the fields of the arts, most of whom were well-known to American readers, audiences and museum-goers. Among them were Sir Adrian Boult, conductor of the London Philharmonic Orchestra; Benjamin Britten, composer; E.M. Forster, novelist; Christopher Fry, playwright; Augustus John, painter; Dame Sybil Thorndike, actress, and Henry Moore, sculptor. From the check marks next to each name on the document—which included the quaint FBI phrase, "Clipped at the Seat of Government"—it was possible to surmise that every one of the sixteen British signers thereafter achieved a dossier of his or her own at the American "Seat of Government": Washington, D.C. One of the scrawled interoffice markings on the page, dated October 16, 1967, referred to Benjamin Britten a second time and indicated that there was still interest in the composer some sixteen years later by the FBI.

The file on Henry Moore offered not a clue to his significance in the world of twentieth-century art; no mention about his valor in the First World War and service as a war artist in the Second; and not a word about the man himself.

A few scraps of paper—in a dossier that had no reason to be in the "Seat of Government" in the first place—showed only a blurred FBI vision of Moore, an artist who, while recognized as a genius in the United States and the rest of the world, somehow was regarded by the G-Men as an "un-American" Briton.

XIV.

RULES OF THE GAME

WEAKENING THE GUIDELINES

In the wake of Watergate and Nixonism, the Privacy Act of 1974 was intended to be a restraining force on the excesses of the FBI and other agencies, particularly in gathering and recording information about individuals. Among those affected were authors and journalists, who frequently grappled with themes that nettled those in positions of power, including public officials.

The purpose of the law, according to Senate Report 93-1183, was "to prevent the kind of illegal, unwise, overbroad investigation and record surveillance of law-abiding citizens produced in recent years from actions of some overzealous investigators, and the curiosity of some government administrators, or the wrongful disclosure and use, in some cases, of the personal files held by federal agencies."

What abuses occurred in the past—and what excesses continue up to the present time?

This book offers evidence from government records that the FBI and other agencies not only exceeded their authority but did so furtively, harmfully and, without exception, unnecessarily. Under the current rules of the game, such abuses supposedly can no longer take place; it is pleasant to think so but an unwarranted assumption. Depending on the administration in power, federal police and intelligence agencies can be encouraged or discouraged to circumvent legal processes. High-level executives in the Reagan administration—some operating inside the White House—proved themselves capable of flouting the laws of the land and resisting the original provisions of the Privacy Act. The Iran-Contra hearings proved that loose cannons in the executive branch knowingly and defiantly shot down the constitutional barriers erected by the legislative branch. Sinclair Lewis' novel, *It Can't Happen Here,* written in the 1930s, came close to life in the 1980s.

Although far from perfect, the Privacy Act was designed to protect Americans from secret gathering of information about them; also, to prevent the creation of secret information systems and data banks by employees of the departments and agencies of the executive branch. The law was supposed to set in motion a long overdue evaluation of the needs of the federal government to acquire and retain personal information by stricter review within agencies of the criteria for collecting and retaining such records. In principle it was expected to promote greater fairness and individual privacy by officials administering institutional and organizational data banks and information records. At the time the proposal was enacted, it was regarded as the first comprehensive federal privacy law since the adoption of the Fourth Amendment to the Constitution that protected persons and their papers against unreasonable searches and seizures.

The Privacy Act established these guidelines:

It permitted an individual to have access to personal information contained in federal agency files and to correct or amend such information; prevented an agency that kept a file from using it or making it available to another agency for a second purpose without the individual's consent; required federal agencies to keep records that were lawful and to disclose the existence of all files and data banks; prohibited agencies from keeping records that described an individual's exercise of First Amendment rights unless the records were authorized by statute or approved by the individual or came within the scope of an official law-enforcement activity; permitted an individual to seek injunctive relief to correct or amend a record maintained by an agency.

It also allowed the recovery of actual damages when an agency acted in a willfully negligent manner; provided that an officer or employee of an agency who violated provisions of the act should be subject to a fine of up to five thousand dollars; prohibited an agency from selling or renting an individual's name or address for mailing list use; made it illegal for any federal, state or local agency to deny an individual any benefit because he refused to disclose his Social Security number; established a privacy protection study commission to provide Congress and the president with information about privacy matters in the public and private sectors.

Seeking reforms after Watergate and the distrust of White House operatives caused by Nixonism, revelations about domestic surveillance and of Americans placed on government "enemies lists," Attorney General Benjamin R. Civiletti issued specific guidelines on criminal investigations of individuals and organizations. These guidelines were formulated near the end of the Carter administration in December 1980—just before President-elect Reagan's inaugural. They were designed to define the work of the FBI and "to give the public a firm assurance that the FBI is acting properly under the law."

This is the question: Have these idealistic guidelines been followed or circumvented during the Reagan administration and the reign of Attorney General Edwin Meese?

The answer becomes clear when one reads relevant excerpts from the 1980 guidelines, including the raison d'etre, and the subsequent changes made to weaken them. Here are the Carter administration guidelines:

"A key principle underlying these practices, and reflected in these guidelines, is that individuals and organizations should be free from law-enforcement scrutiny that is undertaken without a valid factual predicate and without a valid law-enforcement purpose. Such investigative activity poses the risk of undue injury to reputation and increases the chance that an investigative target may be prosecuted for improper reasons.

"No investigation may be based solely on the lawful expression of religious or political views by an individual or group, the lawful exercise of the right to peaceably assemble and to petition the government, or the lawful exercise of any other right secured by the Constitution or by the laws of the United States.

"An investigation is to be conducted with minimal intrusion consistent with the need to collect information or evidence in a timely and effective matter. The seriousness of the alleged criminal activity should be among the factors considered in determining the investigation's proper scope and intrusiveness.

"An investigation should be promptly terminated upon completion of all reasonable and logical investigative steps, and if appropriate, should be presented for prosecutive opinion.

"Whenever an individual is known to be represented by counsel in a particular matter, the FBI shall follow applicable law and [Justice] Department procedure concerning contact with represented individuals in the absence of prior notice to their counsel.

"Before employing an investigative technique in an inquiry, the FBI should consider whether the information could be obtained in a timely and effective way by less intrusive means. Some of the factors to be considered in judging intrusiveness are adverse consequences to an individual's privacy interests and avoidable damage to his reputation.

"The following investigative techniques shall not be used during an inquiry: (a) mail covers; (b) mail openings; (c) nonconsensual electronic surveillance or any other investigative technique covered by Title III of the Omnibus Crime Control and Safe Streets Act of 1968. In setting forth investigative techniques that can be used in an inquiry, the potential subject can be interviewed and also persons able to corroborate the truth or falsity of an allegation, except that this does not include pretext interviews or a potential subject's employer or co-workers unless the interviewee was the complainant.

"Where an inquiry fails to disclose sufficient information to justify an investigation, the FBI should terminate the inquiry and make a record of the closing. In a sensitive criminal matter, the FBI shall notify the United States Attorney of the closing and record the fact of notification in writing."

In addition, only a few weeks before leaving office in January 1981, Attorney General Civiletti tightened up FBI procedures on undercover operations. These guidelines emphasized that before such operations began, what had to be taken into account was "the risk of harm to reputation . . . the risk of invasion of privacy . . . the risk of financial loss to private individuals and businesses . . . the risk of damage liability or other loss to the government."

The Reagan administration set a different tone not long after taking office when it began to undercut these guidelines. In 1983, then Attorney General William French Smith issued new guidelines. He said they were needed "to ensure protection of the public from the greater sophistication and changing nature of domestic groups that are prone to violence." The chief aim of these revised guidelines was to protect against terrorist activities and racketeering, he explained, adding that "the guidelines will adequately protect lawful and peaceful political dissent."

The then director of the FBI, William H. Webster, called the altered guidelines "an extremely balanced and positive law-enforcement initiative." He said that one of the most helpful changes "would permit the FBI to monitor organizations which may be temporarily inactive but whose prior record or stated objectives indicate a need for continued federal interest, so long as the minimum standard for investigation is satisfied." Thereby the door was opened a little wider to surveillance of organizations—and their members—that may have been investigated in the past during the heyday of the Un-American and Internal Security committees.

These Reagan administration changes were made against a background of congressional reforms designed to avoid the excesses of McCarthyism and Nixonism. The Internal Security Act of 1950, also known as the McCarran-Walter Act, required Communist organizations and designated front groups to register with the Attorney General as agents of a foreign power. As amended in 1968, the act eliminated self-registration requirements and authorized only the maintenance of a public list of organizations and individuals found to be Communist-affiliated. In 1974, Executive Order 11785 was issued abolishing the attorney general's list of designated organizations altogether.

On one of the touchiest matters—foreign authors visiting this country who have been denied visas or otherwise harassed by travel limitations and surveillance—the official view of the FBI is that "they are not routinely investigated under the Internal Security Act," according to William M. Baker, assistant director of the Office of Congressional and Public Affairs. "As they relate to the FBI, record checks pertaining to visa and passport matters are conducted primarily at the request of the State Department and that department is guided by directives issued by the executive branch of the government as to whom they may consider for record reviews."

Nevertheless, the practice continues with every exclusion or detention of a foreign author at the borders for ideological reasons an embarrassment to the United States, fully reported, and often ridiculed, here and around the world.

For example, Patricia Lara, a journalist with one of Colombia's leading newspapers, *El Tempo,* had her visa revoked in 1986 because the State Department claimed she might engage in "subversive activities" while here. Ironically, she had been scheduled to attend an awards ceremony at Columbia University celebrating the advancement of inter-American understanding and freedom of information. Instead, Miss Lara, who had received a master's degree in journalism from Columbia University in New York, was arrested and confined, first in the immigration detention center and then in a maximum security federal prison. Assistant Secretary of State Eliott Abrams, one of the Reagan administration's neoconservative idealogues on small wars in Central America and a key figure in the Iran-Contra connection, claimed Miss Lara was expelled because there was evidence that she had been a member of a Colombian terrorist group. Mr. Abrams refused to produce any evidence. Miss Lara maintained that the claims were false and said that the real reason she was jailed and expelled was that she had written a book against American military policies in Latin America.

At the root of such decisions by customs officers, the Immigration and Naturalization Service, the Justice Department and the State Department has been what many consider the Reagan administration's near-paranoia about Cuba and Nicaragua.

The Immigration and Naturalization Service maintains a "Lookout Book" that lists people thought to be potentially dangerous to the United States. A number of internationally published authors have fallen afoul of the McCarran-Walter Act—for ideological, not revolutionary, reasons; they are invited here by their American publishers to bear books, not bombs. For example, Farley Mofat, the Canadian author and naturalist, was barred from undertaking a book tour across the United States.

Dario Fo and Franca Rame, a husband-and-wife team of Italian political satirists who have performed all over Europe and Latin America, were invited in 1983 to perform at the New York Shakespeare Festival and to give lectures at two university drama schools here. But they were turned away: satire can be a security risk in the American "Lookout Book." Only ridicule and protests by the Dramatists Guild, the Center for Constitutional Rights and other civil liberties groups enabled the playwright and his wife to perform here at a later time.

The McCarran Act's most embarrassing feature, Section 28 on ideological exclusion, does appear to be on the way out: Senate and House members are joining forces to repeal the ideological exclusion provisions of the McCarran-Walter Act by prohibiting the government from barring entry on the basis of ideology or affiliation. At the same time they are addressing national security concerns by tightening restrictions on terrorists and excluding anyone expected to commit a dangerous criminal act.

On the sensitive issue of freedom of expression, the attorney general's 1983 revised guidelines sounded reassuring: "It is important that investigations not be based solely on activities protected by the First Amendment or on the lawful exercise of any other rights secured by the Constitution or laws of the United States." This protection was then qualified: "When, however, statements advocate criminal activity or indicate an apparent intent to engage in a crime, particularly crimes of violence, an investigation under these guidelines may be warranted unless it is apparent, from the circumstances or the context in which the statements are made, that there is no prospect of harm."

Attorney General Meese authorized a new policy in 1986 that civil libertarians and some members of Congress immediately interpreted as removing a major deterrent to lawbreaking by the FBI—including in cases involving freedom of expression under the First Amendment. Changing a provision in the Privacy Act that acted as a restraining force, Mr. Meese authorized the government to reimburse Justice Department employees who were sued, and had lost, a case involving violation of a person's civil rights. Mr. Meese said the new policy was needed to allay the fear of personal liability while on the job. (The Supreme Court in 1971 had ruled that persons whose constitutional rights were violated by federal agents could sue the agents as individuals and recover damages in federal courts. Since that decision, thousands of claims had been filed against federal law-enforcement officers.)

The revised Meese guidelines sent out a signal: Justice Department officials and FBI agents would not be obliged to exercise as much caution under the First Amendment (when dealing with individuals speaking, writing or demonstrating); or under the Fourth Amendment (searches and seizures); or the Eighth Amendment (cruel and unusual punishment). Representative Don Edwards, California Democrat and a former FBI agent, said of the Meese policy: "I don't think it's a good idea. It circumvents congressional intent. You and I and everybody else ought to be responsible for our own illegal acts."

On a related matter, where Reagan administration officials weakened guidelines against clandestine subsidies of writing by the government, Congressman Edwards, who is chairman of the House Judiciary Subcommittee on Civil and Constitutional Rights, warned in 1986 against a return to propagandizing by the CIA in the United States. His warning was touched off by the revelation that the CIA, then headed by William J. Casey, who subsequently was deeply involved in the unlawful Iran-Contra scandal, had secretly paid $107,430 to a Harvard professor, Nadar Safran, to underwrite a book, *Saudi Arabia: The Ceaseless Quest for Security.* In response to an inquiry about government surveillance and involvement in writing and publishing, Mr. Edwards said:

"A free society can't work if the government, and especially a secret government security agency, clandestinely publishes books, owns newspapers, and hires professors or clergymen to propagandize the public. The CIA also underwrote with $45,700 a symposium on Islamic fundamentalism organized by Safran, without telling either Harvard or the participants of the CIA involvement. Have we all forgotten that ten years ago this behavior produced a major controversy and the CIA was forced to stop publishing books?

"The public is entitled to know if these are isolated ventures, or are we back to the bad old days when one didn't know which book was a CIA plant or if any particular professor's research was his or her own or was dictated by the Agency. How many books, magazines and newspapers are there in the US that are in reality CIA propaganda? How many professors and clergymen are on its payroll? The Church Committee in 1976 found that prior to 1967 the CIA sponsored, subsidized or produced over one thousand books. The question will always be: Is it honest or is it the CIA?"

The threat to individual rights—including the presumed right to be let alone and not to have an FBI dossier because of unpopular writings, beliefs or associations—continued in the Reagan administration. John B. Crowell, assistant secretary of agriculture, claimed in 1982 that at least two private environmental protection groups, the Audubon Society and the Sierra Club, had been infiltrated by Communists and Socialists. The absurdity of this charge reflected on the kind of thinking that characterized some of the more naive and virulent administration officials. The Heritage Foundation, an ultraconservative think tank with ties to Attorney General Meese and other presidential friends, called upon the administration to lead another campaign alerting the nation to the "reality of subversion." It advocated surveillance of "potentially subversive" political groups, including "antidefense and antinuclear lobbies."

A number of authors, like other citizens, had signed petitions and written and marched against "Star Wars" and other—perceived by them—threats to nuclear sanity and arms limitation treaties, aware that they put themselves in harm's way with government police agencies.

President Reagan issued Executive Order 12356 in 1982 on the matter of classifying government documents. (It was this order that often was cited to deny my requests for information about authors or, when provided, to justify censorship.)

The order ended previous requirements that government officials had to consider the public's right to know before classifying documents and that classification had to be based on "identifiable" potential damage to the national security. A presumption was created that intelligence sources had to be classified and removed the requirement that any doubts had to be resolved in favor of declassification. Security rather than information became the order of the day.

The judiciary has sometimes stood up against the Executive branch on the issue of privacy and recordkeeping. In a 1986 decision written by Judge Abner J. Mikva in the United States Court of Appeals for the District of Columbia *("Jane Doe," Appellant v. United States of America, et al.),* the majority ruled that the Privacy Act imposed a substantial duty on each federal agency "to maintain its records with accuracy and to avoid harming individuals by keeping sloppy or willfully inaccurate records." Judge Mikva added that this duty "cannot be discharged by the maintenance of conflicting reports and the lament that it would be too difficult to determine the truth." The case involved the security clearance of a woman for a Foreign Service position in the State Department. She obtained her dossier and found that it included allegations that she had lied and cheated the government.

In the appellate court's view, "If the individual's right to be protected from McCarthyesque innuendo in government records is to be vindicated, the government cannot casually file damaging reports with merely a nod in the direction of the protesting individual. Without this requirement, the sort of unsubstantiated character assassination that the Privacy Act was, in part, designed to guard against would have a foot in the door of government."

This was one of the strongest judicial defenses of the Privacy Act—as the law was originally conceived—heard against its steady diminution by the Reagan administration.

EXPUNGING RECORDS

On the matter of correcting information, Mr. Baker, the FBI assistant director, said: "Our policy is to consider each request on an individual basis even though the information, to the extent it is subject to the Privacy Act of 1974, is exempt from the correction and amendment provisions of that act. Every effort is made to reach an equitable determination consistent with the best interests of both the individual and the government."

On the matter of expunging records where false accusations exist in an individual's dossier, Mr. Baker said: "The records-destruction programs of the FBI were suspended on January 10, 1980, in response to a preliminary injunction issued by the United States District Court, District of Columbia, in *American Friends Service Committee, et al. v. William H. Webster, et al.* and will continue until a Retention Plan and Disposition Schedule prepared by the National Archives and Records Service (NARS) and the FBI is approved by the court. The Plan and Schedule were delivered to the court on November 9, 1981." No final decision was made regarding the proposed Plan and Schedule. The FBI has been limited to expunging official records under the Privacy Act of 1974. Mr. Baker added that action is taken only after pertinent records have been appraised to determine their historical value.

James K. Hall, chief of the FBI's Freedom of Information-Privacy Acts Section of the Records Management Division, explained the procedures for submitting a "Privacy Correction Request" to the FBI—and only to the FBI. He said: "To make a request for correction or amendment of information in our records, a letter of request should indicate the particular record involved, the nature of the correction sought, and the justification for the correction or amendment. An individual may not request correction or expungement of records of deceased individuals." The rationale for the last exclusion is difficult to understand. The lesson is clear: don't die if you want to reclaim your good name and reputation.

PROFESSOR KIMBALL VINDICATED

The difficulty of correcting and expunging records emerged dramatically after Penn T. Kimball, a distinguished journalist and journalism professor at Columbia University, wrote a personal account of his own ordeal in a book published in 1983 called *The File*—and then went on to challenge the power of the state. For a quarter of a century, the government had kept a dossier on him based on anonymous and false accusations that branded him "a definite security risk" of questionable loyalty. The file harmed his career; it blocked him from government jobs and advancement in his profession. As Anthony Lewis wrote about the case of "Citizen K." in his New York *Times* column, "It did happen here."

Using the Freedom of Information Act, Professor Kimball obtained most of the information—in censored form—that had been kept on him by the State Department and FBI. Senator Lowell P. Weicker, Jr., of Connecticut, who examined the full Kimball file in 1985, said that the information in it was based on "smear tactics" and "guilt by association"—and that the government owed him an apology. Professor Kimball sued the State Department, the FBI and CIA for ten million dollars in damages. The government offered a "settlement" whereby State and the FBI would destroy the file but the CIA might or might not do so in the future. Professor Kimball discovered that the deal was smoke and mirrors. He wrote: "There would be no hearing on the facts. No exoneration. When the CIA file arrived, moreover, I learned that nearly everything the FBI and State Department had offered to send to the shredders had been copied and filed by the Central Intelligence Agency. And the CIA was keeping one document it wouldn't show me at all."

Professor Kimball rejected the compromise and in 1987 continued his efforts in the federal courts. Senator Weicker said that the case illustrated a flaw in the Freedom of Information Act—that in seeking to obtain and correct documents, Professor Kimball had to appeal to the same agency that had created the files, classified them, and reached conclusions about their contents. His case was rare—he had devoted years of his life to appeals, interviews, doublechecking facts, investing his time and resources. A former Rhodes scholar and World War II marine, Professor Kimball's tenacity proved him to be a man of courage willing to take on the government apparatus of secrecy and character assassination and fight alone on the field of principle.

Finally, in October 1987, he accomplished the near-impossible: The federal government acknowledged that, for forty years, its security files had unfairly characterized him. In a settlement approved by United States District Court Judge Whitman Knapp in the Southern District of New York, the FBI, the CIA and the State Department acknowledged that their records contained "no information that the plaintiff, Penn T. Kimball, or his late wife, Janet Fraser Kimball, were ever disloyal to the United States"—despite the fact that he had been denied a security clearance in 1946. The agreement added that "the remaining documents presently available in the records systems of those agencies reflect that, although pre-employment investigations may have been conducted, neither Mr. Kimball nor his wife has been the subject of any criminal, domestic security or internal security investigation." In exchange for the Government's admission, Kimball agreed to drop his suit for money damages; it was too late to assess the possible damages to the career of the seventy-one-year-old writer and teacher. The government also agreed to destroy its security files on the Kimballs. "I'm vindicated," he said. This was the first time that the government had made such an admission about an individual, but it is not likely that the Kimball case will open the gates of truth and provide similar admissions of government guilt-by-file for other maligned authors and artists.

The balance between archival recordkeeping and expunging unnecessary or untruthful documents has weighed in favor of continuing to retain information about individuals—living or dead—with dossiers. Furthermore, since much of the data on "deceased individuals"—including authors and other creators—was accumulated during the most intensive periods of accusation, surveillance and blacklisting, children of the accused do not have the ability to clear family names under the existing procedures of the federal police and intelligence agencies. In effect, once inside there is no legally practical way to disentangle oneself from the web.

XV.

FREEDOM TO CREATE

Many people in the performing arts have traveled and played outside the United States; some have petitioned the federal government to allow professional colleagues from abroad who have been barred to work here. These outspoken Americans have harbored what could be considered dangerous notions about freedom of performance everywhere.

From the patterns developed by the investigative agencies concerning authors, it is reasonable to assume that creators in various fields have been monitored and deemed eligible for their own dossiers in the files of the federal police and intelligence arms.

I asked a prominent American composer and conductor about files on musicians and whether he thought it would be useful to bring some of the old files out into the open today. They too played benefits for causes they believed in, from programs to help the Depression-poor to supporting the Abraham Lincoln Brigade and Spanish War refugees. "Please," he said, "let's not start a second round of blacklisting. A lot of us went through it once and we're still shell-shocked. Don't even bring up the things that happened in the fifties. It could still hurt some of us professionally, or our families, to dig up those old dossiers and committee records."

It is part of the sad, anticreative history of our times that the major Hollywood studios and television networks succumbed and cooperated with government hawkshaws and congressional and State investigative agencies, exposing their own employees to police surveillance, the disapproval of rigid crafts unions, and dismissals. (California's Un-American Activities Committee tarred individuals with an even broader brush than Washington's.) Yet despite the best efforts of such publicity-seeking investigative agencies, no convincing proof could ever be produced that scenarists and directors—as if they could—served a foreign enemy or ideology.

It was not only the "Hollywood Ten" who were watched by the FBI and other agencies; those who supported their constitutional rights were also inscribed in the government records. That wonderful humorist, S. J. Perelman, who wrote memorable pieces for the New Yorker and some of the Marx Brothers movies, might have muttered an elegant obscenity in print had he known that, during his lifetime, he had his very own three-page dossier (and possibly more; only three pages were released to me). He was listed as one of the "leading figures" who supported a review by the Supreme Court of the contempt conviction against the "Hollywood Ten" writers and directors. Among other items in Perelman's file—he belonged to the Artists' Front to Win the War in 1944, cited as a Communist front. Would he have been in the clear had he belonged to a nonexistent organization called Artists Front to *Lose* the War? At least the FBI accurately described him as "a humorist, playwright, and author of *Westward Ha!*"

Hollywood entered an Era of the Ordinary in filmmaking when some of its strongest talents were subjected to loyalty and security tests, held in contempt for exercising their constitutional rights in refusing to answer questions about their political affiliations and, in some cases, jailed. If anything, the radio and television networks displayed even greater cowardice, subjecting their staff members as well as outside authors, directors and performers to "clearances" by private vigilante organizations, notably Red Channels. The networks also employed their own in-house security and censorial officialdom, disguised under such euphemistic departmental names as "Program Practices."

In broadcasting, the so-called Golden Age of original drama on television turned to dross when scores of leading authors, actors and directors were blacklisted. American dramatic television has never recovered its originality and sense of purpose since then; rather, the commercial networks have become an all-too-visible branch of marketing and advertising. On the publicly franchised airwaves, freedom to see has become freedom to sell.

This writer does not believe that authors are wiser or more talented than any other creators in this country; nor should they be singled out as privileged characters. Many professions make equally important contributions to the nation's knowledge and well-being. However, there is one major difference that distinguishes the role played by the press, literature and printing from other professions. The framers of the Constitution built the First Amendment guarantee of freedom of expression—without abridgment of any kind—into the democratic structure of the new Republic. Also, to encourage their survival and creativity, authors were recognized in the body of the Constitution (Section 8) as the "exclusive" owners of their writings—the basis for the copyright law. These free-

doms and rights were accorded to authors not for purposes of personal gain but as part of the very foundation of the government.

Clearly, the constitutional aims of the framers were not recognized or respected by police-minded government officials in our time. The McCarthys and Hoovers thought they were saving the nation by exposing and harassing creative individuals. But they did not know their own country's values—nor do their present-day successors. By inscribing names and works in dossiers, in effect they were and are placing these individuals on trial with a presumption of guilt: openly in hearings, secretly in files. These government vigilantes ignored the written provisions of the Constitution that, over the years, have been underlined and magnified by decisions of the Supreme Court.

Justice Oliver Wendell Holmes (*Abrams v. United States,* 1919) declared it to be "the theory of our Constitution" that "the ultimate good desired is better achieved by free trade in ideas." Justice Louis D. Brandeis wrote (*Whitney v. California,* 1927) that "those who won our independence knew that order cannot be secured merely through fear of punishment for its infraction; that it is hazardous to discourage thought, hope, and imagination; that repression breeds hate; that hate menaces stable government; that the path of safety lies in the opportunity to discuss freely supposed grievances and proposed remedies."

Early in this century, the American muckrakers courted official presidential censure for exposing corporate practices and excesses that endangered the health and welfare of workers and the public. The FBI's hidden power had not yet developed when Upton Sinclair wrote *The Jungle,* a novel that led to federal regulation of the meat-packing industry. However, by the time John Steinbeck wrote *The Grapes of Wrath,* which helped bring awareness of the plight of migratory workers and some improvement in their conditions, the FBI recordkeepers were inscribing his name as an author to be watched. In their myopic vision of the country's diversity and freedom, Steinbeck was regarded as a suspicious, untrustworthy American because of what he had written.

Of course, American authors do enjoy enormous freedom. Only rarely are books burned, though even once is more than enough; Kurt Vonnegut's *Slaughterhouse Five* was consigned to the flames in a school furnace in Drake, North Dakota, on instructions from the school committee there, which found the novel "unwholesome." But the real and perhaps unavoidable pressures in American book publishing, in this writer's view, are more subtle. They are the inhibitions caused by commercialism in a marketplace increasingly dominated by depersonalizing conglomerates, including several foreign-owned American publishing houses, whose interests have little to do with literature and almost everything to do with comparative currency values and restrictive antitrust laws in their own countries. Some authors have also been requested by their publishers to make changes in their textbooks in order to gain acceptance by narrow-minded school boards. Literature that does not pay is too often passed by or too frequently permitted to go out of print.

Again, to put the American cases of censorship in perspective, it should be stressed that nothing perpetrated by school boards can be compared to repressive Soviet censorship or the official bonfires lit in Nazi Germany, where books written by foes of the Third Reich—including Jewish authors, anti-Fascists, Americans and radicals—were publicly torched. Among the authors whose books were burned in front of the University of Berlin, while Joseph Goebbels, Hitler's minister of public enlightenment, delivered an address on the "symbolic significance of the gesture," were Sholem Asch, John Dos Passos, Albert Einstein, Maxim Gorky, Heinrich Heine,

Ernest Hemingway, Helen Keller, Jack London, Rosa Luxemburg, Thomas Mann, Erich Maria Remarque and Upton Sinclair. Some of their names, however, do appear in this book—with American dossiers.

Nevertheless, censorship of reading matter does continue all over the United States today, led by religious pressure groups, often inspired and courted by the Reagan administration. (His political antagonists say that Mr. Reagan owns more tuxedos than books.) The main complaints against books include obscenity, profanity, religious or racial bias, teaching Darwin's theory of evolution without reference to the Biblical account of creation, undermining of "traditional family values," critical views of American historical incidents and personalities. Nothing exposes the minds of the censorial vigilantes more than the removal from the bookshelves to this day, in various parts of the country, of *The Adventures of Huckleberry Finn* because of the "demeaning portrayal of its characters" and, even more absurdly, because of Mark Twain's deliberate use of "bad grammar."

AN ALIEN STATE

The federal government itself has also been known to police and purge bookshelves. United States Information Agency libraries abroad have banned certain books and authors. For example, James Baldwin's *Tell Me How Long the Train's Been Gone* was removed, despite the fact that it explained the views of a respected black writer, because the book included this sentence: "My countrymen impressed me simply as being, on the whole, the emptiest and most unattractive people in the world." Not flattering, but less captious when taken in context. George R. Stewart's *Not So Rich as You Think* was found unacceptable because, the USIA said, "The book just wouldn't help to glamorize our program, nor will it help other nations prevent or solve similar problems." Henry Steele Commager's *Freedom and Order* was not permitted on government bookshelves, said the USIA, because "the value of the rest of the book does not begin to overcome the liability of the thirty-plus pages condemning American policies in Vietnam."

Under the Reagan administration respect for the USIA, headed by Charles Wick—one of the president's political cronies and fundraisers without any known literary credentials—has diminished. Some authors have declined the opportunity to participate in the USIA's overseas programs because, they feel, the agency has become politicized.

Despite the cold warriors and the risk of finding themselves condemned by their governments, American authors and dramatists have participated in conferences with fellow writers from the Soviet Union, China and other countries not consistently approved in official circles. Yevgeny Yevtushenko, the renowned poet who has been in and out of favor in the Soviet Union—his country tends to honor poetry and some poets but has been known to jail others for "antigovernment activities" because of their critical, prematurely glasnost, writing—is well-qualified to speak across international boundaries:

"Great literature is always a great warning," he said in the United States not long ago. "If we see some danger, we must prophylactically write about it. Even if it's very painful. This literature must be like acupuncture. We mustn't be afraid to put needles into the most painful points of the conscience. It's painful, it's unpleasant, but you might be saved. That's why I don't like so-called pleasant art. There is a beautiful South American expression: 'Where are the incendiaries now? The incendiaries of all the revolutionary fires. Where are they?

They are working as firemen. They are all in the firemen's service now.' I am absolutely convinced that all poets, all real poets, are rebels. I don't demand that all poets write political poetry, political declarations. Any kind of honesty is rebellion."

The open and covert investigation by the FBI of authors, journalists and other professionals continues up to our time—mostly because so many are dissenters and hold independent views that they express in their writings. They may not be tracked as authors per se; but to this day they can be watched and kept on file through what I consider is a wide opening in the back door of the guidelines.

The FBI's domestic security guidelines sound as though they protect political dissent, requiring as they do "evidence of a criminal act committed for political purposes." The guidelines state that domestic security investigations are not to be undertaken unless persons are engaged in "an enterprise for the purpose of furthering political or social goals wholly or in part through activities that involve force and violence and a violation of the criminal laws of the United States." But there is recent evidence that these guidelines have been ignored and that the FBI has continued domestic security investigations. For example, in the summer of 1987 the FBI dismissed one of its veteran special agents because he refused to begin an investigation of individuals associated with such organizations as Veterans Fast for Life and the Silo Plowshares—antiwar groups. The special agent, John Ryan of the FBI's Peoria office, was ordered to do so by the Chicago Bureau. He replied that "the acts performed by Plowshares have been consistently nonviolent symbolic statements against violence." He pointed out that the word "plowshares" derived from the Old Testament injunction in Isaiah: "They shall beat their swords into plowshares, and their spears into pruninghooks: nation shall not lift up sword against nation, neither shall they learn war any more." In addition, this agent said, "I believe that in the past members of our government have used the FBI to quell dissent, sometimes where the dissent was warranted."

According to the Center for Constitutional Rights, a legal and educational organization that monitors abuses and defends accused individuals subjected to harassment by the government, the Reagan administration has set a high priority for the FBI on watching dissenters—especially those with opinions of their own about warlike American policies in Central America.

Such surveillance was underscored by the House Subcommittee on Civil and Constitutional Rights held on February 19–20, 1987, in Washington, D.C. The FBI questioned more than one hundred people from the United States after they had visited Nicaragua. Agents also tracked others involved in protest rallies against the Reagan administration. Customs agents have copied and seized personal written material and subjected travelers to questioning and verbal abuse. Copies of personal papers have been sent to the FBI and retained for use in its investigation of protest groups. Individuals who have traveled to Central America have been audited by the Internal Revenue Service. Many also reported that their mail had been tampered with. An administration that created and supported a secret war in Nicaragua financed in part by Saudia Arabia and other nations, and run by private arms merchants with the approval of presidential operatives in the White House in defiance of Congress, not surprisingly has had little hesitation in harassing comparatively "unimportant" individuals, including authors.

When it comes to the suppression of literature, censorial minds in dissimilar nations can sometimes find common cause. It is interesting to recall that Nathaniel Hawthorne's great American novel about the hypocrisy of Puritanism, *The Scarlet Letter,* was banned by Nicholas I during the "censorship terror" in mid-nineteenth–century Russia. In twentieth-century America a film version of the same novel was distorted on orders of the official censorship office in Hollywood so that Hester Prynne ended up married. The Russian Tsar also banned Hans Christian Andersen's *Wonder Stories,* an act almost equaled in the State of Illinois during the McCarthy era when the book was stamped "For Adults Only" to make it "impossible for children to obtain smut."

There are novelists and dramatists and essayists and poets who hope that their words and ideas can enlighten and reform. Risk-taking is a noble part of the republic of letters, and not just in our time. Socrates was indicted in 399 B.C. for "impiety," accused of corrupting the young and neglecting the Gods. He treated the charges with contempt—not unlike, in manner, the "Hollywood Ten" who defied their accusers and risked their necks. As a condemned man, the Athenian philosopher "drank the hemlock." What he said and did, he did openly; the surveillance of American authors, whose names are placed in police files, is done covertly. In some cases, their lives have also been poisoned.

Independent opinions, unpopular ideas, political dissent and the freedom to be let alone are embedded as rights in the American Constitution and in our tradition of due process by law. Secretly policing authors and their writings are the dreaded hallmarks of an alien police state.

XVI

HOW TO GET YOUR OWN DOSSIER

Ever since the theme of *Dangerous Dossiers* first came to public notice, the author has heard from colleagues, students, and strangers from around the country, all asking the same question: How can I find out if I have a file—and what do I have to do to get it?

The aim of this new supplement is to help remove some of the mystery. The facts are based on the latest government information and on my experience in requesting and obtaining more than a hundred dossiers over the past five years from various federal agencies.

Under the government's Freedom of Information Act and Privacy Act, any citizen can request his or her own government records. Getting your own dossier—if you have one—does not require hocus-pocus, a lawyer, or writing to your congressman. It does require patience and persistence because of the great number of requests.

Many people wonder if they are doing something wrong by

asking for their own files or for other information. But they certainly should not feel that they are inconveniencing a busy government with a personal request. The Freedom of Information Act (FOIA) established a presumption that records held by agencies and departments of the executive branch of the United States government ought to be accessible to the public. Before the enactment of the Freedom of Information law in 1966, the burden was on the individual to establish a right to examine government records. Now, the burden has shifted from the individual to the government. The "need to know" has been replaced by the "right to know."

The Privacy Act that was passed in 1974 is a companion to the FOIA. It regulates federal agency record keeping and disclosure practices. It allows most people to seek access to federal agency records about themselves. (I cannot ask for your file and you cannot ask for my file without obtaining specific permission and proof that it's a valid request.) Together with the FOIA, the Privacy Act permits disclosure of personally identifiable information by federal agencies. Both acts allow disclosure of most personal files to the individual who is the subject of the file, but they restrict disclosing personal information to others when it would violate an individual's right of privacy.

The law allows the subject of a record to challenge the accuracy of the information; this, however, takes some doing. As with the FOIA, the Privacy Act provides civil remedies for a person whose rights have been violated.

While neither law grants a person an absolute right to examine government documents, both laws provide a right to request records and to receive a prompt response. If a requested record cannot be released, the requester is entitled to a reason for the denial. There is a right of appeal. It usually first goes to a higher authority within the agency—in the FBI, for example, an appeal would go to the Office of Legal Policy.

If information is still denied, there is a second, costlier step that could take years—the courts. Judicial review is available in the United States District Court for the judicial district in which you reside or have your principal place of business, or in the District of Columbia, where most of the federal records are located.

Both laws recognize the legitimate need to restrict disclosure of certain information. There are two general exemptions under the Privacy Act. The first applies to all records maintained by the Central Intelligence Agency. The second concerns selected records kept by an agency whose principal function involves criminal law enforcement. In addition, there are more specific exemptions, including medical and litigation records.

Under the Freedom of Information Act, there are nine statutory exemptions. The first says that agencies may withhold information classified "in the interest of national defense or foreign policy"—an all-embracing, vague phrase that can be used to deny access to almost any document. But sometimes classified documents—even those once stamped "secret"—can become declassified.

Other exemptions include internal personnel rules and practices; government laws that restrict the availability of information—the provision of the Tax Code, for instance, that prohibits public disclosure of someone else's tax returns; confidential business information—such as a trade secret that would give away the recipe for a commercial food product; internal government communications—a memorandum from an agency employee to his supervisor describing options for conducting the agency's affairs; personal privacy—this exemption covers personnel, medical, and other intimate details that would constitute an unwarranted invasion of someone's privacy; law enforcement—this protects investigation records, conceals the identity of confidential sources and informants, and prevents disclosure of police methods; financial institutions—such as the records of the Federal Reserve; and geological information—this rarely used exemption covers such data as maps about the location of wells.

When a record contains some information that qualifies as exempt, the entire record is not necessarily withheld. Instead, the FOIA specifically provides that any reasonably segregable portions of a record must be provided to a requester after the deletion of the exempt pages, paragraphs or words. With each exemption, the agency must give the reason why.

The essential feature of both laws is that they make federal agencies accountable for information without hiding behind secrecy or confidentiality. Government information cannot be controlled by arbitrary or unreviewable actions. The access provisions of the FOIA and the Privacy Act sometimes overlap; information exempt under one law may be disclosable under the other. That is why, when you request information, both laws should be cited. (The letters FOIPA stand for Freedom of Information and Privacy Act.) Congress intended that the two laws be considered together in processing requests.

In general, I have found the government officials concerned with searching and forwarding the dossiers dedicated and cooperative. Of course, what should be realized is that these officials are civil servants, and they are obliged to uphold the law. They cannot refuse requests outright; it's their job to treat all applicants for information equally.

By comparison, the Federal Bureau of Investigation is the most helpful among the government agencies. The Central Intelligence Agency and the State Department are less forthcoming when it comes to how much material to part with. In my experience, the least cooperative are the intelligence branches of the armed forces; apparently, they don't like to pass on too much information from their files to civilians.

Sometimes it seems as if they're playing the old army game; doing it by the numbers.

After receiving a letter, an agency is required to determine within ten days (excluding weekends and holidays) whether to comply with the request. Theoretically, the actual disclosure of the documents is required to follow promptly. If a request for records is denied, the agency must give the reasons why. And the agency must also tell the requester that he or she has a right of appeal if documents have been withheld or censored.

Delays by all agencies are routine—anywhere from a month to a year from the time you make a request. Response time depends on the number of requests ahead of yours; where information about you is located; the number of pages that concern you and how far back they go; whether the file is of such size that a photocopying fee will be required; the nature of the file itself—if it contains a lot of censorable material; it will take longer for the anonymous government elves to black out the pages.

A request for information from the Federal Bureau of Investigation should be addressed to the Chief, Freedom of Information–Privacy Acts Section, Records Management Division, FBI, Department of Justice, Washington, D.C. 20535. The FBI is the usual starting point unless you have reason to believe that your request should go to some other agency; the FBI's domestic surveillance and record keeping reach back into the first quarter of this century.

Then, again, you may be seeking information not about yourself but about a subject, such as some aspect of the environment. In that case, the Environmental Protection Agency would be the agency to turn to.

Your request will be acknowledged and a number assigned to your name. You will be given a specific number that simply says: FOIPA No. 000,000. The initial response of the form letter will read: "We are currently conducting a search of the indices to our central records system files at FBI headquarters to determine if we have the records you are seeking. Upon completion of this review, you will be informed." Or, with luck, a sentence will be checked on the form letter that says: "We have located documents which may pertain to your request."

In either case, this paragraph will be included in the acknowledgment: "As a result of the large number of FOIPA requests received by the FBI, we may encounter some delay in processing your request(s). The FBI has allocated substantial resources, including manpower, to insure that delays in responding to FOIPA requests are minimized. We solicit your understanding and assure you that we will process your request(s) as soon as possible. Your continued patience will be appreciated."

A little later—weeks or, more likely, months—a letter may arrive saying that documents have been found and they will be sent along to you as soon as they are processed. There may be a photocopying fee, in which case the FOIPA office will ask if you are willing to pay. Then, after the passage of more time, the documents—duly declassified and probably censored in part—will be forwarded to you.

An individual seeking records about himself or herself under the FOIA should not be charged review charges. As for photocopying or research fees, the rules vary, depending on the requester. Both could be costly if the file is large. According to the Government Information subcommittee of the House of Representatives Committee on Government Operations, these factors would determine the costs under the 1986 amendments to the Freedom of Information and Privacy laws:

> Representatives of the news media and most academic requesters may only be charged copying fees. Commercial users

> may be charged search and review fees as well as copying fees. All other requesters may be charged search and copying fees. Except for commercial users, no fees may be charged for the first two hours of search time or for the first one hundred pages of photocopying.

Fees for all requesters may be waived or reduced if disclosure of the information is in the public interest. The reason for this exception, according to the congressional subcommittee overseeing the law, is that it is likely to contribute significantly to public understanding of the operations or activities of the government and is not primarily in the commercial interest of the requester.

The original fee structure, initiated during the Reagan administration, erected financial roadblocks for many people seeking to obtain government information under the law. In addition, a 1982 executive order restricted freedom of information. It was described by a former member of the Department of Justice, Quinn Shea, who had served as director of the FOIA appeals office under presidents Ford and Carter, as "a sell-out to secrecy freaks."

After complaints were voiced to Congress from all over the country, amendments were made to the FOIA in 1986. A new fee structure lowered the costs for many requesters. The requester has the burden of demonstrating to the agency that he falls into a favorable fee category.

Under the laws, requesters must ask for existing records and "reasonably describe" what is being sought. It is important to spell out as carefully as possible exactly what you are looking for to help speed the process. Because different agencies organize and index records in different ways, one agency may consider a request to be reasonably descriptive while another may reject a similar request as too vague.

The FBI has a central name index for its primary record

system. That is why the bureau is able to search for records about a specific person. (If you are inquiring about your own records, it would be useful to put down your date and place of birth, military service, your occupation, perhaps other identifying data such as if you've held a government job, but it isn't necessary to tell your life story in the request.) Other agencies that do not maintain a central index may be unable to conduct the same kind of search with alacrity.

If you are doing research for a college paper on, for example, the environment, it may take not only patience but a little creativity. Assuming that you want to obtain a list of toxic waste sites near your home or school, a request to the Environmental Protection Agency for all records on toxic waste would cover too much. The fees for such a request could be prohibitive; it is possible that such a request might be denied as too vague. A request for all toxic waste sites within three miles of a particular place would be more specific, but it is unlikely that the agency would have an existing record organized in such a way. That request, too, might be denied because of its narrow grounds.

Your request might do better if you asked for a list of toxic waste sites in your city, county or state. It is more likely that existing records might contain this information. The requests might also tell the agency exactly what information is desired. It is to everyone's advantage to be as narrow and precise as possible. Some people have been known to include their telephone numbers with their requests. Questions about the scope of a request can be resolved quickly when the agency employee and the requester have a chance to talk.

All agencies normally require that requests be in writing. If you do not know beforehand which agency has the desired records, consult a government directory, such as the United States Government Manual, which you can find at a public library. There is nothing to prevent you from making the same request to more than one agency simultaneously. But it is advisable not to make several requests on different subjects in the same letter; each one should be listed separately so that they are not linked in a search, which could cause delays.

Here is a sample request letter, prepared by the congressional subcommittee on Government Information, that I have modified:

Agency Head (Or Freedom of Information Act Officer)
Name of Agency
Address and zip code

Re: Freedom of Information and Privacy Act Request

Dear Sir or Madam:

This is a request under the Freedom of Information and Privacy laws.

Without limitation, I request a copy of any documents (or name specific records) about me in your records.

To help you locate my records and determine my fee status, here is information about me:

I was born in (name of city) on (date) and live at the above address. I am an American citizen; served in the (military branch and regiment); am now a graduate student (or name profession) who seeks this information for the purpose of research (or whatever, but not merely idle curiosity).

This request is made for a scholarly or scientific purpose and not for commercial use.

I am willing to pay fees up to a maximum of $00. If you estimate that the fees will exceed this limit, please let me know.

If true, you have the option of including the following paragraph:

I request a waiver of all fees for this request. Disclosure of the requested information to me is in the public interest because it is likely to contribute significantly to public understanding of the operations or activities of the government and is not primarily in my commercial interest.

(Also optional): Enclosed is (a notarized signature or other identifying document) that will verify my identity.

Thank you.

Sincerely,

Name, address, and daytime telephone number

EVIDENCE AND READINGS

The documents obtained under the Freedom of Information Act that form the basic evidence for this book, together with correspondence and notes, interviews with former government officials and other research material, will be deposited in the author's existing personal papers in the Manuscript Division of the New York Public Library. There is one exception: I am withholding the list containing the names of living authors and creators in other fields that exist in certain government archives. This is done to protect their privacy and also because I was given access to these records in Washington on condition that I would not reveal the source.

The citations on privacy and the law and other related legal issues can be found in several of the books listed below, including *The Tree of Liberty* and *Encyclopedia of the American Constitution.* In addition to the writings by and about the authors and creators included, the following is a bibliography of some of the works consulted that scholars and others exploring this theme and the times may find useful:

Baker, Carlos. *Ernest Hemingway: A Life Story.* (Scribners, 1969.)

Benson, Jackson J. *The True Adventures of John Steinbeck, Writer.* The Viking Press, 1984.

Berthoud, Roger. *The Life of Henry Moore.* Faber & Faber, 1987.

Blotner, Joseph. *Faulkner: A Biography.* Random House, 1984.

Brian, Denis. *The True Gen: An Intimate Portrait of Ernest Hemingway by Those Who Knew Him.* Grove Press, 1988.

Carr, Virginia Spencer. *Dos Passos.* Doubleday, 1984.

Cogley, John. *Report on Blacklisting: I. Movies. II. Radio-Television.* Fund for the Republic, 1956.

Commager, Henry Steele, ed. *Documents of American History.* F. S. Crofts, 1947.

———, Leuchtenberg, William E., and Samuel Eliot Morison. *A Concise History of the American Republic.* Oxford University Press, 1977.

Cook, Fred J. *The FBI Nobody Knows.* Macmillan, 1964.

Donald, David Herbert. *Look Homeward: A Life of Thomas Wolfe.* Little, Brown, 1987.

Dugger, Ronnie. *On Reagan: The Man and His Presidency.* McGraw-Hill, 1983.

Edwards, Anne. *Early Reagan.* William Morrow, 1987.

Fadiman, Clifton, ed. *Fifty Years: Borzoi Books, 1915–1965.* Alfred A. Knopf, 1965.

Farand, Max, and James H. Hutson, eds. *Records of the Federal Convention of 1787.* Yale University Press, 1987.

Fowler, Doreen, and Ann J. Abadie, eds. *Faulkner and Race.* University of Mississippi Press, 1988.

Garbus, Martin. *Traitors and Heroes.* Atheneum, 1987.

Ginsberg, Allen. *White Shroud: Poems 1980–1985.* Harper & Row, 1986.

Gitlin, Todd. *The Sixties.* Bantam Books, 1987.

Goldsmith, John, ed. *Stephen Spender: Journals 1939–1983.* Random House, 1986.

Haight, Anne Lyon, and Chandler B. Harris. *Banned Books.* R.R. Bowker, 1978.

Harris, Richard. *Justice.* E. P. Dutton, 1970.

Harrison, Gilbert A. *The Enthusiast: A Life of Thornton Wilder.* Ticknor & Fields, 1983.

Johnson, Diane. *Dashiell Hammett: A Life.* Ballantine Books, 1985.

Kimball, Penn. *The File.* Harcourt Brace Jovanovich, 1983.

Kittrie, Nicholas N., and Eldon D. Wedblock, Jr. *The Tree of Liberty.* Johns Hopkins University Press, 1986.

Kluger, Richard. *The Paper: The Life and Death of the New York Herald Tribune.* Knopf, 1986.

Lehan, Richard, ed. *Theodore Dreiser.* Library of America, 1987.

Levy, Leonard W., ed. *Encyclopedia of the American Constitution.* Macmillan, 1986.

Lewis, Anthony. *Portrait of a Decade.* Random House, 1964.

Lowenthal, Max. *The Federal Bureau of Investigation.* William Sloane, 1950.

Mauldin, William. *Bill Mauldin in Korea.* W. W. Norton, 1952.

———. *Up Front.* W. W. Norton, 1968.

Meade, Marion. *Dorothy Parker: What Fresh Hell Is This?* Villard Books, 1988.

Meyers, Jeffrey. *Hemingway: A Biography.* Harper & Row, 1985.

Miller, Arthur. *Timebends: A Life.* Grove Press, 1987.

Mitgang, Herbert, ed. *The Letters of Carl Sandburg.* Harcourt Brace Jovanovich, 1968.

Nichols, David, ed. *Ernie's War: Ernie Pyle's World War II Dispatches.* Random House, 1986.

Nobile, Philip, and Eric Nadler. *United States of America v. Sex: How the Meese Commission Lied About Pornography.* Minotaur Press, 1986.

O'Reilly, Kenneth. *Hoover and the Un-Americans.* Temple University Press, 1983.

Peeler, David P. *Hope Among Us Yet.* University of Georgia Press, 1987.

Powers, Richard Gid. *Secrecy and Power: The Life of J. Edgar Hoover.* The Free Press, 1987.

Reagan, Ronald, and Richard Hubler. *Where's the Rest of Me?* Dell, 1965.

Rogin, Michael. *Ronald Reagan, The Movie and Other Episodes in Political Demonology.* University of California Press, 1987.

Scales, Junius Irving, and Richard Nickson. *Cause at Heart: A Former Communist Remembers.* University of Georgia Press, 1987.

Shannon, William V. *The Heir Apparent: Robert Kennedy and the Struggle for Power.* Macmillan, 1967.

Smith, Bradley F. *The War's Long Shadow.* Simon & Schuster, 1986.

Sullivan, William C. *The Bureau: My Thirty Years in Hoover's FBI.* W. W. Norton, 1979.

Theiner, George, ed. *They Shoot Writers, Don't They?* Faber & Faber, 1984.

Theoharis, Athan. *Spying on Americans: Political Surveillance from Hoover to the Houston Plan.* Temple University Press, 1978.

———. *Beyond the Hiss Case: The FBI, Congress and the Cold War.* Temple University Press, 1982.

Turner, Stansfield. *Secrecy and Democracy: The CIA in Transition.* Houghton Mifflin, 1985.

Welch, Neil J., and David W. Marston. *Inside Hoover's FBI.* Doubleday, 1984.

Westin, Alan F., project director. *Databanks in a Free Society.* Quadrangle Books, 1972.

Wheeler, Stanton, ed. *On Record.* Transaction Books, 1976.

Wills, Garry. *Reagan's America.* Doubleday, 1987.

Wright, Peter. *Spy Catcher.* Viking Press, 1987.

Wright, William. *Lillian Hellman: The Image, the Woman.* Simon and Schuster, 1986.

INDEX